पुरातत्त्व
पुरातत्त्व
PURĀTATTVA

Bulletin of the Indian Archaeological Society

No. 20 1989-90

Editor
S.P. Gupta

Jt. Editor
Makkhan Lal

D.K. Printworld (P) Ltd.
New Delhi

Cataloging in Publication Data — DK
[Courtesy : D.K. Agencies (P) Ltd. <docinfo@dkagencies.com>]

Purātattva : bulletin of the Indian Archaeological Society, no. 20, 1989-90 / editor, S.P. Gupta ; jt. editor, Makkhan Lal.
p. cm.
Includes bibliographical references.
ISBN 81-246-0295-6

1. Archaeology — India — Periodicals. 2. India — Antiquities — Periodicals. 3. India — Civilization — Periodicals. I. Gupta, S.P. II. Indian Archaeological Society.

First Published in 1991
First Reprinted in 2005
ISBN 81-246-0295-6
Price for volume 20 (1989-90): Rs. 800 US $ 40

Reprint authorised by
Indian Archaeological Society
New Delhi - 110 016

The Editors are not responsible for the opinions expressed by the Contributors.

Purātattva is published annually.

Manuscripts (whether in the form of articles or notes or book reviews) offered for publication should be sent to the Editor, Purātattva, Indian Archaeological Society, B-17, Qutab Institutional Area, New Delhi - 110 016.

Published and printed by:
D.K. Printworld (P) Ltd.
'*Srikunj*,' F-52, Bali Nagar
New Delhi – 110015
Phone : (011) 2545 3975, 2546 6019 Fax : (011) 2546 5926
E-mail : dkprintworld@vsnl.net
www. dkprintworld.com

PURATATTVA

CONTENTS

EDITORIAL v

ARTICLES

PAGES

1. Evidence of Social Differentiation and Sociopolitical Organization during Megalithic Period in South India — 1
   Udairavi S. Moorti
2. Deogarh Acheulian Assemblage: A Preliminary Report — 65
   Makkhan Lal & Salahuddin
3. Dholavira: A New Horizon of the Indus Civilization — 71
   R.S. Bisht
4. The Chalcolithic Culture of South Bihar as Revealed by the Explorations and Excavations in district Rohtas — 83
   Birendra Pratap Singh
5. Archaeology of Wardha and Wain Ganga Divide — 93
   Amarendra Nath
6. The Keshtrapala Shrine at Kandhar — 99
   M. K. Dhavalikar & A.P. Jamkhedkar
7. An Early Temple in Gujarat - Excavations at Goraj (Mahadevapura) — 107
   B.M. Pande & Narayan Vyas

NOTES AND NEWS

8. Iron and Gem Stone Industries as Revealed from Kodumanal Excavations — 111
   K. Rajan
9. A Rare Image of Avalokiteswar from Eastern India — 113
   Shashi Asthana
10. Archaeometallurgical studies at Kankarjhor and Dhuliapar — 115
    S. De and *P.K. Chattopadhyaya*
11. Archaeometallurgical study of Iron Pillar at Dhar — 118
    B. Prakash

BOOK REVIEWS

12.	Stone Age of India by S.A. Sali *B.B. Lal*	123
13.	Encylopaedia of Indian Archaeology. Two Volumes Edited by A. Ghosh *Y.M. Chitalwala*	123
14.	The External Trade of Indus Civilization by Dilip K. Chakrabarti *S.P. Gupta*	124
15.	One World Archaeology Series From Unwin Hyman, London. General Editor Peter J. Ucko *Makkhan Lal*	125

PURATATTVA

Number 20 1989-90

Editorial

Like in the previous numbers of *Puratattva*, we have tried to accommodate articles ranging from Palaeolithic to Medieval period covering the various facets of archaeology. On palaeolithic period Deogarh assamblage has been discussed. On Neolithic and Bronze age the papers on Dholavia, a Harappan site in Gujarat and excavations at Senuwar and exploration in adjoining areas in S. Bihar throw light on various aspects of the cultures. The discovery of Harappan inscription at Dholavira, each letter upto to 37 cm. in height and 27 cm. in width, is an important discovery. Articles on Iron Age include the one on megalithic culture of S. India. The analysis of excavated material and presentation of basic data in form of self explainatory tables should be welcomed. The excavation reports on Adam and Goraj contain the material on ancient and early medieval periods. Also the papers on iron technology enhance our knowledge about composition of metal and smelting and foraging techniques.

Needless to say that main emphasis in the selection of papers for publication has been the presentation of new source material, new archaeological discoveries and fresh interpretation of existing data and it shall continue to be the criteria for inclusion of papers in the *Puratattva*. We would like to mention to our contributors that without their continued support the journal cannot be brought out regularly. However, we shall be grateful if the contributions reach us by the end of June if the authors want that their papers should be considered for the journal coming out at the end of same year. This will not only give us time to plan better but also authors may have a chance to see the final proofs themselves.

The Indian Archaeological Society would like to express its gratitude to the Archaeological Survey of India and Indian Council of Historical Research for their financial support towards the publication cost of this number. Thanks are due to Dr. Salahuddin for his help in various ways.

Editors

EVIDENCE OF SOCIAL DIFFERENTIATION AND SOCIO-POLITICAL ORGANISATION DURING THE MEGALITHIC PERIOD IN SOUTH INDIA

Udayaravi S. Moorti*

Decoding the organisational aspects of past societies through a study of their mortuary practices has been in the forefront of Archaeology for the last two decades. The literature brought out by American and European archaeologists in recent years on this aspect is quite considerable. The studies concerning the application of funerary analysis to the problem of social reconstruction fall in two groups viz., those concerned with evidences of social differentiation at a single site and those that assess social systems using groups of sites. The studies of Shennan (1975), Chapman (1977), Hodson (1977), van de Velde (1979) fall in the first group and those of Renfrew (1973), Randsborg (1973, 1975), Peebles and Kus (1977), Tainter (1977), Kristiansen (1984), O'Shea (1984) and Sjorgen (1986) in the second group, to quote a few. Mention may be made of Kendall (1971), Doran (1972) and Tainter (1975), which are of the seriation studies carried out to understand the diachronic changes in the mortuary occurrences. The central theme of all these studies is the assumption that an individual's treatment at death bears some predictable relationship to the individual's status in life and the organisation of the society to which the individual belonged.

Of the above mentioned studies, the works of Saxe (1970), Binford (1972), Peebles and Kus (1977), Tainter and Cordy (1977), Brown (1981) and Alkeshin (1983) have a strong generalising character of this important archaeological pradigm and hence more useful in understanding the archaeological representation of mortuary differentiation, variability and societal organisation. These studies have demonstrated the existence of regularities linking aspects of the living society and its procedure for the disposal of the dead. The core observations of these studies as summarised by O'Shea (1984:21) are as follows:

1. Mortuary differentiation is patterned, and its elements are integrated with other aspects of the sociocultural system.
2. The mortuary differentiation accorded to an individual, although not necessarily isomorphic, is consistent with his social position in the living society.
3. The complexity of the system of mortuary differentiation will increase with the complexity of the society at large.

Binford (1962: 217-225), while reviewing the artifact assemblages of a cultural system brings out three major functional sub-classes of material culture viz., technomic, socio-technic and ideo-technic items, each with its own distinctive formal properties. The following definitions have been made by Binford (1962: 219-20) for artifacts of each category.

Technomic artifacts

"Technomic signifies those artifacts having their primary functional context in coping directly with the physical environment".

Socio-technic artifacts

"These artifacts were the material elements having their primary functional context in the social sub-systems of the total cultural system" (i.e., those artifacts which signify the social status of an individual.

Ideo-technic artifacts

"Items of this class have their primary functional context in the ideological component of the social system. These are the items which signify and symbolize ideological rationalizations for a social system and further provide the symbolic milieu in which individuals are enculturated, a necessity if they are to take their place as functional participants in the social system."

Using Bindord's above criteria of the artifact usage as a means of defining the nature of burial inclusions, Peebles (1971 : 69) refined the definition of sociotechnic artifacts in terms of their ability to symbolise differentiation or ranking. He makes two subcategories viz., supralocal and local symbols, the former defined as symbols that are recognized over a wide area and likely to cut across a number of ethic boundaries and the latter defined as those sociotechnic artifacts that serve to rank or differentiate individuals only within a given locality (1971 : 69).

Peebles and Kus (1977) further attempted to define general criteria for the recognition of sociol ranking within an archaeological context. They put forward two independent dimensions in the symbolic representation of an individual's *social persona* viz., a superordinate dimension and a subordinate dimension. According to them, the former dimension pro-

* Visiting Fellow, Faculty of Archaeology and Anthropology, Downing Street, Cambridge CB2 3DZ.

duces a partial ordering of the graves through energy expenditure or symbols that is not simultaneously based on age and sex; and the latter dimension produces a partial ordering of graves that is generally based on age and sex, or achievements during an individual's life history (Peebles and Kus 1977 : 431). They asserted that only in a ranked society both dimensional effects are observed.

The following points summarises the criteria Peebles and Kus (1977:431) expect for superordinate and subordinate dimensions of mortuary differentiation in a ranked society:

Superordinate dimension

1. Some infants, some children, and some adults will be found in every scale category except the paramount category.
2. The apical class will contain only adults, and probably only adult males.
3. Some infants and children will have greater amounts of energy expended in their treatment than some men.
4. The numbers of burials in each scale category will markedly decrease as one goes higher on the scale, thereby reflecting the rank pyramid.

Subordinate dimension

1. As the chronological age of the individual buried increases, so will the energy expended in that individual's burial.
2. Children and infants will have some items as grave goods that will not be shared by adults; women will have some items as grave goods not shared by men.
3. Energy expended in the lowest level of the superordinate dimension will be greater than that exparded in the highest level of the subordinate dimension.
4. The number of individuals in each scale category of the subordinate dimension should reflect the age and sex pyramid of the population through time.

Sears' (1961) caution on the dangers of an exclusive use of mortuary data for obtaining an accurate and reasonably precise portrait of past socièties has to be kept in mind. To quote him, "The funerary context, although offering a unique view of past social and economic organization, cannot realistically be analysed to the exclusion of other contexts" (p.229). Hence, in the present study settlement and other data have also been utilised.

With this background we shall be analysing the mortuary and other related data to undersand the socio-political organisation of the Megalithic society of South India.

SOCIAL DIFFERENTIATION AS OBSERVED IN THE MORTUARY DATA OF MEGALITHIC PERIOD

The mortuary data brought out by different excavators for 29 Megalithic sites has been analysed here. There are many other Megalithic sites where only a single burial was excavated. In such cases it is difficult to make any inter- site or intra-site comparisons of mortuary patterns. Hence, such sites have not been included in our anylysis. So far, more than 504 burials and 52 non-sepulchral monuments (i.e., which are commemorative or memorial in nature) of Megalithic period (see Table) have been excavated in South India. However details to some extent are available only in respect of 205 burials. And even out of these 205 burials, 19 were previously disturbed (but have been excavated). Hence, we have detail, if not complete information only in respect of 186 burials (see Table 31). Although information regarding the disturbed burials has been provided in our tables they have not been considered for our analysis as they do not provide the original condition of the burial and the burial goods.

What follows is an analysis of mortuary data from only 29 sites wherein a total of 186 burials have been excavated and concerning which there is detail information to some extent. The sites considered for our analysis are: Khairwada, Bhagi Mahari, Borgaon Khurd, Naikund, Mahurjhari, Rajpur- Hingura, Gangapur, Takalghat-Khapa (all in Maharashtra); Yalleshwaram, Nagarjunakonda, Peddamarur, Uppalapadu, Satanikota, Agiripalli (in Andhra Pradesh); Jewargi, Maski, Brahmagiri, Terdal Halingali, Tadakanahalli, Jadigenhalli, Savandurga, Heggedehalli (in Karnatak); Kunnathur, Sanur, Odugattur, Sittannavasal, Pancha-Pandavar-Mettu, Vellur Adichanallur (in Tamil Nadu) and Machad (in Kerala). The total

Table: Statewise statistical breakup of excavated burials in south India.

Sl. No.	Name of State	Total no. of Megalithic sites	Total no. of excavated Megalithic sites	Total no. of burial monuments at these excavated sites	Total no. of excavated burials
I	Maharashtra	91	12	>2643	40+
II	Andhra Pradesh	300	58	>4908	174+
III	Karnataka	665	50	>2294	92+
IV	Tamil Nadu (including the union territory of Pondicherry	607	122	> 880	157+
V	Kerala	270	41	> 128	41+

number of burials at these sites and the number of burials excavated at these sites and other details are mentioned in Table 31.

To understand mortuary differentiation through a study of artifacts interred in the burial, the functional subclasses of these artifacts in each burial type, alongwith information on the size of burial, sex and age of the individual/s has been analysed. The quantification of the interred burial goods, specially sociotechnic artifacts as an indicator of social differentiation, has enabled us to ascribe the burials either as belonging to superordinate, or subordinate group of the social dimension.

As noted earlier the categorisation of artifacts into three functional subgroups, viz., technomic, sociotechnic and ideotechnic is useful in understanding their functional role in a cultural system. The megalithic artifacts can be grouped under following heads:

Technomic artifacts

Axes, adzes, chisels, wedges, points, pokers, plough-share tips, hoes, sickles, pickaxes, billhooks, crowbars, bars with a pointed tip and socketed end, scrapers, awls/needles, sharp-edged cutters (of Iron); spatula (of Copper); fishhooks of (Copper/Iron), spindle-whorls (of terracotta have been considered as artifacts belonging to this category.

Sociotechnic artifacts

Under this head two subgroups viz., Sociotechnic-A and Sociotechnic-B have been made. The sociotechnic-A group includes all the status goods whereas sociotechnic-B group includes only weapons of offence and defence. Our interest in making sociotechnic-B group as a separate category was to see whether all the burials contain such artifacts, or not.

Horse, horse trappings (of Iron): horse ornaments (of Gold, Copper and Iron); rings, chains, spiral rings, leaves, strips, wire, necklaces, ear ornaments, sheet rings with punched decoration, beads, diadems (of Gold); spacers (of Silver); bowls, pots, lids with finials having different motifs, dishes, cup with side handles (of Copper); stands with various decorative motifs, lids, bowls, vessels, cups, jars, small water-vessels or small water vessels or *lotas*, sieves, strainers bulb objects (of Bronze); bangles, convex discs, long objects with closed and pointed ends, each with an encased iron rod, perforated discs with decorations, cigar-shaped pieces, triangular chips (of Conch-shell); bangles (of Glass); halberd/plough-coulter (?), dagger with a copper fillet on the guard, dagger with an iron blade and a copper hilt (of Iron have been considered as artifacts belonging to this category i.e., sociotechnic-A group).

Spearheads, arrowheads, daggers, spikes, tridents, javelins, swords, spike-studded lance, lances, pikes (of Iron) are considered as artifacts belonging to sociotechnic-B group).

Ideotechnic artifacts

Identifying artifacts carrying symbolic value and meaning in the material repertoire of a culture is the most difficult task to deal with. For example dress pattern differentiation has been considered by social anthropologists as a distinguishing feature in the identification of status in a society. Unfortunately, we have no access to this information from burials because of environmental conditions of this region. However, a few material objects found in the burials which seem to carry symbolic value are grouped under this head. They are as follows:

Turtle motif (of copper); sarcophagus rim luted with a figurine possibly of a buffalo, horn-shaped vessels (cornucopia?), figurines of animals (of T.C.); rattle having the decoration of a grotesque human face (of Bronze); plates of various shapes and dimensions having either conical/flat disc (one was bird shaped) attached to them (of copper/bronze).

Burial interments consist varieties of artifacts ranging from pottery to precious metal objects. Many of the artifacts which may be of domestic or personal use (such as pottery, iron tripods, steatite beads) have not been considered in our analysis as they are of secondary importance in the functional subgrouping of artifacts.

Details of the excavated burials at 29 megalithic sites are given in Tables 1 to 29. These tables carry information on skeletal remains and associated artifacts found in each burial, functional breakup of burial goods and the ascribed social dimension of the individual/s buried in the respective grave.

The site of Khairwada, which falls in the physical zone of Wardha-Penganga has a total number of 1496 burials. Only 6 burials have been excavated at this site (*IAR* 1981-82 : 51- 52; Walimbe, 1989: 61-71). Our analysis shows that out of 6 excavated burials only two burials viz., Br. Nos. 2 (Loc. I) and 1 (Loc. III) fall in superordinate group and the rest viz., Br. Nos. 1, 3 (Loc. I), 1 (Loc. II), 3 (Loc. III) fall under subordinate group (Table 1).

The site of Bhagi Mahari, falling in the physical zone of Wainganga basin has more than 70 burials. The total number of excavated burials at this site is 5 (*IAR* 1982-83 : 61; *IAR* 1983-84 : 57-58; Deo, pers. comm.). Our present analysis shows that of the excavated 5 burials, Br. Nos. 1 and 3 can be grouped under superordinate category and the remaining three burials viz., Br. Nos. 2, 4 and 5 under subordinate category (see Table 2).

From the site of Borgaon Khurd (in the physical zone of Wainganga basin) a total of 48 burials have been reported. And out of these, 4 burials have been excavated (*IAR* 1980-81: 40; Deo, pers. comm.; Walimbe, 1989: 61-71; Thomas, pers. comm.). Table 3 shows that Br. Nos. 3 and 35 belong to superordinate group and Br. Nos. 7 and 36 to subordinate group.

Coming under the same physical zone as the above two sites, is the site of Naikund which has a total of 70 burials. Out of these, 6 burials have been excavated (Deo and Jamkhedkar, 1982: Kennedy *et. al.*, 1982: 49-51; Badam, 1982: 70-91). Table 4 shows that Br. Nos. 3 and 7 (Loc. I) can be ascribed to superordinate category while Br. Nos. 8 (Loc. I), 1 (Loc. II), 1 (Loc. III) and 13 (Loc. IV) to that of subordinate category.

Table 5 gives details on the site of Mahurjhari, which also falls in the physical zone of Waingagna basin. From this site a total of 300 burials have been reported and out of these, 26 burials have been excavated (Deo, 1973a; Rao, 1973 : 63-76; *IAR* 1978-79: 71).Of the excavated 26 burials Br. No.1 (Loc. I) was a previously disturbed. Our analysis shows that Br. Nos. 1, 2 (Loc. II), 4 (of 1971-72 exc. season), 7, 11 and 29 (of 1978-79 exc. season) can be ascribed to superordinate category whereas Br. Nos. 2, 3 (Loc. I), 1, 2, 3, 5, 6, 7, 8, 9 (Loc. III), 1 (Loc. IV) (of 1971-72 exc. season) and Br.Nos. 1, 2, 3, 4, 5, 8, 9, 10 (of 1978-79 exr. season) come under subordinate category.

The next site in the same physical zone, is Raipur-Hingna which has a total of 360 burials. Only 4 burials have been excavated (*IAR* 1984-85: 53-55; Walimbe, 1989: 61-71) Table 6 gives details on the excava.ed burials and their contents. Out of the excavated 4 burials, Br. No.2 (Loc. IV) can be ascribed as belonging to superordinate category while the remaining three, viz. Br. Nos. 3, 4 (Loc. III) and 1 (Loc. IV) are ascribable to subordinate category.

Gangapur, another site falling in the same physical zone has 30 burials. Three burials were excavated at this site (Deo, 1970; Rao, 1970: 60-77). Table 7 gives details on these excavated burials and it is obvious from the table that all the three, i.e. Br. Nos. 2, 3 (Cl. I) and 1 (Cl. II) can be ascribed to subordinate category.

From the site of Takalghat-Khapa (again in Wainganga basin) a total of 14 burials have been reported of which 9 were excavated (Deo, 1970; Rao, 1970 : 60-77). Table 8 shows that except two burials, i.e, Br. Nos. 1 and 6 (Cl. I) which can be ascribed to superordinate category, others i.e., Br. Nos. 4, 7, 8 (Cl. I), 2, 3 (Cl. II), 5 and 9 (Cl. III) belong to subordinate category.

Table 9 gives information on the site of Yelleswaram. The site fall in the physical zone of Telangana peneplain. Information is not available on the total numbers of burials existing at this site but 5 burials have been excavated here (Khan, 1963 : Gupta and Dutta, 1962 : 19-34; Sarkar, 1972 : 20-40; Alur, 1979a: 127-134). None of these excavated burials i.e, Br. Nos. I, III (YLM-A), II, IV (YLM-A ?) and V (YLM-B) could be ascribed to superordinate category and all fall under subordinate category.

Next four site, viz. Nagarjunakonda, Peddamarur, Uppalapadu and Satanikota, to be described in the following paragraphs, come under the physical zone of the Middle Krishna Valley.

Fifteen burials were excavated, out of a total of 21 occurring at Nagarjunakonda (Subrahmanyam, 1975l; Sarkar, 1972 : 19-20 ; Nath, 1968: 9-10; Anth. Survey of India, 1975: 185-195). And details on these burials and their contents have been shown in Table 10. The table evidently reveals that only Br. No. XIV (site 63) can be ascribed to superordinate category and the rest 14 burials, i.e. Br. Nos. II, III, IV, V, VI, VIII, X, XI, XII, XIII, XV, IX, VII (site 63) and I (site 44) fall under subordinate category.

Altogether four burials were excavated at Ped damarpur (*IAR* 1977-78 : 12-13); Krishnasastry, 1983: 60-67). Information regarding the total number of burials occuring at the site has not been provided in the report. Table 11 gives the details of these excavated burials. All the excavated four burials, i.e. Br. Nos. I, II, III and IV can be ascribed to subordinate category.

A total of 21 burials were excavated at Uppalapadu (*IAR* 1977-78 : 12; *IAR* 1978-79; 65-66; Suryanarayana Raju, 1982: 6-8, Subrahmanyam, pers. comm.). Out of these, Br. Nos. III (site I) and V (site ?) were previously disturbed. Unfortunately, the excavator has not provided the data on the total number of burials occurring at the site. Details on these excavated burials are given in Table 12. An analysis of the interred material shows that only one burial, i.e. Br. No. VI (site I) could be ascribed to superordinate category. Rest of the burials viz., Br. Nos. I, IV, V, IX, VIII (site I), III, IV (site ?), VII, II (site I), I (site ?), Vi (site II), II, VI (site ?), I (site III), I, III, V, IV (site II) fall under subordinate category.

From Satanikota, more than 29 burials have been reported. And out of these, 8 burials have been excavated (Ghosh, 1986: Pal, 1986: 51-60). Of the excavated 8 burials, three [Br. Nos. A I, A II (Cl. A) and B VII (Cl. B)] were previously disturbed. Our analysis (see Table 13) shows that none of them could be ascribed to superordiante category and all i.e., Br. Nos. A III (Cl. A), B VIII, B XVII, B I (Cl. B) and CI (Cl. C) fall under subordiante catogory.

Agiripalli which falls in the phsical zone of Krishna-Godavari delta, has been excavated by Krishnasastry, (1983: 69-72: *IAR*, 1976-77; 5; Rao, Pers. comm.). Information is not available as regards the total number of burials occurring here but in all 7 burials were excavated. Details on these burials are given in Table 14. The burials were very poorly represented and as the table shows that all of them i.e., Br. Nos. I, II, III, IV, V, VI, VII fall under subordinate category.

At Jewargi which is in the physical zone of Gulbarga plain, occur 375 burials. More than 14 burials were excavated at this site (Taylor, 1851 : 179-193; 1853: 380-429 ; 1862: 329-362; Sundara, 1975: 57-62). Of the excavated 14, two [Br. Nos. 3 (fifth Cairn) and 4 (Sixth Cairn)] were previously disturbed and regarding the contents of Br. No. 7 (Cairn C) no information has been provided. Table 15 shows that none of th excavated burials, i.e. Br. Nos. 1 (First Cairn), 2 (Fourth Cairn), 5 (Cairn A), 6 (Cairn B), 8 (Cairn D), 9 (Cairn E), 14, 10 (Second Cairn), 11 (Third Cairn), 12 (Seventh Cairn) and 13 (Eighth Cairn) could be ascribed to superordinate category and they obviously fall in the subordinate category.

Table 16 gives details of the excavated burials at Maski, also known for its Asokan rock edict, which is in Raichur plain. Information regarding the total number of burials occurring at the site was difficult to gather as most of the megalithic burials were covered by later cultural debris. Ten burials have been excavated at this site (Thapar, 1957 : 4-142 ; Sarkar, 1972: 50-123 ; Nath, 1957 : 121-129 ; 1968 : 9). Of these, two were nonsepulchral monuments (i.e., Menhirs). As is clear from the table, all the burials (i.e., Br. Nos. 15, 16, 28, 28A, 30 (MSK-10), 2,1, (MSK-9), 2 (in Durgada Gudda area) fall under subordinate category.

Brahmagiri, known in ancient times as Isila where a rock edict of Mauryan King Asoka has been found, falls in the physical zone of Bellary plain. The site, known for its memorable excavations by Sir Mortimer Wheeler, has more than 309 burials. Ten burials were excavated at this site (Wheeler, 1948 : 181-308; Sarkar, 1972; 124-164; Nath, 1968 : 8). Br. No. III (Area C) was a previously disturbed burial, hence is not considered in our analysis. Our analysis shows (see Table 17) that of the excavated nine burials only one i.e., Br. No. IX (Area C) could be ascribed to superordinate category and the rest i.e., Br. Nos. V, VI, X (Area A), I, VII (Area B), II, IV and VIII (Area C) fall in subordinate category.

From the site of Terdal-Halingali, which is in Bijapur region, 147 burials were reported. Out of these, only 5 have been excavated (Sundara, 1969-70 ; 22-33 ; 1975 ; 99-100). Unfortunately, of the excavated 5 burials four (Br. Nos. Meg. I, II, Meg. 1 and 2) were found to be highly disturbed. Table 18 gives details on these excavated burials. Burial No. (Meg.) III, the only undisturbed burial of the excavated ones. can be ascribed to subordinate category.

Table 19 gives details on the excavated burials at Tadakanahalli, which is in Dharwad plateau region. Altogether four (Br. Nos. I, IV, II, III) burials were excavated at this site (*IAR* 1978-79: 45-46 ; Nagaraja Rao, 1985: 469-470). As regards the total number of burials occurring at the site, there is no information. Our analysis shows that all the excavated four burials fall under subordinate category.

The next two sites viz., Jadigenahalli and Savanadurga fall in the physical zone of Bangalore region.

At Jadigenahalli, four burials were excavated, out of a total of 35 occurring at the site, by Seshadri, (1960). Burial No. IV was a previously disturbed megalith. Table 20 shows that Br. No. II can be ascribd to superordinate category whereas the remaining two i.e., Br. Nos. I and III fall under the subordinate category.

Four burials were excavated at Savandurga (Branfill, 1881 : 1-12). There is no information regarding the total number of burials occurring at the site. Table 21 gives details on the excavated burials and as is clear from the table only one burial (Br. No. 1), out of excavated four, could be ascribed to superordinate category and the remaining three (Br. Nos. 2, 3 and 4) fall under subordinate category.

Table 22 gives details on the excavated burials at Heggedehalli, which is in Soth Malnad region. Altogether four burials were excavated here (Subbayya, 1972: 140-160; Dhavalikar and Subbayya, 1976 : 331-338). There is no information as regards the total number of burials occurring at the site. Burial No. II was a previously disturbed burial and Br. Nos. I, IV and III could be ascribed to subordinate category.

Kunnathur, where 8 megalithic burials were excavated (*IAR* 1955-56 : 23 ; *IAR* 1956-57 : 31-34 ; *IAR* 1957-58: 37-38; Sarkar, 1972 : 165-166) falls in the physical zone of Palar- Ponnaiyar basin. No information is given as regards the total number of burials occurring at the site. Of the excavated 8 burials, three i.e., Br. Nos. II, 6 and 9) were previously disturbed. Out of the remaining five considered for our analysis (see Table 23), only one (Br. No.4) could be ascribed to superordinate category, and the rest (Br. Nos. I, III, 5 and 7) fall under the subordinate category.

Another site coming under the same physical zone as is the previous site, is the site of Sanur. A total of 300 burials have been reported from this site. However, only 5 burials have been excavated at this site (Banerjee and Soundara Rajan, 1959 : 4-42; Bose, 1959 : 40-42; Sarkar, 1972 : 166-167). Our analysis of the excavated material from these burials shows (see Table 24) that Br. No.5 can be ascribed to superordinate category and the remaining four i.e., Br. Nos. 2, 1, 3 and 4 belong to subordinate category of social dimension.

At Odugattur, which falls in the physical zone of Mettur-Vellore region, three burials were excavated (Richards, 1924 : 157-165). The report does not mention about the total number of burials occurring at the site. As can be observed from Table 25, only Br. No. 1 could be ascribed to superordinate category and the remaining two excavated burials i.e., 3 and 2 fall under subordinate category.

Four burials were excavated at Sittannavasal (*IAR* 1975-76: 39-42). The site comes under the Cauvery valley and delta physical zone. As is the case with majority of reports, no information has been provided regarding the total number of burials occurring at the site. Burial No.IV (Area III) was a previously disturbed megalith, hence not considered in our present analysis. All the remaining three [Br. Nos. I (Area I), III and II (Area II)] excavated burials can be ascribed to subordinate category (Table 26).

Only two burials were excavated out of a total of 50 occurring at the site of Pancha-Pandavar-Mettu (Aiyappan, 1940-41: 373-397). The site falls in the physical zone of Anaimalai-Palni Hills. As can be observed from Table 27 both the excavated burials [Br. Nos. 1 (Area I) and 2 (Area II)] fall in subordinate category.

Although not less than 50 burials were excavated at Vellur Adichanallur, a well-known archaeological site in the south, it is a pity that no accurate information followed after quite extensive excavations by Rea (1902-03 : 111-143; 1915: 1-49). The site falls in the physical zone of the Vaigai-Tambraparani basin. Hundreds of burials have been reported from this site, but it is difficult to get an exact total because it is an urn burial site, with no surface indications left. It is obvious from the published reports that the context of most of the excavated material is missing. However, with great difficulty details could be collected atleast for 5 excavated burials to some extent (see Table 28). The shows that only Br. No. 3 could be ascribed to subordinate category, whereas the remaining burials, i.e., Bur. Nos. 1, 2, 4 and 5 fall under subordinate category.

The last site to be considered for our analysis was that of Machad where to burials have been excavated (Mehta and George, 1978). The site fall in the physical zone of North Malabar. Information regarding the total number of burials is not available. Table 29 gives details regarding these two excavated burials. Both the excavated burials (Br. Nos. II and II) can be ascribed to subordinate category.

It is obvious from the above discussions that significant differences to occur in the burial interments. The following pages probe further into the aspect of quantitative differences in burial interments and how this can be understood in the background of social differentiation as observed in the mortuary practices.

As mentioned earlier, mortuary data from 29 Megalithic sites have been considered in our present analysis. Table 31 provides a list of all these sites along with information concerning the total number of burials occurring at each site, number of excavated burials, number of previously disturbed burials and also non-sepulchral monuments (but which have been excavated) and the number of excavated non-sepulchral monuments. Out of 29 sites considered, information is not available in respect of 13 sites regarding total number of burials. However, from the remaining 16 sites we have a total of more than 3654 burials. A total of 186 burials (and 3 non-sepulchral monuments) have been excavated from all these 29 sites. There were 19 burials which were previously disturbed (but have been excavated) and these are not considered in our analysis for want of primary information. Hence, information available from 186 burials forms the basis of our analysis.

Out of 186 excavated burials (Table 32), 32 did not contain any skeletal remains and were obviously symbolic burials. For 71 burials unfortunately, we do not have information regarding the human skeletal remains, as either they have not been studied or the skeletal remains were too fragmentary for analysis. So, from the remaining 83 burials we have a total of 184 individuals who have been represented in different types of burial, viz., single (where only a single individual is buried), double (where two individuals are buried together), and multiple (where more than two individuals are buried together) burials, Out of 29 sites mentioned earlier, only at 19 (see Table 33) this breakup can be observed. Of the 156 burials excavated at these 19 sites, where in all 184 individuals are represented, we have 40 (25.64%) single burials, 17 (10.4%) double burials, 26 (16.67%) multiple burials, and 22 (14.1%) symbolic burials (see also Fig. 7). There were 51 (32.69%) burials containing skeletal remains, but information is not available regarding the total number of individual/s buried in them and also age and sex of the individuals.

Sexwise and agewise distribution of the 184 individuals is given in Table 34 (see also Figs. 8 and 9). It is clear from the table that out of 184 individuals there are 27 (14.67%) males and 17 (9.24%) females and for the remaining 140 we have no information. The agewise[1] distribution of the individuals shows that infants are not represented in the burials. There are 11 (5.98%) children, 5 (2.72%) adolescents, 99 (53.8%) young adults and 2 (1.1%) middle aged/old adults. For 67 (36.41%) individuals information is not available in respect of their age.

The distribution pattern of single, double, multiple and symbolic burials at 29 Megalithic sites along with information on ascribed social dimensional category to which they belong and also the age and sex of the individuals is brought out in Table 35. The next table i.e., Table 36 shows the number of burials in each category (viz., single, double, multiple and symbolic) and sex and agewise breakup of individuals falling in the above mentioned categories. It isevident from the table that in single burials category 40 burials represent 40 individuals, 17 double burials represent 34 individuals and 26 burials represent 110 individuals in multiple burial category. There are 32 symbolic burials. There were also 71 burials containing skeletal remains but information is not available regarding the total number, age and sex of the individuals represented in them.

Of the 40 individuals representing 40 single burials (Table 36 and Fig. 11), 10 (25.0%) are males and 2 (5.0%) are females. For remaining 28 (70.0%) individuals information is not available. The agewise grouping (Table 36 and Fig. 10) shows that of these 40 individuals, 4 (10.0%) are children, 1 (2,5%) is adolescent and 26 (65.0%) are young adults. Infants and middle age/old adults are not found in this category and information is not available in the case of 9 (22.5%) individuals.

In double burials, out of 34 individuals which are represented in this category, 6 are males and 4 are females. And for the remaining 24 individuals information is not available regarding their sex. The age grouping shows that of the 34, there is one child, one middle aged/old adult and 20 young adults. For the remaining 12 individuals there is no information regarding their age.

As mentioned earlier, 26 burials represent a total of 110 individuals in multiple burial category. Of these 110 individuals, 11 are males and another 11 females, and the sex of remaining 88 individuals is not known. Out of these 110 individuals, there are 6 children, 4 adolescents, 53 young adults and one middle aged / old adult. Age of remaining 46 individuals is not known.

Table 37 shows the number of superordinate and subordinate burials of ascribed social dimension within each burial category. It also includes information regarding the sex and agewise distribution of individuals in the respective burial categories.

As can be observed from Table 37, out of 40 single burials 12 burials fall in superordinate category and 28 in subordinate category. Of the 12 superordinate burials represented by 12 individuals, there is one of a male and another of a female. Sex of the remaining 10 individuals is not known. Again of these 12 individuals, 10 are adults, one is adolescent and age of the remaining one individual is not known. Of the 28 subordinate burials (represented by 28 individuals) there are 9 males and 1 female. Sex of the remaining 18 individuals is not known. Of these 28 individuals, 4 are children and 16 are young adults. Age of the remaining 8 individuals is not known.

Of the 17 double burials, only one burial falls in the superordinate category and the rest (16) come under subordinate category. The lone double burial coming under superordinate category is represented by two individuals; both are adults but their sex is not known. Out of the 16 double burials belonging to subordinate category (represented by 32 individuals) 6 are male and 4 are females. Sex of the remaining 22 individuals is not known. However, the age grouping shows that there is one child, 18 young adults and one middle aged/old adult. Age of the rest 12 individuals is not known.

Out of a total of 26 multiple burials, only one could be ascribed to superordinate category and the rest (25) fall under subordinate category. The burial falling under superordinate category has three individuals represented in it. The age of only one individual could be known. It is of a young adult. Age of the remaining two individuals and sex of all the three is not known. Now the remaining 25 multiple burials which fall under subordinate category, are represented by a total of 107 individuals. Out of these 107 individuals, 11 are males and another 11 are females. Information regard-

---

Note : The standard anthropological age categorisation followed is as below:

<u>Between the age group of</u>

0-1 yr.	Infant
2 - 11 yrs.	Child
12-16 yrs.	Adolescent
17 - 35 yrs.	Young adult
36 - 46 yrs. &* above	Middle Aged/ Old Adult

ing the sex of remaining 85 individuals is not available. Age grouping of these 107 individuals shows that there are 6 children, 4 adolescents, 52 young adults and one middle aged/old adult. Information concerning the age of remaining 44 individuals is not available.

As mentioned earlier there are altogether 32 symbolic burials. Of these 32, 4 burials could be ascribed to superordinate category and 28 burials to subordinate category.

There are 71 burials which contained skeletal remains but unfortunately no information is available on this lot. Without a detailed osteological report of the interred skeletal remains, the study of such burials becomes meaningless. However, as is evident, quite a large number of burials were of this category. Therefore, we have considered these burials too in our analysis. In this group, there are 8 burials which fall in superordinate category and remaining 63 burials could be ascribed to subordinate category.

Now, we shall move to a detailed description of individual burials at different Megalithic sites, falling either in superordinate or subordinate category of ascribed social dimension. Depending on their burial type, i.e., single, double, multiple and symbolic, a detailed account of the type of material interments and functional subgrouping of artifacts along with information regarding the age and sex of the individual/s is provided in Tables 38 to 42.

Table 38 gives details on the single burials at different sites falling either in superordinate or subordinate category. As mentioned earlier a total of 12 single burials can be ascribed to superordinate category. Details regarding the age and sex of individuals found in this category has already been mentioned (cf. Table 35). In these 12 superordinate single burials more than 1055 artifacts were interred as grave goods. Of these, 130 artifacts could be ascribed to a technomic category, 310 artifacts to sociotechnic-A category, 48 artifacts to sociotechnic-B category and 3 artifacts to ideotechnic category.

The remaining 28 burials of single burial type which can be ascribed to subordinate category, contained more than 605 artifacts interred as burial goods. Of these, 20 artifacts could be ascribed to technomic category, 8 artifacts to sociotechnic-A category and 19 artifacts to sociotechnic-B category.

The distribution of artifacts in their functional subgrouping in single burials, according to different age- groups within respective ascribed social dimension, has been shown in Fig.12. In superordinate dimension an adolescent burial had 3.0 artifacts each in technomic and sociotechnic-A category, and 1.0 sociotechnic-B artifacts. There were no ideotechnic artifacts. In the same social dimension the adult group has per burial 12.4 technomic artifacts, 27.3 sociotechnic-A artifacts, 4.4 sociotechnic-B artifacts and 0.3 ideotechnic artifacts.

In the subordinate dimension of the above burial type, the child group has per burial 1.25 technomic artifacts, 2.75 sociotechnic-A artifacts, 0.5 sociotechnic-B artifacts. There were no ideotechnic artifacts. The adult group of this social dimension has 0.8 technomic artifacts, 0.06 sociotechnic-A artifacts and 0.9 sociotechnic-B artifacts per burial. This group did not contain any ideotechnic artifacts.

The sex wise distribution of single burials of superordinate and subordinate dimension along with their artifactual functional subgroupings is brought out in Fig.13. In superordinate dimension male group has 37.0 technomic artifacts, 34.0 sociotechnic-A artifacts, 12.0 sociotechnic-B artifacts and no ideotechnic artifacts. In the same social dimension female group has 3.0 technomic artifacts, 55.0 sociotechnic-A artifacts. Artifacts of sociotechnic-B and ideotechnic category could not be found in this group.

The male group of the subordinate dimension of the above burial type has 0.4 technomic artifacts, 0.1 sociotechnic-A artifacts and 0.5 sociotechnic-B artifacts per burial. No ideotechnic artifacts have been found in this group. The female group of this dimension contained only 1.0 sociotechnic-B artifacts and in remaining functional subgroups it has nil per burial.

Details on burials belonging to double burial type along with a statistical count of different types of material interred as burial goods (including their functional) subgrouping) and the ascribed social dimension of respective burials is brought out in Table 39. There is only one double burial which could be ascribed to superordinate category and it contained more than 40 artifacts as burial goods. Out of these 40 artifacts, 3 artifacts each belonged to technomic and sociotechnic-A categories and 2 artifacts to that of sociotechnic-B category.

These are 16 double burials falling in subordinate category and there is no need to recount here the age and sex of the individuals found in them as it has already been mentioned earlier. They had in them more than 722 artifacts as burial goods. The number of technomic, sociotechnic-A, sociotechnic-B and ideotechnic artifacts out of a total of 722 burial goods was 39, 25, 46 and 1, respectively.

Table 40 deals with multiple burials along with details on burial interments, their functional subgrouping, sex and age of the individuals found in these burials and the ascribed social dimension of the burials. Out of 26 multiple burials, only one could be ascribed to superordinate category and it contained a total of 163 artifacts as burial goods. Of these 163, 6 artifacts were of technomic category, 19 artifacts were of sociotechnic-A category and 10 artifacts were of sociotechnic-B category.

Twenty five multiple burials, ascribed to subordinate social dimension were having in them more than 516 artifacts as burial goods. Out of these 516 artifacts, 64 artifacts could be ascribed to technomic category, 24 artifacts to sociotechnic-A category, 31 artifacts to sociotechnic-B category and 3 artifacts to ideotechnic category.

There are 4 symbolic burials ascribed to superordinate category and 28 burials of subordinate category. Material- wise account of the burial interments and their functional subgroupings is brought out in Table 41. The number of artifacts interred as burial goods in 4 superordinate symbolic burials is more than 192. Out of these 192 artifacts, 45 artifacts were technomic items, 23 artifacts were sociotechnic-A category items and 18 artifacts were sociotechnic-B category items.

More than 486 artifacts had been interred as burial goods in 28 symbolic burials belonging to subordinate category. Out of these 486 artifacts, 49 artifacts could be ascribed to technomic category, 4 artifacts to sociotechnic-A category, 25 artifacts to sociotechnic-B category and one artifact to ideotechnic category.

Table 42 gives details on those burials wherein human skeletal remains have been reported but not studied. The table carries information on the number of burial interments of different material, their functional subgrouping and ascribed social dimension of these burials. Out of a total of 71 burials, 8 burials could be ascribed to superordinate category. More than 341 artifacts were found interred in these 8 burials as burial goods. Of these 341 artifacts, 61 were technomic artifacts, 63 were sociotechnic-A artifacts and 25 were sociotechnic-B artifacts.

More than 1269 artifacts were found to be interred as burial goods in 63 subordinate burials of this group. Out of these 1269 artifacts, 108 artifacts were of technomic category, 57 artifacts of sociotechnic-A category, 61 artifacts of sociotechnic-B category and one of ideotechnic category.

Fig. 14 provides an overall picture of the distribution of technomic, sociotechnic and ideotechnic artifacts burial typewise and social dimension categorywise.

There are 12 single burials of superordinate dimension. They contain a total of 130 technomic artifacts, 310 sociotechnic-A artifacts, 48 sociotechnic-B artifacts and 3 ideotechnic artifacts. The above figures show that per burial it comes to 10.8 technomic artifacts, 25.8 sociotechnic-A artifacts, 4.0 sociotechnic-B artifacts and 0.2 ideotechnic artifacts.

The total number of subordinate burials of the above burial type in 28. From them 20 technomic, 8 sociotechnic-A, 19 sociotechnic-B artifacts have been reported. The did not contain any ideotechnic artifacts. Per burial it comes to be 0.7 technomic artifacts, 0.2 sociotechnic-A artifacts and 0.6 sociotechnic-B artifacts. No ideotechnic artifacts were found in this group.

There is one double burial of superordinate dimension. The number of technomic, sociotechnic-A, sociotechnic-B artifacts found in it were, 3, 3 and 2 respectively. It did not have any ideotechnic items. Per burial it comes to the same, i.e., 3.0 technomic artifacts, 3.0 sociotechnic-A artifacts and 2.0 sociotechnic-B artifacts.

There are altogether 16 double burials of subordinate dimension. A total of 39 technomic artifacts, 25 sociotechnic-A artifacts, 46 sociotechnic-B artifacts and 1 ideotechnic artifact were found in these 16 burials. So, per burial the number of technomic, sociotechnic-A, sociotechnic-B and ideotechnic artifacts comes to be 2.4, 1.5, 2.8 and 0.06, respectively.

Of the 26 multiple burials, only one burial could be ascribed to superordinate dimension. This burial contains 6 technomic artifacts, 19 sociotechnic-A artifacts and 10 sociotechnic-B artifacts. No ideotechnic artifacts were found in this burial. As it is obvious, per burial it comes to the same i.e., 6.0 technomic artifacts, 19.0 sociotechnic-A artifacts and 10 .0 sociotechnic-B artifacts.

From the remaining 25 burials of the subordinate dimension of the above burial type, a total of 64 technomic artifacts, 24 sociotechnic-A artifacts, 31 sociotechnic-B artifacts and 3 ideotechnic artifacts could be found. The number of technomic, sociotechnic-A, sociotechnic-B and ideotechnic artifacts per burial of this category comes to be 2.5, 0.9, 1.2 and 0.1, respectively.

As mentioned earlier, altogether there are 32 symbolic burials. Of these, 4 burials could be ascribed to superordinate dimension. These four burials yielded a total of 45 technomic artifacts, 23 sociotechnic-A artifacts and 18 sociotechnic-B artifacts. No ideotechnic artifacts were recovered from these burials. So, per burial there were 11.2 technomic artifacts, 5.7 sociotechnic-A artifacts and 4.5 sociotechnic-B artifacts.

In the subordinate dimension of the above burial type there are 28 burials. They contain in them a total of 49 technomic artifacts, 4 sociotechnic-A artifacts, 25 sociotechnic-B artifacts and 1 ideotechnic artifact. So, per burial the number of technomic artifacts is 1.7, 0.1 of sociotechnic-A artifacts, 0.8 of sociotechnic-B artifact and 0.03 of ideotechnic artifacts.

A clear-cut differentiation in artifactual associations in the burials of superordinate and subordinate dimension can be seen in Tables 4.1 to 4.29. Out of a total of 186 burials considered for our analysis 26 burials could be ascribed to superordinate dimension and remaining 160 to that of subordinate dimension.

The 26 burials of superordinate dimension represent 17 individuals. From these 26 burials a total of 245 technomic artifacts, 418 sociotechnic-A artifacts, 103 sociotechnic-B artifacts and 3 ideotechnic artifacts could be recovered. In this social dimension per burial the amount of technomic artifacts is 9.4, that of sociotechnic-A artifacts is 16.0, for sociotechnic-B artifacts it is 3.9 and for ideotechnic artifacts 0.1.

Out of 160 burials of subordinate dimension, the number of individuals represented in 167. These burials contain a total of 280 technomic artifacts, 118 sociotechnic-A artifacts, 182 sociotechnic-B artifacts and 6 ideotechnic artifacts. So, per burial it comes to be 1.7 technomic artifacts, 0.7 sociotechnic-A artifacts, 1.1 sociotechnic-B artifacts and 0.03 ideotechnic artifacts.

The foregoing analysis clearly brings out two facts: first, that significant differences exist in the funerary monuments of this period and in their artifactual associations; and secondly, funerary monuments were used as symbolic carriers of power and social differentiation.

Now, reverting to an important aspect of our study that whether the mortuary data available for this period correlate with the criteria that have been set for observing the mortuary differentiation in the superordinate and subordinate social dimensions of a 'Ranked' society. We shall take up one by one the criteria laid down by Peebles and Kus (1977 : 431-433) for the above mentioned social dimensions and see whether our data fulfills these criteria:

Superordinate Dimension

Criteria 1 : Some infants, some children, and some adults will be found in every scale category except the paramount category.

Our data show (see Table 37) that of the 26 burials (wherein 17 individuals are represented) belonging to the above social dimension there was only one adolescent and the remaining were adults. No infants were reported from any of these burials.

Criteria 2: The apical class will contain only adults, and probably only adult males.

In very clear terms this aspect has been reflected in our data. Of the 17 individuals represented in 26 burials, 13 were adults and one is an adolescent. Although, we expected more number of males, unfortunately, information regarding the sex of 15 individuals is not available. However, of the two individuals whose sex is known, one is male and the other a female. We hope, if large samples are taken up for anthropological analysis, it will most likely show that males outnumber females in significant proportion in this category. The significance of a female burial in this social dimension will be explained at a later stage.

Criteria 3 : Some infants and children will have graeter amounts of energy expended in their treatment than some men.

This criteria could not be applied, as in our data infant and child burials were not noticed.

Criteria 4 : The numbers of burials in each scale category will make markedly decrease as one goes higher on the scale thereby reflecting the rank pyramid.

This aspect is clearly brought out in Table 37. Out of 40 single burials, 12 are of superordinate dimension. In double burials out of 17, only one burial comes under this dimension, and so is the case with multiple burials where out of 26 burials only one burial is of superordinate dimension. Even in symbolic burials (4 superordinate burials out of 32) this could be noticed. The overall picture of the mortuary data from 186 burials clearly shows that only 26 burials fall under superordinate dimension and the remaining 160 belong to subordinate dimension thereby reflecting the rank pyramid.

Subordinate Dimension

Criteria 1 : As the chronological age of the individual buried increases, so will be energy extended in that individual' burial.

On analysis of associated artifacts in child, adolescent, young adult and middle age/old adult burials shows significant variations in the number of technomic, sociotechnic-A, sociotechnic-B and ideotechnic category artifacts (Tables 38, 39 and 40) interred as burial inclusions. The following table brings out this aspect.

Age group	No. of artifacts (per burial)			
	Technomic	Socio-technic-A	Socio-technic-B	Ideo-technic-C
Child	0.8	0.5	0.5	0.02
Adolescent	1.3	0.4	0.2	-
Young Adult	1.7	0.7	1.4	0.04
Middle Aged/ Old Adult	-	11.0	3.0	

An increase in the associated artifacts of technomic, sociotechnic-A and sociotechnic-B significance according to the chronological age of the individual is clearly evident from the above table. Even where the difference in the number of associated artifacts is less (e.g., in sociotechnic-A and B category of child and adolescent group) it is negligible from statistical count. What is more important is that the number of sociotechnic artifacts show a marked increase from child age group to that of middle aged/ old adult group. This shows differences in the energy expenditure in the burials of different age groups.

Criteria 2 : Children and infants will have some items as grave goods that will not be shared by adults; women will have some items as grave goods not shared by men.

It was difficult to securely substantiate the above criteria from the available data from megalithic burials. The differences in the different burial goods associated with child/adolescent burials (occurring singly or in association with skeletons of other age groups) and those of other age groups are sporadic and do not occur as a general rule. However , a few occurrences are noteworthy. Occurrence of the skeletal remains of a calf and a bovine (in Br. No. XII at Nagarjunakonda), of ram/goat (in Br. No. C I at Satanikota and also in some of the child/adolescent burials at Ramapuram); some burial goods such as spherical stone balls (in Br. Pit 30 at Maski), a thin, shallow dish like object (of iron), a large fragmentary ring with two nails affixed (of iron) (in Br. No. VII at Brahmagiri, a copper jingle (in Br. No.9 at Mahurjhari), a unique fusiform sarcophagus (of T.C.), a spatula (of iron), a cable type nail (of iron) rivetted to a copper ring (in Br. II at Peddamarur), miniature vases (in Br. No. B XVII at Satanikota), copper necklaces (in Br. No. 1 at Raipur-Hingna), a pottery disc (hopscotch ?) (in Br. No. C I at Satanikota) merit our attention.

Some of the female burials (occurring singly or in association with male skeletons) have yielded a few interesting objects. The occurrence of artifacts like the long digging implements (crowbars ?) (of iron), spiral earrings (of gold), small spacers (of silver) (in Br. No. XIV at Nagarjunakonda), a circular earthen stand with rows of triangular and rectangular perforations and a large sized dish fitted to it with a funnel-shaped lid having a hollow knobbed ring terminal (in Br. No. III at Yelleswaram), whorl-beads (in Br. No. 2 at Sanur) and copper bangles (in Br. No. 8 at Mahurjhari) are noteworthy.

At the moment we can not say how valid is this criterion in our context, but this aspect needs to be probed further with large sample data coming either from a single site or from a cluster of closely knit sites.

Criteria 3 : Energy expended in the lowest level of the superordinate dimension will be greater than that expended in the highest level of subordinate dimension.

In our case this criterion could not be applied at each site level as the number of excavated burials and the sample data available are very meagre compared to the total number of burials occurring at each site. So, instead of skipping this criterion for want of data, if we consider the differences evidenced in the artifactual associations as a major signifier of energy expenditure in burials of both superordinate and subordinate dimension, it seems to be more useful. Our analysis of the total material assemblage (see Fig. 15) clearly shows that the energy expended in the superordinate burials in the form of technomic artifacts (per burial 9.4), sociotechnic-A artifacts (per burial 16.0), sociotechnic-B artifacts (per burial 3.9) and ideotechnic artifacts (per burial 0.1) is significantly more as against the burials of subordinate dimension where it is 1.7 (per burial) in case of technomic artifacts, 0.7 (per burial) in case of sociotechnic-A artifacts, 1.1 (per burial) in case of sociotechnic-B artifacts and 0.03 (per burial) in case of ideotechnic artifacts.

Criteria 4 : The number of individuals in each scale category of the subordinate dimension should reflect the age and sex pyramid of the population through time.

Out of 186 burials considered for the present analysis, 160 burials could be classed as those belonging to subordinate category of social dimension. Leaving aside 28 symbolic burials and 63 burials containing skeletal remains but regarding which anthropological information is not available, 69 burials of this category represent a total of 167 individuals (refer to Table 37). Information regarding the sex of the individuals is available in 42 cases and age of the individuals in 103 cases. out of 167 individuals found in this social dimension 26 are males, 16 are females and for remaining 125 individuals information is not available. Again, the agewise breakup of 167 individuals shows that of these 86 are young adults, 11 are children, 4 are adolescents and 2 middle aged/old adults. The above figures indicate that the high figures available for males and young adults in the sex and age categories of subordinate population indeed reflect the social preferences and priorities in according mortuary treatment to certain specific age and sex groups.

Some Archaeological Correlates Of Ranked Societies

In the foregoing pages we have already seen that the first archaeological correlate of ranked societies proposed by Peebles and Kus (1977 : 431) i.e., "there should be clear evidence of nonvolitional, ascribed ranking of persons" is explicitly tested for our mortuary data and results are positive.

There are four more archaeological correlates which Peebles and Kus (1977 : 431-433) have proposed as major areas of variability distinctive of ranked societies. These archaeological correlates are as follows:

Second : There should be a hierarchy of settlement types and sizes, and the position of settlements in hierarchy should reflect their position in the regulatory and ritual net-work.

Third : All other things being equal, settlements should be located in areas which assure a high degree of local subsistence sufficiency.

Fourth: There should be evidence of organized productive activities which transcend the basic household group.

Fifth : There should be a correlation between those elements of the cultural system's environment which are of a frequency, amplitude and duration to be dealt with but which are least predictable and evidence of society-wide organizational activity to buffer or otherwise with these perturbations.

We shall test the above propositions one by one against the data available for Megalithic period and find out whether our hypothesis is valid or not.

Of the reported 1933 Megalithic sites, 399 sites are settlement sites. Of these information is available only for 116 sites. Of these information is available only for 116 sites regarding the size of the settlements. As mentioned elsewhere (Moorti, 1989: 95-96) the task of building a site typology for Megalithic sites, suffers from serious limitations because of totally inadequate data. However, analysis of whatever meagre information we have shown that there are atleast 26 larger settlements (which are above 5 ha.) and 90 smaller settlements (which are below 5 ha. in extent) (Moorti, 1989: Table 2.7). Since detailed information is available regarding the size of settlements atleast for 54 sites, they can be categorized as given below:

Size of settlements	No. of settlements
Below 1 ha.	9
1 - 1.99 ha.	7
2 - 2.99 ha.	3
3 - 3.99 ha.	3
4 - 4.99 ha.	5
5 - 5.99 ha.	2
6 - 6.99 ha.	1
7 - 7.99 ha.	1
Above 8 ha.	23

However, the figures indicated above, against extent of each settlement category should not be considered as a general patterning of settlement sizes. Although a hierarchy of settlement types and sizes is clearly evident, the position of these settlements in the hierarchy and their role in the regulatory and ritual net-work, at the moment is not clear. This is mainly because no detailed studies have been carried out on the settlement pattern of these sites. However, a preliminary analysis has shown (Moorti, 1989:93-95) that most of the larger settlements (some of them in all probability serving as regional centres) was situated on the known major trade and communication routes of early historic India. This may be just a small clue, but it does open up an avenue to understand the functional role of these settlement in the regulatory and ritual net-work. However, what is more important is that disparity in the type and size of settlements does occur and the locational significance of larger settlements itself fulfils (howsoever partial it may seem) the second parameter of ranked societies.

Now, coming to the third parameter that the settlements should be located in areas which assure a high degree of local subsistence sufficiency is very well brought out in the study done by the author on the locational analysis and subsistence strategies (Moorti, 1989: Table 2.1, 3.3 and 3.1). The concentration of maximum number of Megalithic sites in the regions of Wardha-Penganga plain Waingana basin, Middle Krishna valley, Rayalaseema plateau, Andhra Ghats, south, Dharwad plateau, Mysore region, Mattur-vellore region, coimbatore uplands, the Palar-Ponnaiyar basin, the Vaigai- Tambraparani basin, South Malabar, Telagana peneplain, Andhra Ghats north, Hyderabad plateau, Rayalaseema peneplain, Gulbarga plain, Bijapur region, shows their location in varied ecozones. Many of these zones form agriculturally fertile areas. The concentration of Megalithic sites in zones having black soil, red sandyloamy soil, loamy soil, loamy or clayey black soil, ferruginous sandy soil, alluvial rendzinas, black-brown soil on trap, clay-loamy alluvial soil covers and in rainfall zones ranging from 600-1500 mm clearly indicates their adaptive mature to varied environments.

It is often emphasized that the evidence of organised activities transcending the basic household group can be obtained atleast from two areas which are archaeologically recognisable. The first one is in the construction of monuments, which on account of their size and complexity, require planning and a labour force, and second in the organised part-time rudimentary craft specialisation. The occurrence of a large number of commemorative/memorial monuments like stone alignments, avenues, menhirs or for that matter the burials themselves strongly indicate that they were the products of intercommunity cooperation. Although studies estimating number of man-hours required to construct such monuments have not been conducted in India, yet if this aspect is observed in the background of contemporary tribal practice of erecting megaliths, it clearly highlights both detailed planning and intercommunity cooperation.

Our analysis of the distribution of Megalithic sites in relation to metal and mineral resources has shown that only 40% of these are located in resource zones and the remaining 60% of the sites are located where there are no mineral resources in the vicinity. Secondly, not an all the settlement sites did we notice activities connected with smithery. Of the 399 settlement sites reported so far, only at 85 sites one notices archaeological traces of these productive activities (Moorti, 1989: Table 2.3). However, at present it is not clear how these activities were organised; whether at interhousehold level or on intercommunity basis.

Another area that we need to consider here is the warfare. The occurrence of a large number of socio-technic-B artifacts, i.e., weapons in the material repertoire of this period is not without significance. Out of a total 1896 burials considered for analysis, 92 burials have yielded weapons in varying quantities. From these 92 burials 285 weapons were recovered. Warfare appears to have increased during this period probably to control resource-rich zones if large aggregation of cemetery in some of these resource rich zones (e.g., in Wainganga basin, Raichur region, Middle Krishna Valley, Kolar region and Coimbatore uplands) is any indication.

Unfortunately, as no large-scale horizontal excavations have been conducted to understand the lay-out of both residential and defensive structures it is not possible to substantiate the present point further. It is commonly held that in sharp contrast to egalitarian systems, ranked institutions are more successfully expansionist, both territorially and demographically. An increase in the number of settlement and cemetery sites from the preceding Neolithic/Chalcolithic phases very much seems to indicate this development. These are only a few of evidences of society's organizational activity. However, if aspects like degree of food production and its redistribution, defence organization and intersocietal exchange net-work are studied with more sound data, it is likely to reveal many interesting aspects of adaptive strategies (both to environmental and cultural) of the Megalithic society.

The foregoing discussion attempts to demonstrate that mortuary differentiation is patterned and its elements are integrated with other aspects of the socio-cultural system. Granted the assumption that an individual's *social persona* (the sum of the statuses and roles played) in life is reflected in the mortuary ritual, that it i s clear from the above discussion that the prehistoric Megalithic population of south India was organised into a ranked society.

LIST OF ABBREVIATIONS

A(s)	Adult (s)
Ad	(Adolescent)
AI	Ancient India
Br (s)	Burial (s)
c.	circa
C	Child/Young
circ.	circumference
Cl.	Cluster
dia.	diameter
exc.	excavation/excavated
F	Female
Hab.	Habitation
Hab.-cum-Br.	Habitation-cum-burial
IAR	*Indian Archaeology-A Review*
INA	Data/Information Not Available
Loc.	Locality
M	Male
M. Adult	Mature Adult
Meg.	Megalith
N.A.P.	Not Applicable
N.A.V.	Data Not Available
O	Old
Pd.	Period
PGW	Painted Grey Ware
Rect.	Rectangular platform
S. Adult	Sub-adult
Sar.	Sarcophagus
Semiprec. stone	Semiprecious stone (s)
sk.	skeletal

T.C.	Terracotta
Y. Adult	Young Adult
*	Disturbed burial
+	Denotes the presence of a specified characteristic or trait/ item
-	Denotes the absence of a specified characteristic of trait/item
>	greater than/above
<	less than/ below

REFERENCES

Aiyappan, A. 1940-41. "Rude Stone Monuments of the Perumal Hills, Kodaikanal", *Quarterly Journal of the Mythic Society* XXXI (Krishnaraja Memorial Number): 373-397.

Alekshin, V.A., 1983. "Burial Customs as an Archaeological source", *Current Anthropology* 24(2) : 137-150.

Alur, K.R., 1979. "Animal Remains from Yelleswaram", *Andhra Pradesh Journal of Archaeology* 1 (2): 127-134.

Subrahmanyam, R. (ed.) 1975. "Skeletal Remains" In *Nagarjunakenda* (1954-60), New Delhi: *Memoirs of the Arch. Surv.* of India, No. 75, pp. 185-195.

Badam, G.L. 1982. "Animal Remains from Naikund with special Reference to Domestication", In *Excavations at Naikund 1978-80*, Deo, S.B. and A.P. Jamkhedkar, Bombay and Deccan College, Pune, Appendix VII, pp. 70-90.

Banerjee, N.R. and K.V. Soundara Rajan, 1959. "Sanur 1950- 1952: A Megalithic site in District Chingleput" *Ancient India* 15: 4-42.

Binford, L.R., 1962. "Archaeology As Anthropology", *American Antiquity* 28(2) : 217-225.

Binford, L.R., 1972. "Mortuary practices: Their study and their potential" In *An Archaeological Perspective*, Binford, L.R., New York: Seminar press, pp. 208-243.

Bose, H.K., 1959. "Preliminary Report on Skeletal Remains", In "Sanur - 1950 to 1952. A Megalithic site in District Chingleput", *Ancient India* 15: 40-42.

Branfill, B.R., 1881. "On the Savandurga Rude Stone Cemetery, Central Maisur", *Indian Antiquary* X : 1-12.

Brown, J.A., 1981. "The search for rank in prehistoric burials", In *The Archaeology of Death*, Chapman, R., I. Kinnes and K. Randsborg (eds.) New York: Cambridge Univ. Press, pp. 25-38.

Chapman, R.W., 1977. "Burial Practices: An Area of Mutual Interest", In *Archaeology and Anthropology: Areas of Mutual Interest*, Spriggs,M. (ed.), BAR Supplementary Series 19, Oxford: British Archaeological Reports, p. 19-33.

Deo, S.B., 1970. "*Excavations at Takalghat and Khapa (1968-69)*, Nagpur: Nagpur Univ.

Deo, S.B., 1973. "*Mahurjhari Excavation (1970-72)*, Nagpur: Nagpur University.

Deo, S.B. and A.P. Jamkhedkar, 1982. *Excavations at Naikund (1978-80)*, Bombay : Department of Archaeology and Museums.

Dhavalikar, M.K. and K.K. Subbayya, 1976. "Excavations at Heggadahalli: A Megalithic site in Coorg", *Journal of Andhra Historical Research Society* XXXV: 331-338.

Doran, J. 1972. "Computer models as tools for archaeological hypothesis formation", In *Models in Archaeology*, Clarke, D.L. (ed.), London: Methuen, pp. 425-452.

Ghosh, N.C., 1986. "*Excavations at Satanikota (1977-80)*, New Delhi: *Memoirs of the Archaeological Survey of India No.82.*

Gupta, P. and P.C. Dutta, 1962. "Human Remains excavated from Megaliths at Yelleswaram (Andhra Pradesh)", *Man in India* 42: 19-34.

Hodson, F.R. 1977. "Quantifying Hallstatt: Some initial results", *American Antiquity* 42: 394-412.

Kendall, D.G., 1971. "Seriation from abundance matrices", In *Mathematics in the Archaeological and Historical Sciences*, Hodson, F.R., D.G. Kendall and P. Tautu (eds.), Edinburgh: Edinburgh University Press, pp. 215-252.

Kennedy, K.A.R., C. Burrow and J.R. Lukacs, 1982. "Note on the Human skeletal specimen from Naikund". In *Excavtions at Naikund* (1978-80), Deo, S.B. and A.P. Jamkhedkar, Bombay: Dept. of Arch. & Museums, Appendix I, pp. 49-51.

Khan, M.A.W., 1963. "*A Monograph on Yeleswaram Excavations*, Hyderabad: Andhra Pradesh Archaeological Series No. 14.

Krishnasastry, V.V., 1983. *The Protoand Early Historical Cultures of Andhra Pradesh*, Hyderabad: Govt. of Andhra Pradesh.

Kristiansen, K., 1984: "Ideology and Material Culture: An Archaeological Perspective", In *Marxist Perspectives in Archaeology*, Spriggs M. (ed.), Cambridge: Cambrdige Univ. Press, pp. 72-100.

Mehta, R.N. and K.M. George, 1978. "*Megalithis at Machad and Pazhayannur, Talppally Taluka, Trichur District, Kerala, State*, Baroda: M.S. University Series No.15.

Moorti, U.S., 1989. "*Megalithic Culture of South India: Socio-Economic-Perspectives*, unpublished Ph.D. thesis, Poona: University of Poona.

Nagaraja Rao, M.S. 1985: "The Earliest Iron Age Graves in Karnataka", In *Recent Advances in Indo-Pacific Prehistory*, Misra, V.N. and P. Bellwood (eds.), New Delhi: Oxford & IBH Pub. Co., pp 469-470.

Nath, B., 1957. "Animal Remains from Maski", *Ancient India* 13: 121-129.

Nath, B. 1968. "Advances in the study of Prehistoric and Ancident Animal Remains in India: A Review", *Records of the Zoological Survey of India* 61 (1 & 2) : 1-63.

O'Shea, J.M., 1984. *Mortuary Variability: An Archaeological Investigation*, London: Academic Press.

Pal, A., 1986. "Skeletal Remains", In *Excavations at Satanikota (1977-80)*, Ghosh, N.C., New Delhi: *Memoirs of the Archaeological Survey of India No.82*, pp. 51-60.

Peebles, C.S. 1971. "Moundville and surrounding sites: Some structural considerations of mortuary practices", In *Approaches to the social Dimensions of Mortuary Practices*, Brown, J.A. (ed.), *Memoirs of the Society for American Archeology* 25· 69-91.

Peebles, C.S. and S.M. Kus, 1977. "Some Archaeological Correlates of Ranked Societies", *American Antiquity* 42: 421-448.

Rao, V.V., 1970. "Skeletal Remains from Takalghat and Khapa Excavations", In *Excavations at Takalghat and Khapa (1968- 69)*, Deo, S.B., Nagpur: Nagpur Univ., Appendix I, pp. 60-77.

Rao, V.V., 1973. "Skeletral Remains from Mahurjhari", In *Mahurjhari Excavation (1970-72)*, Deo, S.B.. Nagpur: Nagpur Univ., Appendix 1, pp. 63-76.

Randsborg, K.,1973. "Wealth and Social Structure as reflected in Bronze Age Burials - A Quantitative Approach", In *The Explanation of Culture Change - Models in Prehistory*, Renfrew, C. (ed.), London: Duckworth, pp. 565-570.

Randsborg, K., 1975. "Population and Social Variation in Early Bronze Age Denmark: A Systemic Approach", In *Population, Ecology and Social Evolution*, Polgar, S.(ed.), Hague: Mouton Pub., pp. 139-166.

Rea, A. 1902-03. "Prehistoric Antiquities in Tinnevelly", *Annual Report of the Archaeological Survey of India for the year 1902-03*: 111-143.

Rea, A. 1915. "*Catalogue of the Prehistoric Antiquities from Adichanallur and Perumbair*, Madras: Government Press.

Renfrew, C., 1973. "Mounuments, Mobilisation and social Organisation in Neolithic Wessex", In *The Explanation of Culture Change: Models in Prehitory*, Renfrew, c. (ed.), London: Duckworth, pp. 539-558.

Richards, F.J. 1924. "Note on some Iron Age Graves at Odugattur, North Arcot District, South India", *Journal of Royal Anthropological Institute of Great Britain and Ireland* 54: 157-165.

Sarkar, S.S., 1972. "*Ancient Races of the Deccan*, New Delhi: Munshiram Manoharlal.

Saxe, A., 1970. "*Social Dimensions of Mortuary Practices*, Ph.D. dissertation, Univ. of Michigan, Ann Arbar: Univ. Microfilms.

Sears, W.H., 1961. "The Study of Social and Religious systems in North American Archaeology", *Current Anthropology* 2: 223- 246.

Seshadri, M., 1960. "*Report on the Jadigenahalli Megalithic Excavations for the year 1957*. Mysore Dept. of Archaeology, Govt. of Mysore.

Shennan, S., 1975. "The Social Organisation at Branc", *Antiquity*, 49: 279-288.

Sjogren, K.G., 1986. "Kinship Labour and Land in Neolithic South West Sweden: Social Aspects of Megalithic Graves", .pa

Subbayya, K.K., 1972. *Archaeology of Coorg with Special Reference to Megaliths*, Unpublished Ph.D. thesis, Univ. of Poona, Pune.

Subrahmanyam, R., 1975. *Nagarjunakonda (1954-60), Memoirs of the Archaeological Survey of India No. 75*, New Delhi.

Sundara, A., 1969-70. "A New Type of Neolithic Burial in Terdal, Mysore State", *Puratattva* 3: 23-33.

Sundara, A., 1975. *The Early Chamber Tombs of South India - A Study of the Iron Age Megalithic Monuments of North Karnataka*, Delhi.

Suryanarayana Raju, J., 1982. "Excavtions at uppalapadu, District Mahbubnagar", In *Annual Report of the Dept. of Archaeolgoy and Museums for the year 1977-78*. Govt. of Andhra Pradesh, pp. 6-8.

Tainter, J.A., 1975. "Social inference and mortury practices: An experiment in numerical classification", *World Archaeology* 7(1) : 1-15.

Tainter, J.A. 1977. "Modeling change in prehistoric social systems", In *For theory building in Archaeology*. Binford, L. (ed.) New York: Academic Press, pp. 327-351.

Tainter, J. and R. Cordy, 1977. "An archaeolgical analysis of social ranking and residence groups in prehistoric Hawaii", *World Archaeology* 9: 94-112.

Taylor, M., 1851. "Ancient Remains at the village of Jiwargi, near Ferozabad on the Bhima", *Journal of the Bombay Branch of the Royal Asiatic Society* III (2) 179-193.

Taylor, M., 1953. "Notices of Cromlechs, Cairn and other Ancient Scytho-Druidical Remains in the principality of Shorapur", *Journal of the Bombay Branch of the Royal Asiatic Society* IV: 380-429.

Taylor, M., 1862. "Descrition of Cairns, Cromlechs, Kistvaens and other Celtic, Druidical or Scythian Monuments in Dekhan", *Transactions of the Royal Irish Academy, Antiquities*, XXIV (3): 329-362.

Thapar, B.K. 1957. "Maski 1954 - A Chalcolithic site of the Southern Deccan", *Ancient India* 13: 4-142.

Van de Velde, P., 1979. "The Social anthropology of a Neolithic cemetery in the Netherlands", *Current Anthropology* 20: 37-58.

Walimbe, S.R., 1989. "Human Skeletal Remains from Megalithic Vidarbha", *Puratattva* 18: 61-71.

Wheeler, R.E.M., 1948. "Brahmagiri and Chandravalli 1947: Megalithic and other cultures in the Chitaldrug District, Mysore State", *Ancient India* 4: 181-308.

Table 4.1 : Technomic and sociotechnic artifacts with respect to social dimension of the individual(s) buried at Khairwada

Site : KHAIRWADA
Physical zone : Wardha-Penganga plain (040102)

Total no. of burials : 1496
No. of burials excavated : 6

Burial no.	Burial type	Size	Total no. of indivi-duals	Sex	Age	Total no. of artifacts							Technomic artifacts	Sociotechnic artifacts		Ascribed social dimension	
						Pott-ery	Metal	Stone	Semi-prec. stones	T.C.	Bone	Shell		A	B	Super-ordinate	Sub-ordinate
1 (Loc.I)	Pit Circle	INA	1	Male(?)	Adult	INA	1	-	-	-	-	1	-	Horse	-	-	Yes
2	Pit Circle	INA	1	INA	Adult (25 yrs)	INA	36+	-	8	-	-	-	Axe(2), Adze(4), Chisel(3)	Horse; Horse trappings of iron (2), Gold ring, Copper bowl (2)	Spearhead (3), Arrowhead, Dagger, Spike(2)	Yes	-
3	Pit Circle	INA	?	INA	INA	INA	18+	-	-	-	-	-	Adze(6), Point(2)	Horse trappings of iron (2), Copper pot	-	-	Yes
1 (Loc.II)	Pit Circle	INA	1	INA	Adult	INA	8	-	1	-	-	-	Adze(4)	-	-	-	Yes
1 (Loc.III)	Pit Circle	INA	1	INA	Adult	INA	17+	-	5	-	-	-	Adze(4) Chisel	Horse; Gold ring, Piece of gold chain	Arrowhead	Yes	-
3	Pit Circle	INA	?	INA	INA	INA	2+	-	-	-	-	-	Adze	-	-	-	Yes

Table 2 : Technomic and sociotechnic artifacts with respect to social dimension of the individual(s) buried at Bhagi Mahari

Site : BHAGI MAHARI (Also Bhagi Mohari) Total no. of burials : >70

Physical zone : Wainganga basin or Nagpur plain (040201) No. of burials excavated : 5

Burial no.	Burial type	Size	Total no. of individuals	Sex	Age	Total no. of artifacts: Pottery	Metal	Stone	Semi-prec. stones	T.C.	Bone	Shell	Technomic artifacts	Sociotechnic artifacts: A	B	Ascribed social dimension: Super-ordinate	Sub-ordinate
1	Chamber burial	INA	?	INA	INA	INA	92+	2	37	1	-	-	Axe (8), Adze (10), Chisel (13), Hoe, Sickle	Horse (?)	Spike (4), Dagger, Spear	Yes	-
2	Pit burial	INA	?	INA	INA	INA	29	-	2	-	-	-	Axe (6), Adze (4), Chisel (3)	Horse (?)	Spearhead (2), Spike, Dagger	-	Yes
3	Pit burial	INA	?	INA	INA	INA	38+	-	1	-	-	-	Adze (9)	Horse (?); Gold spiral ring, Gold ring	Dagger (2), Spike (5)	Yes	-
4	Pit burial	INA	?	INA	INA	INA	3+	-	-	-	-	-	Adze	-	-	-	Yes
5	Pit burial	INA	?	INA	INA	INA	3	-	-	1	-	-	Adze	-	Spearhead	-	Yes

Table 3 : Technomic and sociotechnic artifacts with respect to social dimension of the individual(s) buried at Borgaon Khurd

Site : BORGAON KHURD Total no. of burials : 48

Physical zone : Wainganga basin or Nagpur plain (040201) No. of burials excavated : 4

Burial no.	Burial type	Size	Total no. of individuals	Sex	Age	Total no. of artifacts: Pottery	Metal	Stone	Semi-prec. stones	T.C.	Bone	Shell	Technomic artifacts	Sociotechnic artifacts: A	B	Ascribed social dimension: Super-ordinate	Sub-ordinate
3	Pit Circle	INA	1	INA	Adult	INA	25	2	-	-	-	-	Axe (6), Hoe (2)	Horse; Gold Ring (2)	-	Yes	-
7	Pit Circle	INA	1	INA	Child (10 yrs)	INA	+	-	243	-	-	-	-	-	-	-	Yes
35	Pit Circle	INA	-	-	-	INA	44+	2	-	-	-	-	Axe (5), Adze (5), Chisel (5), Hoe	Horse trapping (1), Copper bowl, Bowl with parrot motif, Dish (2)	Spike (2) Arrowhead, Trident, Spearhead	Yes	-
36	Pit Circle	INA	?	INA	INA	INA	12	-	-	-	-	-	Axe (3), Adze (4), Chisel (2), Sickle	Copper bowl, Lid with a finial of peacock motif	-	-	Yes

Table 4 : Technomic and sociotechnic artifacts with respect to social dimension of the individual(s) buried at Naikund

Site : NAIKUND

Physical zone : Wainganga basin or Nagpur plain (040201)

Total no. of burials : 70

No. of burials excavated : 6

Burial no.	Burial type	Size	Total no. of individuals	Sex	Age	Total no. of artifacts							Technomic artifacts	Sociotechnic artifacts		Ascribed social dimension	
						Pottery	Metal	Stone	Semi-prec. Stones	T.C.	Bone	Shell		A	B	Super-ordinate	Sub-ordinate
3 (Loc.I)	Pit Circle	12.80m dia.	?	INA	INA	22	6	-	-	-	-	-	Axe, Adze Chisel, Hoe	Horse; Small strips of gold leaf	Dagger	Yes	-
7	Pit Circle	21.5m dia.	?	INA	INA	30	21+	-	-	-	-	-	Axe (3)	Horse; Copper bowl (3), Lipped bowl, Cup with conical bottom & side handle, Dish, Pots (2), Lid with a finial of four birds, Lid with a finial of bud, Horse ornament pieces (?) (3), Spiral ornament of gold wire	-	Yes	-
8	Pit Circle	9.10m dia.	?	INA	INA	30	2+	-	-	-	-	-	-	Horse; Copper pot, Bird finials	-	-	Yes
1 (Loc.II)	Pit Circle	13.50m dia.	?	INA	INA	37	12	-	-	-	-	-	Axe (2), Adze, Chisel (2)	Horse; Copper dish, Lid with a bird finial, Horse ornament	Dagger (?), Spear (?) (2)	-	Yes
1 (Loc.III)	Pit Circle	26.30m dia.	?	INA	INA	-	1	-	-	-	-	-	-	Horse (?)	-	-	Yes
13 (Loc.IV)	Pit Circle	12.00m dia.	1	INA	Child (7 yrs)	32	11	-	1	-	-	-	Axe (3), Adze	Horse (?); Copper ornaments of horse (5)	-	-	Yes

Table 5 : Technomic and sociotechnic artifacts with respect to social dimension of the individual(s) buried at Mahurjhari

Site : MAHURJHARI
Physical zone : Wainganga basin of Nagpur plain (040201)
Total no. of burials : 300
No. of burials excavated : 15 + 11 = 26

Burial no.	Burial type	Size	Total no. of indi-viduals	Sex	Age	Total no. of artifacts (7)							Technomic artifacts	Sociotechnic artifacts (9)		Ascribed social di-mension (10)	
						Pott-ery	Metal	Stone	Semi-prec. stones	T.C.	Bone	Shell		A	B	Super-ordinate	Sub ordinate
(1)	(2)	(3)	(4)	(5)	(6)	(7a)	(7b)	(7c)	(7d)	(7e)	(7f)	(7g)	(8)	(9a)	(9b)	(10a)	(10b)
*1 (Loc.I)	Pit Circle	12.90m dia.	-	-	-	-	1	-	2	-	-	-	-	-	Dagger/ Spear head	-	-
2	Pit Circle	18.15m dia.	2	INA	Adult (17 yrs)	15+	7	2	5+	-	-	-	Axe, Chisel (2)	Horse; Copper lid with a finial hav-ing a motif of 8 buds	Dagger, Spike	-	Yes
3	Pit Circle	16.05m dia.	1+	INA	Aged	16+	36+	-	296	-	-	-	-	Gold strips (11), Leaf pieces	Dagger (3)	-	Yes
1 (Loc.II)	Pit Circle	15.17m dia.	1	INA	Young (Adolescent)	9+	8+	1	-	-	-	-	Axe (3)	Horse; Circular gold leaf, Fragment of a wire	Spike	Yes	-
2	Pit Circle	14.15m dia.	INA	INA	INA	3+	6+	-	-	-	-	-	-	Gold leaf, Circular discs of very thin leaf	-	Yes	-
1 (Loc.III) (1971-72 season)	Pit Circle	14.82m dia.	INA	INA	INA	+	12+	-	2		-	-	Adze (?) (2), Chisel	-	Dagger, Spike, Arrow-heads	-	Yes
2	Pit Circle	12.15m dia.	1	INA	INA	2+	3+	-	+	-	-	-	Axe, Chisel	Horse	Arrow head, Spear-heads	-	Yes
3	Pit Circle	11.70m dia.	2	a. Male b. INA	a. Adult b. Adult	8+	9+	1	-	-	-	-	Axe, Chisel, Hoe	Horse	Dagger, Spike	-	Yes

						(7)								(9)		(10)	
(1)	(2)	(3)	(4)	(5)	(6)	(7a)	(7b)	(7c)	(7d)	(7e)	(7f)	(7g)	(8)	(9a)	(9b)	(10a)	(10b)
4	Pit Circle	13.25m dia.	1	INA	Adult	18+	25+	-	+	-	-	-	Axes, Adze, Chisels	Horse; Necklace of gold wire, Spiral ear-rings (5), Ear ornament of gold debased with Silver, Gold sheet rings with punched decoration, Horse trappings of Iron (5), Copper bowl with a finial of 6 budded motif, Earthen lid with a finial in the shape of a goat, Lid with a finial of four birds (2)	Spears, Javelins	Yes	-
5	Pit Circle	8.23m dia.	INA	INA	INA	3+	7+	-	-	-	-	-	Axes, Chisel (2), Hoe	-	Dagger Spike (2)	-	Yes
6	Pit Circle	11.54m dia.	2	a. Male b. INA	a. Adult b. Adult	7+	8+	2	-	-	-	-	-	Dagger with an iron blade & a copper hilt, Gold ear ornaments debased with Silver (2), Gold necklaces	Spike (2)	-	Yes
7	Pit Circle	9.92m dia.	2	a. INA b. INA	a. Adult b. Adult	+	4+	-	-	-	-	-	Adzes, Chisel	Horse	Dagger, Spearhead	-	Yes
8	Pit Circle	12.70m dia.	3	a. INA b. INA c. INA	a. Adult b. Adult c. Adult	3+	20+	-	1	-	-	-	Adze, Chisels	Horse; Horse trappings of iron (2), Copper ornaments for horse (7), Gold necklace, Circular beads (5)	Spike	-	Yes

						(7)								(9)		(10)	
(1)	(2)	(3)	(4)	(5)	(6)	(7a)	(7b)	(7c)	(7d)	(7e)	(7f)	(7g)	(8)	(9a)	(9b)	(10a)	(10b)
9	Pit Circle	16.45m dia.	2	a. INA b. INA	a. Adult b. Adult	6+	6+	-	-	-	-	-	Axes, Adzes, Chisels	Horse; Horse trapping of iron (1), Gold necklace, Spiral ear-rings	Spike (3)	-	Yes
1 (1978-79 season)	Pit Circle	INA	-	-	-	INA	34+	1	8	-	-	-	Axe, Adze (10), Pick-axe (?), Chisel	-	Arrowhead (3)	-	Yes
2	Pit Circle	INA	-	-	-	INA	14+	-	1	-	-	-	Axe, Adze, Chisel (2)	-	Spike (2)	-	Yes
3	Pit Circle	INA	5	a. Male b. INA c. Female? d. Female? e. Female?	a. Adult (27-32 yrs) b. INA c. Y.Adult (18-22 yrs) d. Y.Adult (16-20 yrs) e. Y.Adult (18-22 yrs)	INA	63+	2	-	2	-	-	Axe (6), Adze (11), Chisel (10)	Horse; Horse trappings of iron (1)	Spearhead (4), Spike (3)	-	Yes
4	Pit Circle	INA	-	-	-	INA	45+	1	3	-	-	-	Axe (2), Adze (7), Chisel (5), Hoe	Copper dish (2)	Dagger, Spike (4), Arrowhead	-	Yes
5	Pit Circle	INA	2	a. INA b. INA	a. Adult b. Adult (24-28 yrs)	INA	13	-	-	-	-	-	Adze (3), Chisel, Hoe	-	Spearhead	-	Yes
7	Pit Circle	INA	1	Male?	Y.Adult (18-22 yrs)	INA	176+	2	-	-	-	2+	Axe (4), Adze (22), Chisel (9), Sickle, Scraper	Horse; Horse trappings of iron (2), Copper bowl (2), Lid (1), Bird motif (4), Bud motif, pot, Horse ornaments (12), Gold strip (2), Spiral ear ring (3), Ring (2), Silver ring, shell bangles (2)	Arrowhead, Spearhead (5), Spike (6)	Yes	-

(1)	(2)	(3)	(4)	(5)	(6)	(7) (7a)	(7b)	(7c)	(7d)	(7e)	(7f)	(7g)	(8)	(9) (9a)	(9b)	(10) (10a)	(10b)
8	Pit Circle	INA	4	a. Female? b. INA c. Male? d. Female?	a. Y.Adult (18-22 yrs) b. S.Adult (12-15 yrs) c. Y.Adult d. Y.Adult	INA	34+	-	-	-	-	-	Axe (4), Adze (6), Chisel (4)	Copper ornament of horse, Bowl (2)	Spike (2)	-	Yes
9	Pit Circle	INA	3	a. Female? b. INA c. INA	a. Y.Adult (17-20 yrs) b. INA c. Child	INA	28+	-	-	-	-	-	Adze (4), Chisel, Sickle	-	Spearhead	-	Yes
10	Pit Circle	INA	1	Male	M.Adult (24-28 yrs)	INA	7	-	-	-	-	-	Adze (2)	-	-	-	Yes
11	Pit Circle	INA	-	-	-	INA	87+	-	-	1	-	-	Axe (8), Adze (7), Chisel (8), Hoe	Horse; Horse trappings of iron (4), Iron dagger with copper hilt, copper bowl (3), Dish, Gold ring (2), Wire	Spike (4)	Yes	-
29	Pit Circle	INA	1	INA	Y.Adult (18-22yrs)	INA	243+	1	53 (?)	-	-	-	Axe (8), Adze (16), Chisel (14), Hoe	Horse; Horse trappings of iron (5), Copper ornaments of horse (102), Bowl, Dish, Lid, Gold ring	Spike (3), Spearhead (2)	Yes	-
1 (Loc. IV) (1971-72 season)	Pit Circle	14.55m dia.	1	INA	Adult	4+	14+	-	+	-	-	-	Axe, Chisels	-	Daggers, Spearheads	-	Yes

Table 6 : Technomic, sociotechnic and ideotechnic artifacts with respect to social dimension of the individual(s) buried at Raipur-Hingna

Site : RAIPUR-HINGNA
Physical zone : Wainganga Basin or Nagpur plain (040201)

Total no. of burials : 360
No. of burials excavated : 4

urial no.	Burial type	Size	Total no.of indivi-duals	Sex	Age	Total no. of artifacts: Pott-ery	Metal	Stone	Semi-prec. Stones	T.C.	Bone	Shell	Technomic artifacts	Sociotechnic artifacts: A	B	Ideotechnic artifacts	Ascribed social dimension: Super-ordinate	Sub-ordinate
3 Loc.III)	Pit circle	15.30m dia.	?	INA	INA	INA	50+	1	36	-	-	-	Axe (2), Adze (11), Chisel	Horse; Horse trappings of iron (2)	Spearhead, Spike	-	-	Yes
4	Pit Circle	10.40m dia.	INA	INA	INA	INA	3	-	-	-	-	-	Axe (2), Hoe	Horse		-	-	Yes
1 (Loc.IV)	Chamber br.	180 x 60cm. 15.00m dia.	2 (+ ?)	a. INA b. INA	a. Adolescent (<16 yrs) b. Adult	INA	37	-	-	-	-	-	Adze (5)	Horse; Gold bead, Earthen lid with the finial of bird motif	Arrowhead	-	-	Yes
2	Chamber br.	140 x 215cm 16.35m dia.	1	INA	Adult	INA	89+	-	134	-	-	-	Axe (2), Adze (8), Chisel (3)	Horse; Horse trappings of iron (2), Copper ornaments of horse (25) Gold ring (2)	Spike	Turtle motif of copper	Yes	-

Table 4.7 : Technomic and sociotechnic artifacts with respect to social dimension of the individual(s) buried at Gangapur

Site : GANGAPUR
Physical zone : Wainganga basin or Nagpur Plain (040201)

Total no. of burials : 30
No. of burials excavated : 3

Burial no.	Burial type	Size	Total no. of indi-viduals	Sex	Age	Total no. of artifacts: Pott-ery	Metal	Stone	Semi. Proc. Stones	T.C.	Bone	Shell	Technomic artifacts	Sociotechnic artifacts: A	B	Ascribed Social dimension: Super-ordinate	Sub-ordinate
2 (Cl.I)	Pit Circle	11.97m dia.	?	INA	INA	8+	16+	-	1	-	-	-	Axe (2), Adze, Chisel	-	Spearhead, Arrowhead (2)	-	Yes
3	Pit Circle	12.12m dia.	?	INA	INA	5+	2	-	+	-	-	-	Chisel	-	-	-	Yes
1 (Cl.II)	Pit Circle	9.60m dia.	?	INA	INA	2+	10+	-	21	-	-	-	Chisel, Poker, Fish-hook	Copper bowl	Spike	-	Yes

Table 8 : Technomic and sociotechnic artifacts with respect to social dimension of the individual(s) buried at Takalghat-Khapa

Site : TAKALGHAT-KHAPA — Total no. of burials : 14

Physical zone : Wainganga basin or Nagpur plain (040201) — No. of burials excavated : 9

Burial no.	Burial type	Size	Total no. of indivi-duals	Sex	Age	Total no. of artifacts							Technomic artifacts	Sociotechnic artifacts		Ascribed Social dimension	
						Pott-ery	Metal	Stone	Semi. Prec. Stones	T.C.	Bone	Shell		A	B	Super-ordinate	Sub-ordinate
1 (Cl.I)	Pit Circle	25.25m dia.	2	a. INA b. INA	a. Adult (> 17 yrs) b. Adult (> 17 yrs)	18	19+	-	2+	-	1	-	Axe(2), Adze, Chisel	Horse; Copper lid having a finial of four birds, knobbed lid	Dagger, Sword(?)	Yes	-
4	Pit Circle	12.00m dia.	-	-	-	+	-	-	2	-	-	-	-	-	-	-	Yes
6	Pit Circle	17.45m dia.	1	INA	Adult (> 17 yrs)	+	16	-	-	-	-	-	Chisel(2), Fish-hook	Horse; Copper ornaments of horse (10)	Dagger	Yes	-
7	Pit Circle	17.05m dia.	?	INA	INA	+	5+	-	13	-	-	-	Adze	Horse trappings of iron (1)	-	-	Yes
8	Pit Circle	13.00m dia.	-	-	-	-	-	-	-	-	-	-	-	-	-	-	Yes
2 (Cl.II)	Pit Circle	16.00m dia.	?	-	-	10	10	-	-	-	-	-	Axe(2), Adze	-	Arrowhead, Spike	-	Yes
3	Pit Circle	12.00m dia.	-	-	-	4	2	1	1	-	-	-	-	Copper lid with ring hold	Dagger	-	Yes
5 (Cl.III)	Pit Circle	11.80m dia.	?	-	-	8	4+	-	6+	-	-	-	Chisel	Copper dish with a finial having a motif of four birds	-	-	Yes
9	Pit Circle	13.20m dia.	-	-	-	1+	5+	-	-	-	-	-	Axe, Fish-hook	-	-	-	Yes

Table 9 : Technomic and sociotechnic artifacts with respect to social dimension of the individual(s) buried at Yelleswaram

Site : YELLESWARAM
Physical zone : Telangana peneplain (080202)

Total no. of burials : Inf. not available
No. of burials excavated : 5

Burial no.	Burial type	Size	Total no. of indivi-duals	Sex	Age	Total no. of artifacts							Technomic artifacts	Sociotechnic artifacts		Ascribed Social dimension	
						Pott-ery	Metal	Stone	Semi prec. stones	T.C.	Bone	Shell		A	B	Super-ordinate	Sub-ordinate
I (YLM-A)	Chamber burial	INA	3	a. Male b. Female c. INA	a. M. Adult b. Adult c. Child (3 yrs)	4	-	-	-	-	-	-	-	-	-	-	Yes
II (YLM-A?)	Chamber burial	INA	3	a. Male b. INA c. INA	a. Adult b. Adult c. Adult	5	5	1	-	-	-	-	Hoe	-	Dagger, Sword, Arrowhead	-	Yes
III (YLM-A)	Pit burial	1.80m dia.	2	a. Male b. Female	a. INA b. INA	9	6	-	-	-	-	-	Sickle	A circular earthen stand with rows of triangular & rectangu-lar perfora-tions & a large sized dish fitted to it with a funnel shaped lid with a hollow knobb-ed ring terminal	Dagger, Spike stud-ded lance	-	Yes
V (YLM-B)	Pit burial	INA	1	Male?	Adult	6	1 (+4?)	-	-	-	-	-	Chisel	-	Lance (Meg.5?), Dagger (Meg.5?)	-	Yes
IV (YLM-A?)	Urn burial	INA	1	Female?	Y. Adult?	9	1	-	-	-	-	-	-	-	Dagger	-	Yes

Table 10 : Technomic, sociotechnic and ideotechnic artifacts with respect to social dimension of the individual(s) buried at Nagarjunakonda

Site : NAGARJUNAKONDA
Physical zone : Middle Krishna Valley (080401)

Total no. of burials : 21
No. of burials excavated : 15

Burial no.	Burial type	Size	Total no. of individuals	Sex	Age	Total no. of artifacts							Technomic artifacts	Sociotechnic artifacts		Ideotechnic artifacts	Ascribed social dimension	
						Pottery	Metal	Stone	Semi-prec. stones	T.C.	Bone	Shell		A	B		Super-ordinate	Sub-ordinate
(1)	(2)	(3)	(4)	(5)	(6)	(7a)	(7b)	(7c)	(7d)	(7e)	(7f)	(7g)	(8)	(9a)	(9b)	(10)	(11a)	(11b)
II (Site 63)	Pit circle	6.03m dia.	2(?)	Male(?)	Adult	10	11	-	-	-	-	-	Wedge, Plough-share tip(?)	-	Lance, Lance/Spear, Arrow-head(3), Dagger(2)	-	-	Yes
III	Pit circle	4.27m dia.	-	-	-	-	-	-	-	-	-	-	-	-	-	-	-	Yes
IV	Pit circle	9.15m dia.	-	-	-	1	1	-	-	-	-	-	-	-	-	-	-	Yes
V	Pit Circle	6.79m dia.	1	Male(?)	Adult	26	3	-	-	-	-	-	Adze	-	Sword(2)	-	-	Yes
VI	Pit circle	8.08m dia.	3	a. INA b. INA c. INA	a. Adult b. Adult c. INA	28	3	-	-	-	-	-	-	-	Dagger(?) (2)	-	-	Yes
VIII	Pit circle	7.42m dia.	INA	INA	INA	14	6	-	-	1	-	-	Adze, Spindle Whorl(?)	-	Spearhead (3), Dagger (2)	-	-	Yes
X	Pit circle	7.46m dia.	2	INA	INA	16	6	-	-	-	-	-	Adze(3)	-	Spearhead, Spear(2)	-	-	Yes
XI	Pit circle	3.70m dia.	2	a. Male? b. Female?	a. Adult b. Adult	15	1	-	-	1	-	1	Adze, Spindle Whorl(?)	-	-	-	-	Yes
XII	Pit circle	5.64m dia.	1	INA	Child?	7+	3	-	-	-	-	-	Adze	-	Lance, Dagger	-	-	Yes
XIII	Pit circle	5.72m dia.	1	Male?	Adult?	20	1	-	-	-	-	-	-	-	-	-	-	Yes
XIV	Pit circle	5.36m dia.	1	Female?	Adult	13	58	-	-	-	-	-	Wedge, Crow-bar(?) (2)	Gold spiral ear ring(2), Small cylindrical beads (35), Silver small spacing beads (18)	-	-	Yes	-
XV	Pit circle	4.27m dia.	1	INA	Adult	11	1	-	-	-	-	-	-	-	Dagger	-	-	Yes
IX	Pit circle	5.74m dia.	-	-	-	26	7	-	-	-	-	-	-	-	Dagger, Lance	Incised figures of possibly a bull, horse with a rider & figures of indeterminate shapes	-	Yes
VII	Chamber br.	1.70 x 0.50 x 0.70 m; 5.49 m dia.	INA	INA	INA	30+	4	-	-	-	-	-	Wedge	-	-	-	-	Yes
I (Site 44)	Chamber br.	1.90 x 0.42 x 0.70 m; 5.49 m dia.	6	a. Male? b. INA c. INA d. INA e. INA f. INA	a. Adult b. INA c. INA d. INA e. INA f. INA	24	4+	1	-	1	-	-	Adze, Spindle, Whorl(?) (T.C.)	-	Daggers, Spearhead, Lance(2)	Incised figure of a rectangular pattern which had been bisected by another line	-	Yes

Table 11 : Technomic, sociotechnic and ideotechnic artifacts with respect to social dimension of the individual(s) buried at Peddamarur

Site : PEDDAMARUR
Physical zone : Middle Krishna Valley (080402)

Total no. of burials : Inf. not available
No. of burials excavated : 4

Burial no.	Burial type	Size	Total no. of individuals	Sex	Age	Total no. of artifacts							Technomic artifacts	Sociotechnic artifacts		Ideotechnic artifacts	Ascribed social dimension	
						Pottery	Metal	Stone	Semi-prec. stones	T.C.	Bone	Shell		A	B		Superordinate	Subordinate
I	Chamber br. (along with sarcophagus)	2.35 x 1.95 x 1.33 m ; Circle dia.?	INA (Multiple br. ?)	INA	INA	65+	2	-	2	-	-	-	Bill-hook (?)	-	-	-	-	Yes
II	Chamber br. (along with sarcophagi)	2.45 x 2.00 x 0.60 m Circle dia.?	6	a. INA b. INA c. INA d. INA e. INA f. INA	a. INA b. INA c. INA d. INA e. INA f. Child	2+	4	-	-	-	-	-	Spatula, A cable type nail rivetted to a copper ring	-	-	The rim of a sarcophagus was luted with a T.C. figurine, possibly of a buffalo	-	Yes
III	Chamber br.	2.30 x 1.85 x 1.00 m ; Circle dia.?	9	INA	INA	1+	4	-	-	-	-	-	Chisel	-	Arrowheads	-	-	Yes
IV	Pit burial	INA	1	INA	INA	1+	-	-	-	-	-	-	-	-	-	-	-	Yes

Table 12 : Technomic and sociotechnic artifacts with respect to social dimension of the individual(s) buried at Uppalapadu

Site : UPPALAPADU
Physical zone : Middle Krishna Valley (080402)

Total no. of burials : Inf. not available
No. of burials excavated : 21

Burial no.	Burial type	Size	Total no. of individuals	Sex	Age	Total no. of artifacts: Pottery	Metal	Stone	Semi-prec. stones	T.C.	Bone	Shell	Technomic artifacts	Sociotechnic artifacts: A	B	Ascribed social dimension: Super-ordinate	Sub-ordinate
I (Site I)	Pit burial	11.00m dia.	INA	INA	INA	+	2	-	-	-	-	-	Chisel	-	-	-	Yes
IV	Pit burial	8.70m dia.	INA	INA	INA	3+	1	-	-	-	-	-	-	-	-	-	Yes
V	Pit burial	9.00m dia.	INA	INA	INA	2+	2	-	-	-	-	-	Chisel (2)	-	-	-	Yes
VI	Pit burial	14.00m dia.	INA	INA	INA	+	22	3+	-	-	-	-	Axe, Chisel (2)	Horse trappings of iron (4)	Dagger (4), Javelin (2)	Yes	-
IX	Pit burial	5.08m dia.	INA	INA	INA	11	3	-	-	-	-	-	Chisel (2)	-	-	-	Yes
VIII	Pit burial	INA	INA	INA	INA	10	+	-	-	-	-	-	-	-	-	-	Yes
III (Site?)	Pit burial	3.34m dia.	-	-	-	-	-	-	-	-	-	-	-	-	-	-	Yes
IV (Site?)	Pit burial	INA	-	-	-	-	-	-	-	-	-	-	-	-	-	-	Yes
VII (Site I)	Pit burial	8.20m dia.	INA	-	-	12	2	2	-	-	-	-	-	-	Sling stone (?)	-	Yes
*III	Chamber burial	1.55 x 0.95 x 0.75 m; 4.20m dia.	INA	INA	INA	+	-	-	-	-	-	-	-	-	-	-	-
II	Chamber burial (along with two ancillary cists)	1.77 x 1.80 m; 2A : 80x35cms; 2B : INA	INA	INA	INA	+	1	-	-	-	-	-	-	-	-	-	Yes

Burial no.	Burial type	Size	Total no. of indivi-duals	Sex	Age	Total no. of artifacts							Technomic artifacts	Sociotechnic artifacts		Ascribed social dimension	
						Pott-ery	Metal	Stone	Semi. prec. stones	T.C.	Bone	Shell		A	B	Super-ordinate	Sub-ordinate
I (Site?)	Chamber br. (along with two anci-llary cists)	Cist:INA; la: 97 x 33x23cms; lb:80 x 30x22cms; Circle dia. 8.0m	12	INA	Adults	3+	2+	-	-	-	-	-	-	-	-	-	Yes
VI (Site II)	Chamber br.	INA	INA	INA	INA	+	-	-	-	-	-	-	-	-	-	-	Yes
II (Site ?)	Chamber br.	INA	5	INA	a. Adult b. Adult c. INA d. INA e. INA	12	-	-	-	-	-	-	-	-	-	-	Yes
*V	Chamber br.	1.90x0.65 x 0.40m; Circle dia.?	INA	INA	INA	-	-	-	-	-	-	-	-	-	-	-	-
VI	Chamber br.	INA	INA	INA	INA	INA	INA	INA	INA	INA	INA	INA	-	-	-	-	-
I (Site III)	Chamber br.	INA	INA	INA	INA	+	-	-	-	-	-	-	-	-	-	-	Yes
I (Site II)	Pit burial	INA	INA	INA	INA	+	+	-	-	-	-	+	-	-	-	-	Yes
III	Pit burial	INA	INA	INA	INA	+	+	-	-	-	-	-	-	-	-	-	Yes
V	Pit burial	INA	INA	INA	INA	+	-	-	-	-	-	-	-	-	-	-	Yes
IV	Pit burial (with three wooden coffins)	INA	INA	INA	INA	INA	INA	INA	INA	INA	INA	INA	-	-	-	-	-
II (Site II)	A platform	INA	-	-	-	-	-	-	-	-	-	-	-	-	-	Possibly meant for the purpose of br.rituals	

Table 13 : Technomic, sociotechnic and ideotechnic artifacts with respect to social dimension of the individual(s) buried at Satanikota

Site : SATANIKOTA
Physical zone : Middle Krishna Valley (080402)

Total no. of burials : 29+
No. of burials excavated : 8

Burial no.	Burial type	Size	Total no. of individuals	Sex	Age	Total no. of artifacts: Pottery	Metal	Stone	Semi-prec. stones	T.C.	Bone	Shell	Technomic artifacts	Sociotechnic artifacts: A	B	Ideotechnic artifacts	Ascribed social dimension: Super-ordinate	Sub-ordinate
*AI (Cl.A)	Chamber br.	1.09 x 1.80 x 1.55 m ; 7.90 m dia.	INA	INA	INA	5	1	1	-	-	-	1	-	Shell bangle	-	-	-	-
*AII	Chamber br. (along with sarcophagus)	2.30 x 2.90 x 1.80 m ; 12.00 m dia.	INA	INA	INA	29	2	-	3	1	-	1	-	Shell bangle, Glass bangle (3)	-	T.C.horn, A bronze rattle having decoration of a grotesque human face	-	-
AIII	Chamber br.	1.7 x 1.4 x 0.92 m ; 6.60 m dia.	INA	INA	INA	26	-	-	-	-	-	-	-	-	-	-	-	Yes
*BVII (Cl.B)	Chamber br.	1.35 x 0.65 x 0.25 m ; 4.15 m dia.	-	-	-	-	-	-	-	-	-	-	-	-	-	-	-	-
BVIII	Chamber br.	1.95 x 0.74 x 0.25 m ; 4.20 m dia.	-	-	-	-	-	-	-	-	-	-	-	-	-	-	-	Yes
BXVII	Chamber br.	1.70 x 1.12 x 0.81 m ; 7.50 m dia.	5	a.Male? b.Male? c.Female? d.Female? e.INA	a.Adult b.Adult c.Adult d.Adult e.Child?	+	1	-	-	-	-	-	-	-	Arrowhead	A shallow pecking on a bounding stone slab (sn.side) forming a wavy design	-	Yes
B I	Pit burial	11.00 m dia.	-	-	-	7	-	-	-	-	-	-	-	-	-	-	-	Yes
C I (Cl.C)	Pit burial	6.80 m dia.	3(?)	a.INA b.INA c.Female	a.Adult (>25 yrs) b.Adult (>25 yrs) c.Teenager (<13 yrs)	16	-	-	-	1	-	-	-	-	-	-	-	Yes

Table 14 : Technomic and sociotechnic artifacts with respect to social dimension of the individual(s) buried at Agiripalli

Site : AGIRIPALLI
Physical zone : The Krishna-Godavari Delta or Middle Coastal Plain (180202)

Total no. of burials : Inf. not available
No. of burials excavated : 7

Burial no.	Burial type	Size	Total no. of individuals	Sex	Age	Total no. of artifacts							Technomic artifacts	Sociotechnic artifacts		Ascribed social dimension	
						Pottery	Metal	Stone	Semi. prec. stones	T.C.	Bone	Shell		A	B	Superordinate	Subordinate
I	Chamber br.	1.60 x 0.75 x 1.15 m; Circle dia. ?	1(?)	INA	INA	11	1	-	-	-	-	-	-	-	-	-	Yes
II	Chamber br.	INA	4	INA	INA	3	-	-	-	-	-	-	-	-	-	-	Yes
III	Chamber br.	3.20 x 0.55 x 1.50 m	1(?)	INA	INA	9	-	-	-	-	-	-	-	-	-	-	Yes
IV	Legged Urn br. (Sarcophagus)	1.37 x 0.45 x 0.4 m	1(?)	INA	INA	-	-	-	-	-	-	-	-	-	-	-	Yes
V	Legged Urn br. (Sarcophagus)	1.12 x 0.45 x 0.50 m	1(?)	INA	INA	3	-	-	-	-	-	-	-	-	-	-	Yes
I	Urn br.	INA	INA	INA	INA	-	-	-	-	-	-	-	-	-	-	-	Yes
[illegible]	Urn br.	INA	INA	INA	INA	-	-	-	-	-	-	-	-	-	-	-	Yes

Table 15 : Technomic and sociotechnic artifacts with respect to social dimension of the individual(s) buried at Jewargi (B.K)

Site : JEWARGI (B.K) | Total no. of burials : 375

Physical zone : Gulbarga plain (060202) | No. of burials excavated : 14+

Burial no.	Burial type	Size	Total no. of indi-viduals	Sex	Age	Total no. of artifacts: Pott-ery	Metal	Stone	Semi. prec. stones	T.C.	Bone	Shell	Technomic artifacts	Sociotechnic artifacts: A	B	Ascribed social dimension: Super-ordinate	Sub-ordinate
(1)	(2)	(3)	(4)	(5)	(6)	(7a)	(7b)	(7c)	(7d)	(7e)	(7f)	(7g)	8	(9a)	(9b)	(10a)	(10b)
1 (First Cairn)	Chamber burial	Chamber: INA; 14.63m dia.	3-5	INA	Adult (1)(?)	8+	4+	-	1	-	-	-	-	-	Spearhead/ Arrowhead, Spearhead (?) (2)	-	Yes
2 (Fourth Cairn)	Chamber burial	1.58 x 0.51 x 0.56 m; 9.75 m dia.	2(?)	INA	INA	3+	6	-	-	-	-	-	Bill-hook (?), Sickle, Hoes (?) (2)	-		-	Yes
*3 (Fifth Cairn)	Chamber burial	INA	3(?)	INA	Adult (1)(?)	+	+	-	-	-	-	-	-	-	-	-	-
*4 (Sixth Cairn)	Chamber burial	1.48 x 0.91m x ?; Circle dia.: INA	3(?)	INA	INA	+	2	-	-	-	-	-	-	-	Spearhead	-	-
5 (Cairn A)	Chamber burial	INA	3	INA	INA	+	3+	-	1	-	-	-	-	-	Spearheads, Arrowheads	-	Yes
6 (Cairn B)	Chamber burial	INA	3	INA	INA	+	2	-	-	-	-	-	Bill-hook, Sickle	-	-	-	Yes
7 (Cairn C)	Chamber br. (?)	INA	INA	INA	INA	INA	INA	INA	INA	INA	INA	INA	-	-	-	-	-
8 (Cairn D)	Chamber burial	1.98 x 0.61m x ?; Circle dia.: INA	3	INA	INA	+	5	-	1	-	-	-	Sickle	-	Arrowhead (2), Sword (?)	-	Yes
9 (Cairn E)	Chamber burial	1.48 x 1.02m x ?	3	INA	INA	+	1	-	-	-	-	-	-	-	-	-	Yes
14	Chamber burial	INA	INA	INA	INA	+	-	-	-	-	-	-	-	-	-	-	Yes
10 (Second Cairn)	Pit burial	7.31m dia.	1	INA	INA	+	3	-	-	-	-	-	-	-	Spearheads	-	Yes
11 (Third Cairn)	Pit burial	4.67m dia.	-	-	-	14	3+	-	-	-	-	-	-	-	Spearhead Sword (?) (2)	-	Yes
12 (Seventh Cairn)	Pit burial	INA	?	INA	INA	+	-	-	-	-	-	-	-	-	-	-	Yes
13 (Eighth Cairn)	Pit burial	INA	1 (?)	INA	INA	+	-	-	-	-	-	-	-	-	-	-	Yes

Table 16 : Technomic and sociotechnic artifacts with respect to social dimension of the individual(s) buried at Maski

Site : MASKI
Physical zone : Raichur plain (060302)

Total no. of burials : Inf. not available
No. of burials excavated : 10

Burial no.	Burial type	Size	Total no. of individuals	Sex	Age	Total no. of artifacts							Technomic artifacts	Sociotechnic artifacts		Ascribed social dimension	
						Pottery	Metal	Stone	Semi-prec. stones	T.C.	Bone	Shell		A	B	Super-ordinate	Sub-ordinate
Pit 15 (MSK-10)	Pit burial	7'4" x 4' x 3'7"	1	Male	Adult	1	-	-	-	-	-	-	-	-	-	-	Yes
Pit 16	Pit burial	7'6" x 3'6" x 5'	1	Male?	Adult	13	2	-	-	-	-	-	-	-	Arrowhead	-	Yes
Pit 28	Pit burial	8' x 5'9" x 6'	1	Male?	Adult	27	1	-	-	-	-	-	-	-	-	-	Yes
Pit 28A	Pit burial	7' x 2'9" x 2'	1	Male?	Adult	-	-	-	-	-	-	-	-	-	-	-	Yes
Pit 30	Pit burial	8' dia.	1	INA	Child (7 yrs)	5	-	5	-	-	-	-	-	-	-	-	Yes
Pit 2 (MSK-9)	Pit burial	8'2" x 4' x 7'9"	1	INA	Adult	63	2	1	-	-	-	-	Axe	-	Dagger	-	Yes
Pit 1	Urn burial	2'9" x 2'9" x 2'	INA	INA	INA	15	-	-	-	-	-	-	-	-	-	-	Yes
Meg.2 (Durgad Gudda area)	Pit burial	7'3" x 2'8" x 6';17'dia.	1	INA	Adult	16	5	-	-	-	-	-	-	-	Lance/Sword, Dagger/Knife, Lance (2)	-	Yes
Meg.1	Menhir	10' x 5'	-	-	-	-	-	-	-	-	-	-	-	-	-	-	-
Meg.3	Menhir	5' x 3'	-	-	-	-	-	-	-	-	-	-	-	-	-	-	-

Table 17 : Technomic and sociotechnic artifacts with respect to social dimension of the individual(s) buried at Brahmagiri

Site : BRAHMAGIRI
Physical zone : Bellary plain (060402)

Total no. of burials : 309+
No. of burials excavated : 10

Burial no.	Burial type	Size	Total no. of indivi-duals	Sex	Age	Total no. of artifacts: Pott-ery	Metal	Stone	Semi-Prec. Stones	T.C.	Bone	Shell	Technomic artifacts	Sociotechnic artifacts: A	B	Ascribed social dimension: Super-ordinate	Sub-ordinate
V (Area A)	Chamber burial	$5\frac{1}{2}'$ x 4'10" x 6';21'dia.	3	INA	a.Adult b.Adult c.Child	6	-	-	-	-	-	-	-	-	-	-	Yes
VI	Chamber burial	$7\frac{1}{4}'$ x 4'7" x 5'8"; $19\frac{1}{2}'$ dia.	INA	INA	INA	10	5	-	-	2	-	-	Ploughshare tips(?) (2), Spindle whorl (2)	-	Knife/ Dagger (2)	-	Yes
X	Chamber burial (along with three ancillary cists)	5'2" x 4'1" x 5'11"; $11\frac{1}{2}'$ dia.	3	INA	Adults	50	1	-	-	-	-	-	-	-	-	-	-
		XA:2' x 1·2' x $1\frac{1}{2}'$; $4\frac{1}{2}'$ dia.	INA	INA	INA	3	-	-	-	-	-	-	-	-	-	-	-
		XB:1' x 1' x $1\frac{1}{2}'$;4' dia.	INA	INA	INA	1	-	-	-	-	-	-	-	-	-	-	Yes
		XC:2' x 11" x $1\frac{1}{2}'$;3' dia.	INA	INA	INA	3	-	-	-	-	-	-	-	-	-		
I (Area B)	Chamber burial	$5\frac{1}{2}'$ x 3'11" x 5'10"; 11' dia.	6	a.Male b.Male c.Male d.Male e.Fe-male? f.INA	a.Adult b.Adult c.Adult d.Adult e.Adult f.Child (12 yrs)	24	1	-	-	-	-	-	Axe	-	-	-	Yes
VII	Pit burial	31' dia.	2	INA	a.Adult b.Child	39	19	-	-	-	-	-	Wedge, Chisel, Sickle, Plough share tips (?) (2)	-	Lance, Knife/ Dagger (5) Spear (?) (2)	-	Yes
II (Area C)	Pit burial	$26\frac{1}{2}'$ dia.	-	-	-	20	14+	1	-	2	-	-	Wedge (2), Chisel (3), Sickle, Plough-share tips (?) (2), Spindle Whorl (2)	Halberd/ Plough coulter (?)	Dagger, Sword, Arrow-head	-	Yes
*III	Pit burial	30' dia.	-	-	-	-	INA	-	-	-	-	-	-	-	-	-	-
IX	Pit burial	20' dia.	1 (?)	INA	INA	30	44	1	1	3	-	1	Wedge, Plough-share tip (?), Spindle Whorl	Gold beads (33); Conchshell ornament	Dagger, spear, Lance	Yes	-
IV	Chamber burial	5'7" x $4\frac{1}{4}'$ x $6\frac{1}{4}'$; 18' dia.	3	INA	a.Adult b.Adult c.Child	50	3	-	39	1	-	-	-	-	-	-	Yes
VIII	Chamber burial	6'5" x 4'4" x $5\frac{3}{4}'$ 15' dia.	2	a.Female b.INA	a.Adult/ Y.Adult b. INA	19	8	-	48	-	-	-	Chisel Plough-share tips (?) (2)	-	Knife/ Dagger (4)	-	Yes

Table 18 : Technomic and sociotechnic artifacts with respect to social dimension of the individual(s) buried at Terdal-Halingali

Site : TERDAL-HALINGALI
Physical zone : Bijapur region (060602)
Total no. of burials : 147
No. of burials excavated : 5

Burial no.	Burial type	Size	Total no. of individuals	Sex	Age	Total no. of artifacts: Pottery	Metal	Stone	Semi-prec. stones	T.C.	Bone	Shell	Technomic artifacts	Sociotechnic artifacts: A	B	Ascribed social dimension: Super-ordinate	Sub-ordinate
*Meg.I	Chamber burial	Chamber: 2m in dia.; Circle dia. 3m; Rect. 6m square	INA	INA	INA	4+	-	-	-	-	-	-	-	-	-	-	-
*Meg.II	Chamber burial	Chamber: 3.45 x 3.40m; Rect. 4m square	INA	INA	INA	2+	-	-	-	-	-	-	-	-	-	-	-
Meg.III	Chamber burial	Chamber: 5.35 x 6.50m; Rect.11.20m square	INA	INA	INA	3+	29	-	-	-	-	-	-	-	-	-	Yes
*Meg.1	Pit burial	5.50m dia.	INA	INA	INA	+	-	-	-	-	-	-	-	-	-	-	-
*Meg.2	Pit burial	INA	INA	INA	INA	+	-	-	-	-	-	-	-	-	-	-	-

Table 4.19 : Technomic and sociotechnic artifacts with respect to social dimension of the individual(s) buried at Tadakanahalli

Site : TADAKANAHALLI
Physical zone : Dharwad plateau (060502)
Total no. of burials : Inf. not available
No. of burials excavated : 4

Burial no.	Burial type	Size	Total no. of individuals	Sex	Age	Total no. of artifacts: Pottery	Metal	Stone	Semi-Prec. Stones	T.C.	Bone	Shell	Technomic artifacts	Sociotechnic artifacts: A	B	Ascribed social dimension: Super-ordinate	Sub-ordinate
I	Pit burial	9.5 m dia.	2	INA	INA	8+	2	-	-	-	-	-	-	Earthen globular pot with four spouts	Dagger, Spearhead	-	Yes
IV	Pit burial	6.0 m dia.	INA	INA	INA	27	4	-	-	-	-	-	-	-	Dagger, Arrowhead (2)	-	Yes
II	Urn burial	9.1 m dia.	INA	INA	INA	34	4+	-	-	-	-	-	Axe	-	Arrowheads, Spearheads	-	Yes
III	Urn burial	11.5 m dia.	INA	INA	INA	36	6	-	-	-	-	-	-	-	-	-	Yes

Table 20 : Technomic and sociotechnic artifacts with respect to social dimension of the individual(s) buried at Jadigenahalli

Site : JADIGENAHALLI
Physical zone : Bangalore region (070302)

Total no. of burials : 35
No. of burials excavated : 4

Burial no.	Burial type	Size	Total no. of indivi-duals	Sex	Age	Total no. of artifacts: Pott-ery	Metal	Stone	Semi-prec. stones	T.C.	Bone	Shell	Technomic artifacts	Sociotechnic artifacts: A	B	Ascribed social dimension: Super-ordinate	Sub-ordinate
I	Legged Urn br. (Sarcophagus)	$6\frac{1}{2}$' x ? x $1\frac{1}{2}$'; 5.18 m dia.	-	-	-	78	7	-	-	-	-	-	Hoes(2), Sickle	-	Sword/ Dagger(2)	-	Yes
II	Legged Urn br. (Sarcophagus)	7' x 1'9" x ?; 6.09 m dia.	-	-	-	22	20	-	-	-	-	-	Chisel, Hoes(3)	Horse trappings (?) of iron	Sword, Dagger, Sword/ Dagger(5) Trident	Yes	-
III	Legged Urn br. (Sarcophagus)	3' x 2' x $1\frac{1}{4}$'; 3.35 m dia.	-	-	-	21	1	-	-	-	-	-	-	-	-	-	Yes
*IV	Legged Urn br. (Sarcophagus)	$5\frac{1}{2}$' x $1\frac{1}{4}$' x1'4"; Circle dia.?	-	-	-	58	2	-	-	-	-	-	-	-	Sword/ Dagger	-	-

Table 4.21 : Technomic, sociotechnic and ideotechnic artifacts with respect to social dimension of the individual(s) buried at Savandurga

Site : SAVANDURGA
Physical zone : Bangalore region (070302)

Total no. of burials : Inf. not available
No. of burials excavated : 4

Burial no.	Burial type	Size	Total no. of indivi-duals	Sex	Age	Total no. of artifacts: Pott-ery	Metal	Stone	Semi-prec. stones	T.C.	Bone	Shell	Technomic artifacts	Sociotechnic artifacts: A	B	Ideotechnic artifacts	Ascribed social dimension: Super-ordinate	Sub-ordinate
1	Chamber br.	9' x 6' x 5'; 7.92 m dia.	1(?)	INA	Adult/ Old(?)	9+	22+	2	-	-	1(?)	-	Iron chisels, Awl/Needle (2), Sharp edged cutt-ers/scrap - ers of small crystal stone(2)	Iron Dagger with a copper fillet on the guard	Dagger, Spearhead, Arrowhead (13+)	T.C.horn-shaped vessels (2)	Yes	-
2	Chamber br.	7'5" x 4'2" x 4'9"	INA	INA	INA	2+	-	1	-	-	-	-	-	-	-	-	-	Yes
3	Chamber br.	8'2" x 4'9" x 5'9"; 7.01 m dia.	INA	INA	INA	10+	2	-	-	-	-	-	-	-	Spearhead	-	-	Yes
4	Chamber br.	7'8" x 4'6" x 5'4"; 5.48 m dia.	INA	INA	INA	32	-	-	-	-	-	-	-	-	-	-	-	Yes

Table .22 : Technomic and sociotechnic artifacts with respect to social dimension of the individual(s) buried at Heggedehalli

Site : HEGGEDEHALLI
Physical zone : South Malnad (050302)

Total no. of burials : Inf. not available
No. of burials excavated : 4

Burial no.	Burial type	Size	Total no. of individuals	Sex	Age	Total no. of artifacts: Pottery	Metal	Stone	Semi-prec. Stones	T.C.	Bone	Shell	Technomic artifacts	Sociotechnic artifacts: A	B	Ascribed social dimension: Super-ordinate	Sub-ordinate
I	Pit burial	7.45 m dia.	-	-	-	23	-	-	-	-	-	-	-	-	-	-	Yes
IV	Pit burial	6.00 m dia.	INA	INA	INA	4	-	-	-	-	-	-	-	-	-	-	Yes
III	Pit burial	3.50 m dia.	-	-	-	1	-	-	-	-	-	-	-	-	-	-	Yes
*II	Chamber burial	2.9 x 1.2 x 1.13 m ; Circle dia.?	-	-	-	-	-	-	-	-	-	-	-	-	-	-	-

Table 4.23 : Technomic and sociotechnic artifacts with respect to social dimension of the individual(s) buried at Kunnathur

Site : KUNNATHUR
Physical zone : The Palar-Ponnaiyar basin or Nn.Coastal plain (170102)

Total no. of burials : Inf. not available
No. of burials excavated : 8

Burial no.	Burial type	Size	Total no. of individuals	Sex	Age	Total no. of artifacts: Pottery	Metal	Stone	Semi-prec. stones	T.C.	Bone	Shell	Technomic artifacts	Sociotechnic artifacts: A	B	Ascribed social dimension: Super-ordinate	Sub-ordinate
1	Pit burial	6.5 m dia.	-	-	-	26+	7	-	-	-	-	-	?	?	+	-	Yes
4	Pit burial	32' dia.	-	-	-	8+	8+	-	-	-	-	-	Axes	Horse trappings of iron (4)	Spear-heads	Yes	-
*II	Chamber burial	8' x 6' x 4'; 5 m dia.	-	-	-	-	2+	-	-	1	-	-	-	-	Sword	-	-
*6	Chamber burial (?)	-	-	-	-	1	-	-	-	-	-	-	-	-	-	-	-
III	Legged Urn br. (Sarcophagus)	Sarcophagus: ? 1.87 m dia.	1	INA	Adult	13	2	-	-	-	-	-	-	-	-	-	Yes
5	Legged Urn br. (Sarcophagus)	Sarcophagus A: 6'6" x 2'8" x ? Sar.B : ? Sar.C : ? Sar.D : ? 33' dia.	?	-	-	2+	6+	-	-	-	-	-	Axes	-	Daggers, Spear-heads, Pike	-	Yes
7	Legged Urn br. (Sarcophagus)	$1'9\frac{1}{2}" \times 1'1\frac{1}{2}" \times 7\frac{1}{2}"$	-	-	-	11	-	-	-	-	-	-	-	-	-	-	Yes
*9	Legged Urn br. (Sarcophagus)	6'3" x 1'9" x ?	INA	INA	INA	4+	5	-	-	-	-	-	Adze, Chisel	-	Dagger (2), Spearhead	-	-

Table 24 : Technomic, sociotechnic and ideotechnic artifacts with respect to social dimension of the individual(s) buried at Sanur

Site : SANUR
Physical zone : The Palar-Ponnaiyar basin or Nn.Coastal plain (170102)

Total no. of burials : 300
No. of burials excavated : 5

Burial no.	Burial type	Size	Total no. of individuals	Sex	Age	Total no. of artifacts: Pottery	Metal	Stone	Semi-prec. stones	T.C.	Bone	Shell	Technomic artifacts	Sociotechnic artifacts: A	B	Ideotechnic artifacts	Ascribed social dimension: Super-ordinate	Sub-ordinate
2	Chamber br. (along with sarcophagi)	Chamber: 6'6"x7'6"x4'; Sar.A: 5'x2'6"x1' Sar.B: 4 ½' x1'x1' Sar C: 3'6"x1'9"x9"; Circle dia. 45'	2(?)	a.Male? b.Female?	a.Adult b.Adult	25+	26	1	-	?	-	-	Bars with a pointed tip & socketed end (of iron) (2), Sickle, T.C. Whorl-beads (Spindle Whorls?)	Horse trappings of iron(1)	Iron Dagger/Knife, Spear/Arrowhead, Arrowhead, Spear/Pike (?), A Spherical ball (Sling stone ?)	T.C. figurine of an animal	-	Yes
1	Chamber br. (along with sarcophagi)	Chamber: 9'x5'6"x3'; Sar.A: 5'x1'9"x1' Sar.B: 4'x1'9"x1' Sar.C: 4'x1'6"x1' Sar.D: 2'x1'1"x9" Sar.E: 1'10"x1'x4"; Circle dia. 33'	INA	INA	INA	50+	19	-	-	-	-	-	-	-	Spear(3), Arrowhead, Dagger/Knife, Dagger	-	-	Yes
3	Chamber br. (along with a sarcophagus)	Chamber: 6'x3'6"x3"; Sarcophagus: 4' x 2' x 1'; Circle dia. 18'3"	-	-	-	45+	3	-	2	-	-	-	-	-	Knife/Dagger	-	-	Yes
4	Chamber br. (along with a sarcophagus)	Chamber: ? ; Sarcophagus: ? ; Circle dia. 23'3"	-	-	-	3+	3	-	-	-	-	-	Chisel(3)	-	-	-	-	Yes
5	Pit burial	50' dia.	3	a. INA b. INA c. INA	a.Y.Adult b. INA c. INA	70	71	4	-	?	-	18	Iron Wedge(3), Chisel, Scraper, T.C. Whorl-beads (Spindle-Whorls?)	Horse trappings of iron (1), Conch shells(3), Circular convex discs (5), Long objects with closed & pointed ends, each with an encased iron rod(2), A disintegrated core(1), Beads (7)	Spears (Pike?)(3), Knife/Dagger, Arrowheads (6)	-	Yes	-

Table 25 : Technomic, sociotechnic and ideotechnic artifacts with respect to social dimension of the individual(s) buried at Odugattur

Site : ODUGATTUR
Physical zone : Mettur-Vellore region (120202)

Total no. of burials : Inf. not available
No. of burials excavated : 3

Burial no.	Burial type	Size	Total no. of individuals	Sex	Age	Total no. of artifacts							Technomic artifacts	Sociotechnic artifacts		Ideotechnic artifacts	Ascribed social dimension	
						Pottery	Metal	Stone	Semi-prec. stones	T.C.	Bone	Shell		A	B		Superordinate	Subordinate
1	Chamber br.	7 1/2' x 3 1/2' x 4'8"; 43' dia.	INA	INA	INA	1	2+	3	-	-	-	10	Iron Axe (2), Stone palette	Shell: Perforated discs with different decorations (4), Cigar shaped pieces used as knife handles (?) (2), Incised chank shell (2), Decorated columella of a chank (2)	Swords, Daggers	-	Yes	-
3	Chamber br.	4'10"x2'9" x 5'2"; 34' dia.	INA	INA	INA	11	3	-	-	-	-	3	Axe (2)	Shell: Circular disc on one side of each six minute triangular flakes have been removed (1), Triangular chips (2)	-	-	-	Yes
2	Chamber br.	6'8"x4'1" x 5'3"; 56' dia.	INA	INA	INA	8	15+	4	-	-	-	-	-	-	Spearheads	Iron plates of various shapes & dimensions having either conical/flat discs attached to them of copper/bronze (one of them had a flat sheet of copper cut rudely in the shape of a bird)	-	Yes

Note : The following material was found in Odugattur burials. But unfortunately, it is not mentioned in Richards' (1924 : 157-165) report from which burial/s they come from :-

a. Large spheroidal jars b. Three legged jar c. Miniature vessel
d. "Spindle whorls" (2) e. Perforated chank shell f. "Sugar-loaf" shaped piece of shell

Table 26 : Technomic and sociotechnic artifacts with respect to social dimension of the individual(s) buried at Sittannavasal

Site : SITTANNAVASAL
Physical zone : The Cauvery Valley and Delta or Central Coastal plain (170201)
Total no. of burials : Inf. not available
No. of burials excavated : 4

Burial no.	Burial type	Size	Total no.of indivi-duals	Sex	Age	Total no. of artifacts: Pott-ery	Metal	Stone	Semi-prec. stones	T.C.	Bone	Shell	Technomic artifacts	Sociotechnic artifacts: A	B	Ascribed social dimension: Super-ordinate	Sub-ordinate
I (Area i)	Chamber br.	7.7 x 6.4 m x ? ; Circle dia.?	-	-	-	3+	-	-	-	-	-	-	-	-	-	-	Yes
*IV (Area iii)	Chamber br.	1.65 x 1.60 x 2.45m; Circle dia. 6.5m	-	-	-	8+	5+	-	-	-	-	-	Sickles	-	Arrowheads, Daggers, Swords	-	-
III (Area ii)	Chamber br.	Chamber ? ; Circle dia. 4.25m	-	-	-	+	4	-	-	-	-	-	Sickle	-	Sword, Dagger	-	Yes
II	Pit burial	2.42m dia.	-	-	-	15	-	-	-	-	-	-	-	-	-	-	Yes

Table 4.27 : Technomic and sociotechnic artifacts with respect to social dimension of the individual(s) buried at Pancha Pandavar-Mettu

Site : PANCHA PANDAVAR-METTU
Physical zone : Anaimalai-Palni Hills (110102)
Total no. of burials : 50
No. of burials excavated : 2

Burial no.	Burial type	Size	Total no.of indivi-duals	Sex	Age	Total no. of artifacts: Pott-ery	Metal	Stone	Semi-prec. stones	T.C.	Bone	Shell	Technomic artifacts	Sociotechnic artifacts: A	B	Ascribed social dimension: Super-ordinate	Sub-ordinate
1 (Area I)	Pit burial	9'3" dia.	-	-	-	1+	1	-	-	-	-	-		-	-	-	Yes
2 (Area II)	Pit burial	9' dia.	-	-	-	18+	-	-	-	-	-	-	-	-	-	-	Yes

Table 4.28 : Technomic and sociotechnic artifacts with respect to social dimension of the individual(s) buried at Vellur Adichchanallur

Site : VELLUR ADICHCHANALLUR
Physical zone : The Vaigai-Tambraparani basin or Sn.Coastal plain (170303)
Total no. of burials : Inf. not available
No. of burial excavated : 5+

Burial no.	Burial type	Size	Total no. of individuals	Sex	Age	Total no. of artifacts							Technomic artifacts	Sociotechnic artifacts		Ascribed social dimension	
						Pottery	Metal	Stone	Semi-prec. stones	T.C.	Bone	Shell		A	B	Super-ordinate	Sub-ordinate
1	Urn burial	INA	INA	INA	INA	+	12	-	-	-	-	-	-	Bronze circular stand, An ornamental surmounting lid, Pots (3), Cylindrical lid, Bowls (2), A Strainer	-	-	Yes
2	Urn burial	INA	INA	INA	INA	+	2+	-	-	-	-	-	-	Bronze stand with four buffaloes stand -ing in a circle facing outwards, Lid, Vessels	-	-	Yes
3	Urn burial	INA	INA	INA	INA	7	34	-	-	-	-	-	Axe, Hoes (5)	Gold diadem, Gold leaves (6), Bronze stand with four animals probably rams, Lids (2), Bowl (7), Vessels (3), Sieve, Cup, Jar	Dagger, Spear, Trident	Yes	-
4	Urn burial	INA	INA	INA	INA	34	18	-	-	-	-	-	Axe, Hoes (4)	An oval ornament of gold, Bronze bowls (2), Sieve, Vase, Vessel, <u>Lota</u>, Cup	Dagger	-	Yes
5	Urn burial	INA	INA	INA	INA	16	34	-	-	1	-	-	Axe, Hoes (5), Sickle	Bronze bowl, Cup, Vessel (5), Bowl with a knobbed lid, Bulb-shaped objects (4)	Trident, Sword (3), Dagger (2), Spear (2), Arrowheads (5)	-	Yes

Table 29 : Technomic and sociotechnic artifacts with respect to social dimension of the individual(s) buried at Machad

Site : MACHAD

Physical zone : North Malabar (160102)

Total no. of burials : Inf. not available

No. of burials excavated : 2

Burial no.	Burial type	Size	Total no. of individuals	Sex	Age	Total no. of artifacts							Technomic artifacts	Sociotechnic artifacts		Ascribed social dimension	
						Pottery	Metal	Stone	Semi-prec. stones	T.C.	Bone	Shell		A	B	Super-ordinate	Sub-ordinate
I	Chamber burial	2.80 x 2.00 x 2.10 m; 9 m dia.	INA	INA	INA	30	6 (?)	1	147	-	-	-	Chisels	-	Dagger	-	Yes
II	Urn burial	Urn: 0.50m ht., 0.25m dia. at mouth, 1.65m cir. at belly; Circle dia. 2.50m	INA	INA	INA	3	5+	-	19	-	-	-	?	-	?	-	Yes

Table 31 : Statistical account of excavated burials and non-sepulchral monuments as against the total number of burials

Sr.no.	Name of Site	Total no. of burials	No. of excavated burials	No. of previously disturbed burials but excavated	No. of excavated non-sepulchral monuments	No. of previously disturbed non-sepulchral monuments but excavated
1	Khairwada	1496	6	-	-	-
2	Bhagi Mahari	>70	5	-	-	-
3	Borgaon Khurd	.48	4	-	-	-
4	Naikund	70	6	-	-	-
5	Mahurjhari	300	25	1	-	-
6	Raipur-Hingna	360	4	-	-	-
7	Gangapur	30	3	-	-	-
8	Takalghat-Khapa	14	9	-	-	-
9	Yelleswaram	INA	5	-	-	-
10	Nagarjunakonda	21	15	-	-	-
11	Peddamarur	INA	4	-	-	-
12	Uppalapadu	INA	19	2	1	-
13	Satanikota	>29	5	3	-	-
14	Agiripalli	INA	7	-	-	-
15	Jewargi	375	12	2	-	-
16	Maski	INA	8	-	2	-
17	Brahmagiri	309	9	1	-	-
18	Terdal-Halingali	147	1	4	-	-
19	Tadakanahalli	INA	4	-	-	-
20	Jadigenahalli	35	3	1	-	-
21	Savandurga	INA	4	-	-	-
22	Heggedehalli	INA	3	1	-	-
23	Kunnathur	INA	5	3	-	-
24	Sanur	300	5	-	-	-
25	Odugattur	INA	3	-	-	-
26	Sittannavasal	INA	3	1	-	-
27	Pancha-Pandavar Mettu	50	2	-	-	-
28	Vellur Adichanallur	INA	5	-	-	-
29	Machad	INA	2	-	-	-
	Grand total	>3654	186	19	3	-

Table 32 : Statistical account of number of individual(s) from the excavated burials

Sr.no.	Name of Site	Total no. of excavated burials	Total no. of individuals found	Inf. not available on no. of excavated burials having sk. remains	No. of excavated burials without sk. remains (Symbolic burials)
1	Khairwada	6	4	2	-
2	Bhagi Mahari	5	-	5	-
3	Borgaon Khurd	4	2	1	1
4	Naikund	6	1	5	-
5	Mahurjhari	25	35+	3	4
6	Raipur-Hingna	4	3+	2	-
7	Gangapur	3	-	3	-
8	Takalghat-Khapa	9	3	4	3
9	Yelleshwaram	5	10	-	-
10	Nagarjunakonda	15	20	2	3
11	Peddamarur	4	16	1	-
12	Uppalapadu	19	17	15	2
13	Satanikota	5	8	1	2
14	Agiripalli	7	8	2	-
15	Jewargi	12	21	3	1
16	Maski	8	7	1	-
17	Brahmagiri	9	20	1	1
18	Terdal-Halingali	1	-	1	-
19	Tadakanhalli	4	2	3	-
20	Jadigenahalli	3	-	-	3
21	Savandurga	4	1	3	-
22	Heggedehalli	3	-	1	2
23	Kunnathur	5	1	1	3
24	Sanur	5	5	1	2
25	Odugattur	3	-	3	-
26	Sittannavasal	3	-	-	3
27	Pancha-Pandavar Mettu	2	-	-	2
28	Vellur Adichanallur	5	-	5	-
29	Machad	2	-	2	-
	Grand total	186	184	71	32

Total no. of excavated burials : 186

Inf. not available on no. of excavated burials having sk. remains : 71

115

Out of these 115 burials 32 burials are Symbolic burials. So, 115 - 32 = 83 burials

Table 33 : Breakup of burials with respect to the number of individuals in each burial category

Sr.no.	Name of Site	Total no. of burials	No. of excavated burials	No. of individuals found	No. of Single burials	No. of Double burials	No. of Multi-ple burials	Inf. not available on no. of excavated burials having sk. remains	No. of burials without sk.remains (Symbolic burials)
1	Khairwada	1496	6	4	4	-	-	2	-
2	Borgaon Khurd	48	4	2	2	-	-	1	1
3	Naikund	70	6	1	1	-	-	5	-
4	Mahurjhari	300	25	35+	7	7	4	3	4
5	Raipur-Hingna	360	4	3+	1	-	1	2	-
6	Takalghat-Khapa	14	9	3	1	1	-	4	3
7	Yelleshvaram	INA	5	10	2	1	2	-	-
8	Nagarjunakonda	21	15	20	5	3	2	2	3
9	Peddamarur	INA	4	16	1	-	2	1	-
10	Uppalapadu	INA	19	17	-	-	[illegible]	15	2
11	Satanikota	>29	5	8	-	-	2	1	2
12	Agiripalli	INA	7	8	4	-	1	2	-
13	Jewargi	375	12	21	2	1	5	3	1
14	Maski	INA	8	7	7	-	-	1	-
15	Brahmagiri	309	9	20	1	2	4	1	1
16	Tadakanhalli	INA	4	2	-	1	-	3	-
17	Savandurga	INA	4	1	1	-	-	3	-
18	Kunnathur	INA	5	1	1	-	-	1	3
19	Sanur	300	5	5	-	1	1	1	2
	Grand total	>3322	156	184	40	17	26	51	22

Table 34 : Sex and Agewise distribution of individuals.

Sr.no.	Name of Site	Total no. of individuals found	Male	Female	Inf. not available on sex	Infant	Child	Adolescent	Young Adult	Middle Aged/ Old Adult	I a o
1	Khairwada	4	1	-	3	-	-	-	4	-	
2	Borgaon Khurd	2	-	-	2	-	1	-	1	-	
3	Naikund	1	-	-	1	-	1	-	-	-	
4	Mahurjhari	35+	6	6	23	-	1	2	27	1	
5	Raipur-Hingna	3+	-	-	3	-	-	1	2	-	
6	Takalghat-Khapa	3	-	-	3	-	-	-	3	-	
7	Yelleshwaram	10	4	3	3	-	1	-	6	1	
8	Nagarjunakonda	20	5	2	13	-	1	-	10	-	
9	Peddamarur	16	-	-	16	-	1	-	-	-	
10	Uppalapadu	17	-	-	17	-	-	-	14	-	
11	Satanikota	8	2	3	3	-	1	1	6	-	
12	Agiripalli	8	-	-	8	-	-	-	-	-	
13	Jewargi	21	-	-	21	-	-	-	1	-	
14	Maski	7	4	-	3	-	1	-	6	-	
15	Brahmagiri	20	4	2	14	-	3	1	14	-	
16	Tadakanahalli	2	-	-	2	-	-	-	-	-	
17	Savandurga	1	-	-	1	-	-	-	1	-	
18	Kunnathur	1	-	-	1	-	-	-	1	-	
19	Sanur	5	1	1	3	-	-	-	3	-	
	Grand total	184	27	17	140	-	11	5	99	2	

Table 35 : Distribution of single, double, multiple and symbolic burials with respect to ascribed social

Sr.no.	Name of Site	Total no.of exc. brs.	No.of Single brs.	Sex	Age	No.of indivi-duals belong-ing to super-ordinate dimension	No. of individu-als be-longing to sub-ordinate dimen-sion	No. of Double brs.	Sex	Age	No. of indivi-duals belong-ing to super-ordinate dimension	No. of individu-als be-longing to sub-ordinate dimen-sion
(1)	(2)	(3)	(4)	(5)	(6)	(7)	(8)	(9)	(10)	(11)	(12)	(13)
1	Khairwada	6	4	-Male	-Adult -Adult -Adult -Adult	2	2	-	-	-	-	-
2	Bhagi Mahari	5	-	-	-	-	-	-	-	-	-	-
3	Borgaon Khurd	4	2	-	-Adult -Child	1	1	-	-	-	-	-
4	Naikund	6	1	-	-Child	-	1	-	-	-	-	-
5	Mahurjhari	25	7	- - - -Male -Male - -	-Young(Ad) -Adult -Adult -Adult -Adult -Adult	4	3	7	- - -M/ -M/ - - -	-A -O -A/A -A/A -A/A -A/A -A/A	-	7
6	Raipur-Hingna	4	1	-	-Adult	1	-	-	-	-	-	-
7	Gangapur	3	-	-	-	-	-	-	-	-	-	-
8	Takalghat-Khapa	9	1	-	-Adult	1	-	1	-	-A/A	1	-
9	Yelleshwaram	5	2	-Male -Female	-Adult -Adult	-	2	1	-M/F	-	-	1
10	Nagarjunakonda	15	5	-Male - -Male -Female -	-Adult -Child -Adult -Adult -Adult	1	4	3	-M/- - -M/F	-A/- - -A/A	-	3
11	Peddamarur	4	1	-	-	-	1	-	-	-	-	-
12	Uppalapadu	19	-	-	-	-	-	-	-	-	-	-
13	Satanikota	5	-	-	-	-	-	-	-	-	-	-
14	Agiripalli	7	4	-	-	-	4	-	-	-	-	-
15	Jewargi (B.K.)	12	2	-	-	-	2	1	-	-	-	1
16	Maski	8	7	-Male -Male -Male -Male - - -	-Adult -Adult -Adult -Adult -Child -Adult -Adult	-	7	-	-	-	-	-
17	Brahmagiri	9	1	-	-	1	-	2	- -F/-	-A/C -A/-	-	
18	Terdal-Halingali	1	-	-	-	-	-	-	-	-	-	
19	Tadakanahalli	4	-	-	-	-	-	1	-	-	-	
20	Jadigenahalli	3	-	-	-	-	-	-	-	-	-	
21	Savandurga	4	1	-	-Adult	1	-	-	-	-	-	
22	Heggedehalli	3	-	-	-	-	-	-	-	-	-	
23	Kunnathur	5	1	-	-Adult	-	1	-	-	-	-	
24	Sanur	5	-	-	-	-	-	1	-M/F	-A/A	-	
25	Odugattur	3	-	-	-	-	-	-	-	-	-	
26	Sittannavasal	3	-	-	-	-	-	-	-	-	-	
27	Pancha-Pandavar Mettu	2	-	-	-	-	-	-	-	-	-	
28	Vellur Adichanallur	5	-	-	-	-	-	-	-	-	-	
29	Machad	2	-	-	-	-	-	-	-	-	-	
	Grand total	186	40	Male:10 Female: 2	Child:4 Ad. :1 Adult:26	12	28	17	Male:6 Female:4	Child:1 Adult:20 Old :1	1	

Legend :

C = Child/Young Ad. = Adolescent A = Adult As = Adults O = Old

M = Male F = Female

dimension etc.

	No. of Multi-ple brs.	Sex	Age	No. of indivi-duals belong-ing to super-ordinate dimension	No. of indivi -duals belong-ing to sub-ordinate dimension	No. of brs. probably with human sk. remains but inf. not available	No. of burials of super-ordinate dimension	No. of burials of sub-ordinate dimension	No. of brs. without sk. remains (Symbolic burials)	No. of burials of super-ordinate dimension	No. of burials of sub-ordinate dimension
	(14)	(15)	(16)	(17)	(18)	(19)	(20)	(21)	(22)	(23)	(24)
	-	-	-	-	-	2	-	2	-	-	-
	-	-	-	-	-	5	2	3	-	-	-
	-	-	-	-	-	1	-	1	1	1	-
	-	-	-	-	-	5	2	3	-	-	-
	4	- -M/-/F/F/F -F/-/M/F -F/-/-	-A/A/A -A/-/A/A/A -A/Ad/A/A -A/-/C	-	4	3	1	2	4	1	3
	1	-	-Ad/A	-	1	2	-	2	-	-	-
	-	-	-	-	-	3	-	3	-	-	-
	-	-	-	-	-	4	-	4	3	-	3
	2	-M/F/- -M/-/-	-O/A/C -A/A/A	-		-	-	-	-	-	-
	2	- -M/-/-/-/-/-	-A/A/- -A/-/-/-/-/-	-	2	2	-	2	3	-	3
	2	- -	-/-/-/-/-/-/C -	-	2	1	-	1	-	-	-
	2	- -	-As (12) -A/A/-/-/-	-	2	15	1	14	2	-	2
	2	-M/M/F/F/- -/-/-/F	-A/A/A/A/C -A/A/Ad	-	2	1	-	1	2	-	2
	1	-	-	-	1	2	-	2	-	-	-
	5	- - - - -	-A/-/-/-/- - - - -	-	5	3	-	3	1	-	1
	-	-	-	-	-	1	-	1	-	-	-
2	4	- - -M/M/M/M/F/- -	-A/A/C -As (3) -A/A/A/A/A/Ad -A/A/C	-	4	1	-	1	1	-	1
-	-	-	-	-	-	1	-	1	-	-	-
1	-	-	-	-	-	3	-	3	-	-	-
-	-	-	-	-	-	-	-	-	3	1	2
-	-	-	-	-	-	3	-	3	-	-	-
-	-	-	-	-	-	1	-	1	2	-	2
-	-	-	-	-	-	1	-	1	3	1	2
1	1	-	-A/-/-	1	-	1	-	1	2	-	2
-	-	-	-	-	-	3	1	2	-	-	-
-	-	-	-	-	-	-	-	-	3	-	3
-	-	-	-	-	-	-	-	-	2	-	2
-	-	-	-	-	-	5	1	4	-	-	-
-	-	-	-	-	-	2	-	2	-	-	-
16	26	Male:11 Female:11	Child:6 Ad. :4 Adult:53 Old :1	1	25	71	8	63	32	4	28

Table 4.38 : Material details of superordinate and subordinate individuals in single burial category

Superordinate burials															
Sr.no.	Name of Site	Burial no.	Sex of the indivi-dual	Age of the indivi-dual	Total no. of artifacts							Functional categories of artifacts			
					Pottery	Metal	Stone	Semi-precious stones	T.C.	Bone	Shell	Technomic	Sociotechnic A	Sociotechnic B
(1)	(2)	(3)	(4)	(5)	(6a)	(6b)	(6c)	(6d)	(6e)	(6f)	(6g)	(7a)	(7b)	(7c)
1	Khairwada	2 (Loc.I)	INA	A	INA	36+	-	8	-	-	-	9	6	7
		1 (Loc.III)	INA	A	INA	17+	-	5	-	-	-	5	3	1
2	Borgaon Khurd	3	INA	A	INA	25	2	-	-	-	-	8	3	-
3	Naikund													
4	Mahurjhari	1 (Loc.II)	INA	Ad	9+	8+	1	-	-	-	-	3	3	1
		4 (Loc.III)	INA	A	18+	25+		+				3+	18	2+
		7 (1978-79 season)	M ?	A	INA	176+	2	-	-	-	2+	37	34	12
		29 (1978-79 season)	INA	A	INA	243+	1	53 (?)	-	-	-	39	112	5
5	Raipur-Hingna	2 (Loc.IV)	INA	A	INA	89+	-	134	-	-	-	13	30	1
6	Takalghat-Khapa	6 (Cl.I)	INA	A	+	16	-	-	-	-	-	3	11	1
7	Yelleshwaram													
8	Nagarjunakonda	XIV (Site 63)	F ?	A	13	58	-	-	-	-	-	3	55	-
9	Peddamarur													
10	Agiripalli													
11	Jewargi (B.K.)													
12	Maski													
13	Brahmagiri	IX (Area C)	INA	INA	30	44	1	1	3	-	1	3	34	3
14	Savandurga	1	INA	A	9+	22+	2	-	-	1 (?)	-	4+	1	15+
15	Kunnathur													
	Grand total	12	M :1 F :1 INA :10	A :10 Ad :1 INA :1	79+	759+	9	201+	3	1	3+	130+	310	48+

Legend :

C = Child/Young Ad.= Adolescent A = Adult O = Old M = Male F = Female

				Subordinate burials							Functional categories of artifacts		
	Burial no.	Sex of the indivi -dual	Age of the indivi -dual	Total no. of artifacts							Tech-nomic	Sociotechnic	
Ideo-technic				Pott-ery	Metal	Stone	Semi-preci-ous stones	T.C.	Bone	Shell		A	B
(7d)	(8)	(9)	(10)	(11a)	(11b)	(11c)	(11d)	(11e)	(11f)	(11g)	(12a)	(12b)	(12c)
-	1 (Loc.I)	M ?	A	INA	1	-	-	-	-	1	-	1	-
-	1 (Loc.II)	INA	A	INA	8	-	1	-	-	-	4	-	-
-	7	INA	C	INA	+	-	243	-	-	-	-	-	-
	13 (Loc.IV)	INA	C	32	11	-	1	-	-	-	4	6	-
-	2 (Loc.III)	INA	INA	2+	3+	-	+	-	-	-	2	1	2+
-	10 (1978-79 season)	M	A	INA	7	-	-	-	-	-	2	-	-
-	h (Loc.IV)	INA	A	4+	14+	-	+	-	-	-	4+	-	2+
-													
1													
-													
	V (YLM-3)	M ?	A	6	5 (?)	-	-	-	-	-	1	-	2 (?)
	IV (YLM-A?)	F ?	A ?	9	1	-	-	-	-	-	-	-	1
-	V (Site 63)	M ?	A	26	3	-	-	-	-	-	1	-	2
	XII (Site 63)	INA	C ?	7+	3	-	-	-	-	-	1	-	2
	XIII (Site 63)	M ?	A ?	20	1	-	-	-	-	-	-	-	-
	XV (Site 63)	INA	A	11	1	-	-	-	-	-	-	-	1
	IV	INA	INA	1+	-	-	-	-	-	-	-	-	-
	I	INA	INA	11	1	-	-	-	-	-	-	-	-
	III	INA	INA	9	-	-	-	-	-	-	-	-	-
	IV	INA	INA	-	-	-	-	-	-	-	-	-	-
	V	INA	INA	3	-	-	-	-	-	-	-	-	-
	10 (Second Cairn)	INA	INA	+	3	-	-	-	-	-	-	-	1+
	13 (Eighth Cairn)	INA	INA	+	-	-	-	-	-	-	-	-	-
	Pit 15	M	A	1	-	-	-	-	-	-	-	-	-
	Pit 16	M ?	A	13	2	-	-	-	-	-	-	-	1
	Pit 28	M ?	A	27	1	-	-	-	-	-	-	-	-
	Pit 28A	M ?	A	-	-	-	-	-	-	-	-	-	-
	Pit 30	INA	C	5	-	5	-	-	-	-	-	-	-
	Pit 2	INA	A	63	2	1	-	-	-	-	1	-	1
	Meg. 2	INA	A	16	5	-	-	-	-	-	-	-	4
-													
2													
	III	INA	A	13	2	-	-	-	-	-	-	-	-
3	28	M :9 F :1 INA:18	A :16 C :4 INA:8	279+	74+	6	245+	-	-	1	20+	8	19+

Table 39 : Material details of superordinate and subordinate individuals in double burial category

Superordinate burials

Sr.no.	Name of Site	Burial no.	Sex of the individual	Age of the individual	Total no. of artifacts: Pottery	Metal	Stone	Semi-precious stones	T.C.	Bone	Shell	Functional categories of artifacts: Technomic	Sociotechnic A	Sociotechnic B
1	Mahurjhari													
2	Takalghat-Khapa	1(Cl.I)	INA	A/A	18	19+	-	2+	-	1	-	3	3	2
3	Yelleshwaram													
4	Nagarjunakonda													
5	Jewargi (B.K.)													
6	Brahmagiri													
7	Tadakanahalli													
8	Sanur													
	Grand total	1	INA:2	A:2	18	19+	-	2+	-	1	-	3	3	2

Legend :

C = Child/Young Ad. = Adolescent A = Adult O = Old

M = Male F = Female

Subordinate burials

Burial no.	Sex of the individual	Age of the individual	Total no. of artifacts: Pottery	Metal	Stone	Semi-precious stones	T.C.	Bone	Shell	Functional categories of artifacts: Technomic	Sociotechnic A	Sociotechnic B	Ideotechnic
Loc.I)	INA	A/-	15+	7	2	5+	-	-	-	3	2	2	
Loc.I)	INA	O/-	16+	36+	-	296	-	-	-	-	11+	3	
Loc.III)	M/-	A/A	8+	9+	1	-	-	-	-	3	1	2	
Loc.III)	M/-	A/A	7+	8+	2	-	-	-	-	-	3+	2	
Loc.III)	INA	A/A	+	4+	-	-	-	-	-	1+	1	2	
Loc.III)	INA	A/A.	6+	6+	-	-	-	-	-	3+	4+	3	
1978-79 season)	INA	A/A	INA	13	-	-	-	-	-	5	-	1	
I(YLM-A)	M/F	INA	9	6	-	-	-	-	-	1	1	2	
(Site 63)	M?/-	A/-	10	11	-	-	-	-	-	2	-	7	
(Site 63)	INA	INA	16	6	-	-	-	-	-	3		3	
(Site 63)	M?/F?	A/A	15	1	-	-	1	-	1	2	-	-	
Fourth Cairn)	INA	INA	3+	6	-	-	-	-	-	4	-	-	
I(Area B)	INA	A/C	39	19	-	-	-	-	-	5	-	8	
II(Area C)	F?/-	A/-	19	8	-	48	-	-	-	3	-	4	
I	INA	INA	8+	2	-	-	-	-	-	-	1	2	
2	M?/F?	A/A	25+	[illegible]	1	-	1	-	-	4+	1	5	1
16	M:6 F:4 INA:22	A:18 O:1 C:1 INA:12	196+	168+	6	349+	[illegible]	-	1	39+	25+	46	1

Table 40 : Material details of superordinate and subordinate individuals in multiple burial category

Superordinate burials														
Sr.no.	Name of Site	Burial no.	Sex of the individual	Age of the individual	Total no. of artifacts: Pottery	Metal	Stone	Semi-precious stones	T.C.	Bone	Shell	Functional categories of artifacts: Technomic	Sociotechnic A	B
(1)	(2)	(3)	(4)	(5)	(6a)	(6b)	(6c)	(6d)	(6e)	(6f)	(6g)	(7a)	(7b)	(7c)
1	Mahurjhari													
2	Raipur-Hingna													
3	Yelleshwaram													
4	Nagarjunakonda													
5	Peddamarur													
6	Uppalapadu													
7	Satanikota													
8	Agiripalli													
9	Jewargi (B.K.)													
10	Brahmagiri													
11	Sanur	5	INA	A/-/-	70	71	4	-		-	18	6+	19	10
	Grand total	1	INA:3	A :1 INA:2	70	71	4	-		-	18	6+	19	10

Legend :

C = Child/Young Ad. = Adolescent A = Adult O = Old M = Male F = Female

	Subordinate burials													
Ideo-technic	Burial no.	Sex of the individual	Age of the individual	Total no. of artifacts: Pottery	Metal	Stone	Semi-precious stones	T.C.	Bone	Shell	Functional categories of artifacts: Technomic	Sociotechnic A	Sociotechnic B	Ideo-technic
(7d)	(8)	(9)	(10)	(11a)	(11b)	(11c)	(11d)	(11e)	(11f)	(11g)	(12a)	(12b)	(12c)	(12d)
	8 (Loc. III)	INA	A/A/A	3+	20+	-	1	-	-	-	2+	16	1	
	3 (1978-79 season)	M/-/F?/ F?/F?	A/-/A/ A/A	INA	63+	2	-	2	-	-	27	2	7	
	8 (1978-79 season)	F?/-/M?/ F?	A/Ad/ A/A	INA	34+	-	-	-	-	-	14	3	2	
	9 (1978-79 season)	F?/-/-	A/-/C	INA	28+	-	-	-	-	-	6	-	1	
	1 (Loc. IV)	INA	Ad/A/-	INA	37	-	-	-	-	-	5	3	1	
	I (YLM-A)	M/F/-	O/A/C	4	-	-	-	-	-	-	-	-	-	
	II (YLM-A?)	M/-/-	A/A/A	5	5	1	-	-	-	-	1	-	3	
	VI (Site 63)	INA	A/A/-	28	3	-	-	-	-	-	-	-	2	
	I (Site 44)	M?/-/-/ -/-/-	A/-/-/ -/-/-	24	4+	1	-	1	-	-	2	-	4+	1
	II	-/-/-/ -/-/-	-/-/-/ -/-/C	2+	4	-	-	-	-	-	2	-	-	1
	III	INA	-/-/-/ -/-/-/ -/-/-	1+	4	-	-	-	-	-	1	-	1+	
	I (Site ?)	INA	A/A/A/A A/A/A/A A/A/A/A	3+	2+	-	-	-	-	-	-	-	-	
	II (Site ?)	INA	A/A/-/ -/-	12	-	-	-	-	-	-	-	-	-	
	B XVII	M?/M?/ F?/F?/-	A/A/A A/C?	+	1	-	-	-	-	-	-	-	1	1
	CI	-/-/F	A/A/Ad	16	-	-	-	1	-	-	-	-	-	
	II	INA	-/-/-/-	3	-	-	-	-	-	-	-	-	-	
	1 (First Cairn)	INA	A?/-/-/-/-	8+	4+	-	1	-	-	-	-	-	3	
	5 (Cairn A)	INA	-/-/-	+	3+	-	1	-	-	-	-	-	2+	
	6 (Cairn B)	INA	-/-/-	+	2	-	-	-	-	-	3	-	-	
	8 (Cairn D)	INA	-/-/-	+	5	-	1	-	-	-	1	-	3	
	9 (Cairn E)	INA	-/-/-	+	1	-	-	-	-	-	-	-	-	
	V (Area A)	INA	A/A/C	6	-	-	-	-	-	-	-	-	-	
	X (Area A)	INA	A/A/A	50	1	-	-	-	-	-	-	-	-	
	I (Area B)	M/M/M/M/F?/-	A/A/A A/A/Ad	24	1	-	-	-	-	-	1	-	-	
	IV (Area C)	INA	A/A/C	50	3	-	39	1	-	-	-	-	-	
	25	M :11 F :11 INA:41	C :6 Ad.:4 A :52 O :1	239+	225+	4	43	5	-	-	64+	24	31+	3

Table 4.41 : Material details of superordinate and subordinate individuals in symbolic burial category

Sr.no.	Name of Site	Burial no.	Sex of the indivi-dual	Age of the indivi-dual	Superordinate burials: Total no. of artifacts: Pott-ery	Metal	Stone	Semi-precious stones	T.C.	Bone	Shell	Functional categories of artifacts: Tech-nomic	Sociotechnic A	Sociotechnic B
(1)		(3)	(4)	(5)	(6a)	(6b)	(6c)	(6d)	(6e)	(6f)	(6g)	(7a)	(7b)	(7c)
1	Borgaon Khurd	35	-	-	INA	44+	2	-	-	-	-	16	5	5
2	Mahurjhari	11 (1978-79 season)	-	-	INA	87+	-	-	1	-	-	24	13	4
3	Takalghat-Khapa													
4	Nagarjunakonda													
5	Uppalapadu													
6	Satanikota													
7	Jewargi (B.K.)													
8	Brahmagiri													
9	Jadigenahalli	II	-	-	22	20	-	-	-	-	-	4	1	8
10	Heggedehalli													
11	Kunnathur	4	-	-	8+	8+	-	-	-	-	-	1+	4	1+
12	Sanur													
13	Sittannavasal													
14	Pancha-Pandavar Mattu													
	Grand total	4	-	-	30+	159+	2	-	1	-	-	45+	23	18+

Subordinate burials													
Burial no.	Sex of the indivi-dual	Age of the indivi-dual	Total no. of artifacts							Functional categories of artifacts			
			Pottery	Metal	Stone	Semi-precious stones	T.C.	Bone	Shell	Technomic	Sociotechnic A	Sociotechnic B	Ideotechnic
(8)	(9)	(10)	(11a)	(11b)	(11c)	(11d)	(11e)	(11f)	(11g)	(12a)	(12b)	(12c)	(12d)
.978-79 season)	-	-	INA	[illegible]4+	1	8	-	-	-	13	-	3	
.978-79 season)	-	-	INA	14+	-	1	-	-	-	4	-	2	
.978-79 season)	-	-	INA	45+	1	3	-	-	-	15	2	6	
:l.I)	-	-	+	-	-	2	-	-	-	-	-	-	
:l.I)	-	-	-	-	-	-	-	-	-	-	-	-	
:l.II)	-	-	4	2	1	1	-	-	-	-	1	1	
I(Site 63)	-	-	-	-	-	-	-	-	-	-	-	-	
(Site 63)	-	-	1	1	-	-	-	-	-	-	-	-	
	-	-	26	7	-	-	-	-	-	-	-	2	1
I(Site ?)	-	-	-	-	-	-	-	-	-	-	-	-	
(Site ?)	-	-	-	-	-	-	-	-	-	-	-	-	
VIII	-	-	-	-	-	-	-	-	-	-	-	-	
I	-	-	-	-	-	-	-	-	-	-	-	-	
(Third Cairn)	-	-	14	3+	-	-	-	-	-	-	-	3	
(Area C)	-	-	20	14+	1	-	2	-	-	10	1	3	
	-	-	78	7	-	-	-	-	-	3	-	2	
I	-	-	21	1	-	-	-	-	-	-	-	-	
	-	-	23	-	-	-	-	-	-	-	-	-	
I	-	-	1	-	-	-	-	-	-	-	-	-	
	-	-	26+	7	-	-	-	-	-			+	
	-	-	11	-	-	-	-	-	-	-	-	-	
	-	-	45+	3	-	2	-	-	-	-	-	1	
	-	-	3+	3	-	-	-	-	-	3	-	-	
(Area i)	-	-	3+	-	-	-	-	-	-	-	-	-	
I(Area ii)	-	-	+	4	-	-	-	-	-	1	-	2	
(Area ii)	-	-	15	-	-	-	-	-	-	-	-	-	
(Area I)	-	-	1+	[illegible]	-	-	-	-	-	-	-	-	
(Area II)	-	-	18+	-	-	-	-	-	-	-	-	-	
8	-	-	317+	146+	4	17	2	-	-	49	4	25+	1

Table 42 : Material details of superordinate and subordinate individual(s) from those burials yielding and/or where such information is not available

			Superordinate burials									
Sr.no.	Name of Site	Burial no.	Total no. of artifacts							Functional categories of artifacts		
			Pottery	Metal	Stone	Semi-precious stones	T.C.	Bone	Shell	Technomic	Sociotechnic A	Sociotechnic B
(1)	(2)	(3)	(4a)	(4b)	(4c)	(4d)	(4e)	(4f)	(4g)	(5a)	(5b)	(5c)
1	Khairwada											
2	Bhagi Mahari	1	INA	92+	2	37	1 *	-	-	33	1	6
		3	INA	38+	-	1	-	-	-	9	3	7
3	Borgaon Khurd											
4	Naikund	3(Loc.I)	22	6	-	-	-	-	-	4	2+	1
		7(Loc.I)	30	21+						3	14	-
5	Mahurjhari	2(Loc.II)	3+	6+	-	-	-	-	-	-	6	-
6	Raipur-Hingna											
7	Gangapur											
8	Takalghat-Khapa											
9	Nagarjunakonda											
10	Peddamarur											

ncomplete physical remains

Subordinate burials								Functional categories of artifacts			
	Total no. of artifacts										
Burial no.	Pottery	Metal	Stone	Semi-precious stones	T.C.	Bone	Shell	Technomic	Sociotechnic A	Sociotechnic B	Ideotechnic
(6)	(7a)	(7b)	(7c)	(7d)	(7e)	(7f)	(7g)	(8a)	(8b)	(8c)	(8d)
3 (Loc.I)	INA	18+	-	-	-	-	-	8	3	-	
3 (Loc.III)	INA	2+	-	-	-	-	-	1	-	-	
2	INA	29	-	2	-	-	-	13	1	4	
4	INA	3+	-	-	-	-	-	1	-	-	
5	INA	3	-	-	1	-	-	1	-	1	
36	INA	12	-	-	-	-	-	10	2	1	
8 (Loc.I)	30	2+	-	-	-	-	-	-	3+	-	
1 (Loc.II)	37	12	-	-	-	-	-	5	4	3	
1 (Loc.III)	-	1	-	-	-	-	-	-	1	-	
1 (Loc.III)	+	12+	-	2	-	-	-	3	-	3+	
5 (Loc.III)	3+	7+	-	-	-	-	-	4+	-	3	
3 (Loc.III)	INA	50+	1	36	-	-	-	14	3	2	
4 (Loc.III)	INA	3	-	-	-	-	-	3	1	-	
2 (Cl.I)	8+	16+	-	1	-	-	-	4	-	3	
3 (Cl.I)	5+	2	-	+	-	-	-	1	-	-	
1 (Cl.II)	2+	10+	-	21	-	-	-	3	1	1	
7 (Cl.I)	+	5+	-	13	-	-	-	1	1	-	
2 (Cl.II)	10	10	-	-	-	-	-	3	-	2	
5 (Cl.III)	8	4+	-	6+	-	-	-	1	1	-	
9 (Cl.III)	1+	5+	-	-	-	-	-	2	-	-	
VIII (Site 63)	14	6	-	-	1	-	-	2	-	5	
VII (Site 63)	30+	4	-	-	-	-	-	1	1	-	
I	65+	2	-	2	-	-	-	1	-	-	

(1)	(2)	(3)	(4a)	(4b)	(4c)	(4d)	(4e)	(4f)	(4g)	(5a)	(5b)	(5c)
11	Uppalapadu	VI(Site I)	+	22	3+	-	-	-	-	3	4	6
12	Satanikota											
13	Agiripalli											
14	Jewargi (B.K.)											
15	Maski											
16	Brahmagiri											
17	Terdal-Halingali											
18	Tadakanahalli											
19	Savandurga											
20	Heggedehalli											
21	Kunnathur											
22	Sanur											
23	Odugattur	1	1	2+	3	-	-	-	10	3	10	2+
24	Vellur Adichanallur	3	7	34	-	-	-	-	-	6	23	3
25	Machad											
	Grand total	8	63+	221+	8+	38	1	-	10	61	63+	25+

(6)	(7a)	(7b)	(7c)	(7d)	(7e)	(7f)	(7g)	(8a)	(8b)	(8c)	(8d)
Site I)	+	2	-	-	-	-	-	1	-	-	
(Site I)	3+	1	-	-	-	-	-	-	-	-	
Site I)	2+	2	-	-	-	-	-	2	-	-	
(Site I)	11	3	-	-	-	-	-	2	-	-	
II (Site I)	10	+	-	-	-	-	-	-	-	-	
(Site I)	12	2	2	-	-	-	-	-	-	1	
(Site I)	+	1	-	-	-	-	-	-	-	-	
(Site II)	+	-	-	-	-	-	-	-	-	-	
(Site ?)	INA	INA	INA	INA	INA	INA	INA	-	-	-	
Site III)	+	-	-	-	-	-	-	-	-	-	
Site II)	+	+	-	-	-	-	+	-	-	-	
(Site II)	+	+	-	-	-	-	-	-	-	-	
Site II)	+	-	-	-	-	-	-	-	-	-	
(Site II)	INA	INA	INA	INA	INA	INA	INA	-	-	-	
II	26	-	-	-	-	-	-	-	-	-	
	-	-	-	-	-	-	-	-	-	-	
	-	-	-	-	-	-	-	-	-	-	
Cairn C)	INA	INA	INA	INA	INA	INA	INA	-	-	-	
	+	-	-	-	-	-	-	-	-	-	
(Seventh Cairn)	+	-	-	-	-	-	-	-	-	-	
1 (MSK-9)	15	-	-	-	-	-	-	-	-	-	
(Area A)	10	5	-	-	2	-	-	4	-	2	
	3+	29	-	-	-	-	-	-	-	-	
	27	4	-	-	-	-	-	-		3	
	34	4+	-	-	-	-	-	1		2+	
	36	6	-	-	-	-	-	-	-	-	
	2+	-	1	-	-	-	-	-	-	-	
	10+	2	-	-	-	-	-	-	-	1	
	32	-	-	-	-	-	-	-	-	-	
	4	-	-	-	-	-	-	-	-	-	
	2+	6+	-	-	-	-	-	1+	-	3+	
	50+	19	-	-	-	-	-	-	-	6	
	11	3	-	-	-	-	3	2	3	-	
	8	15+	4	-	-	-	-	-	-	1+	1+
	+	12	-	-	-	-	-	-	9	-	
	+	2+	-	-	-	-	-	-	3+	-	
	34	18	-	-	-	-	-	5	8	1	
	16	34	-	-	1	-	-	7	12	13	
	30	6 (?)	1	147	-	-	-	1+	-	1	
	3	5+	-	19	-	-	-		-		
	604+	399+	9	249+	5	-	3+	108+	57+	61+	1+

Table 36 : Sex and Agewise account of individuals in different burial categories

Burial type	Total no. of burials	Total no. of individuals found	Male	Female	Inf. not available on the sex of individuals	Infant	Child	Adolescent	Young Adult	Middle Aged/Old Adult	Inf. not available on the age of individuals
Single burials	40	40	10	2	28	-	4	1	26	-	9
Double burials	17	34	6	4	24	-	1	-	20	1	12
Multiple burials	26	110	11	11	88	-	6	4	53	1	46
Burials probably with human sk. remains but inf. not available	71	INA	-	-	-	-	-	-	-	-	-
Symbolic burials	32	-	-	-	-	-	-	-	-	-	-

Table 4.37 : Sex and Agewise breakup of superordinate and subordinate individuals

Burial type	Total no. of burials	No. of Superordinate burials	Sex	Age	No. of Subordinate burials	Sex	Age
Single burials	40	12	Male : 1 Female : 1	Adolescents:1 Adults :10	28	Male : 9 Female : 1	Children : 4 Adults :16
Double burials	17	1	INA	Adults : 2	16	Male : 6 Female : 4	Child : 1 Adults :18 Old : 1
Multiple burials	26	1	INA	Adult : 1	25	Male : 11 Female : 11	Children : 6 Adolescent:4 Adults :52 Old : 1
Burials probably with sk. remains but inf. not available	71	8	INA	INA	63	INA	INA
Burials without sk. remains (Symbolic burials)	32	4	-	-	28	-	-
Grand total	186	26	Male : 1 Female : 1	Adolescents: 1 Adults :13	160	Male : 26 Female : 16	Children :11 Adolescents: 4 Adults :86 Old : 2

Fig.7 Percentage of different burial categories based on excavated data

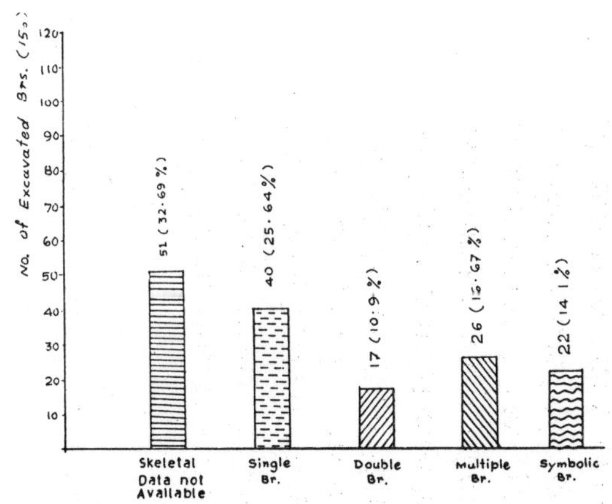

Fig.8 Age-wise distribution of individuals

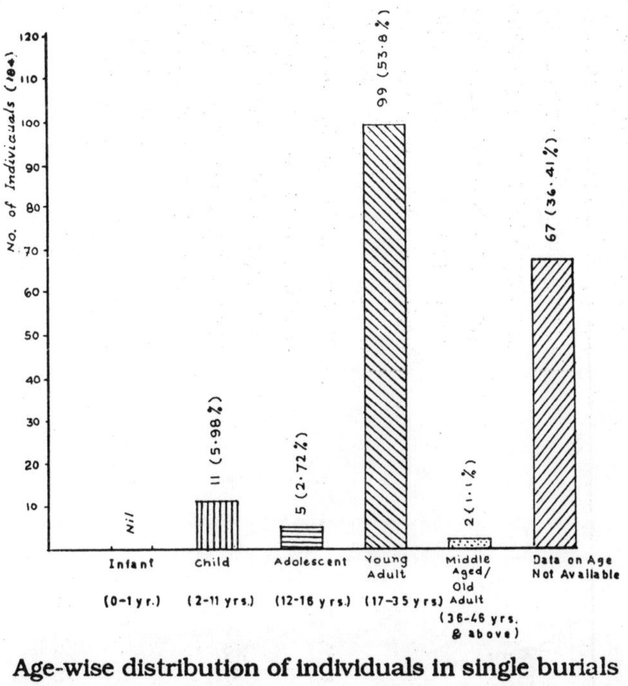

Age-wise distribution of individuals in single burials

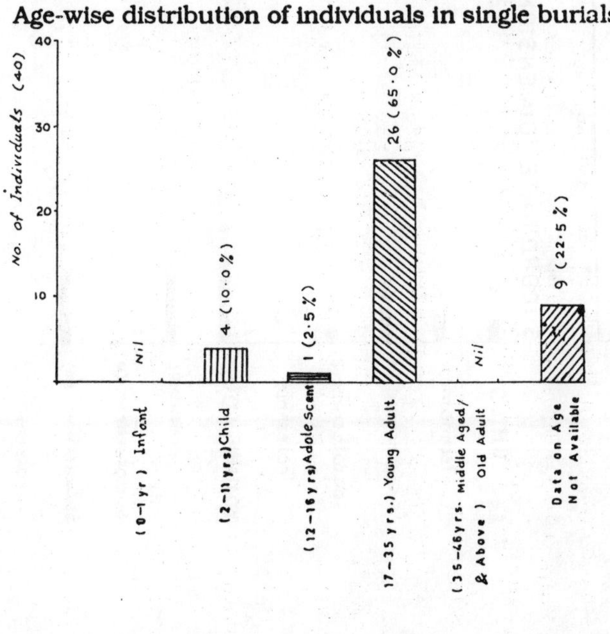

Sex-wise distribution of individuals

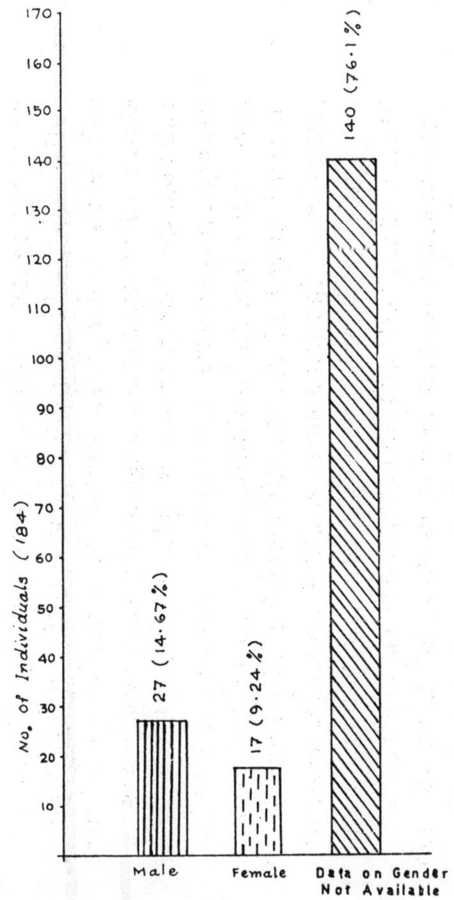

Sex-wise distribution of individuals in single buri

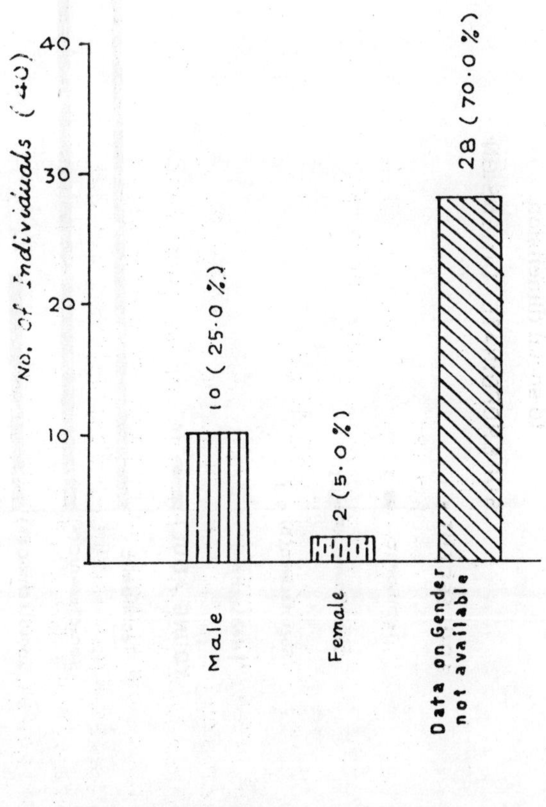

Fig.12 Age-wise distribution of single burials along with functional categories of entered burial goods with respect to social dimension

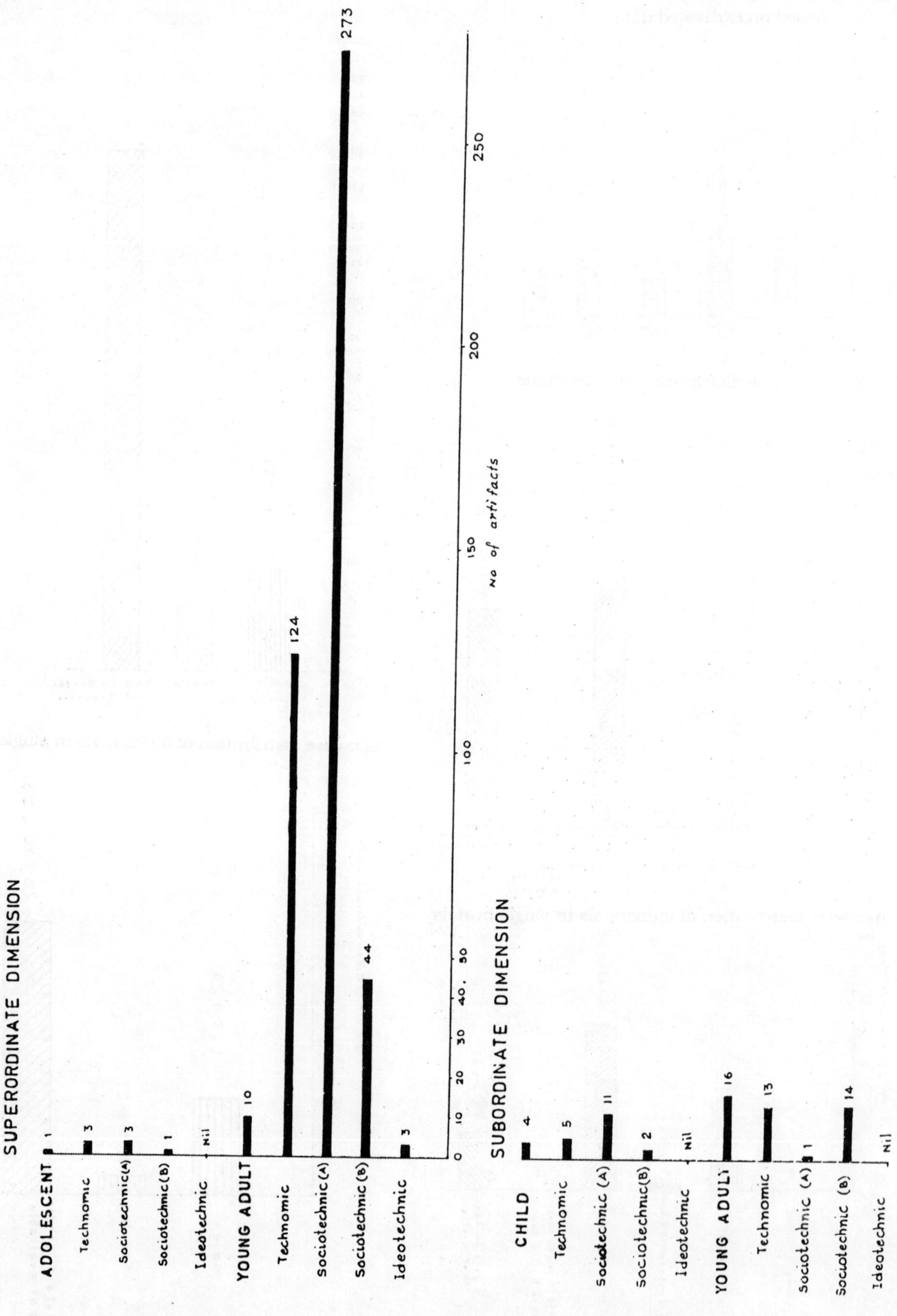

Fig. 13 Distribution of single burials along with functional categories of entered Burial goods with respect to Social dimension

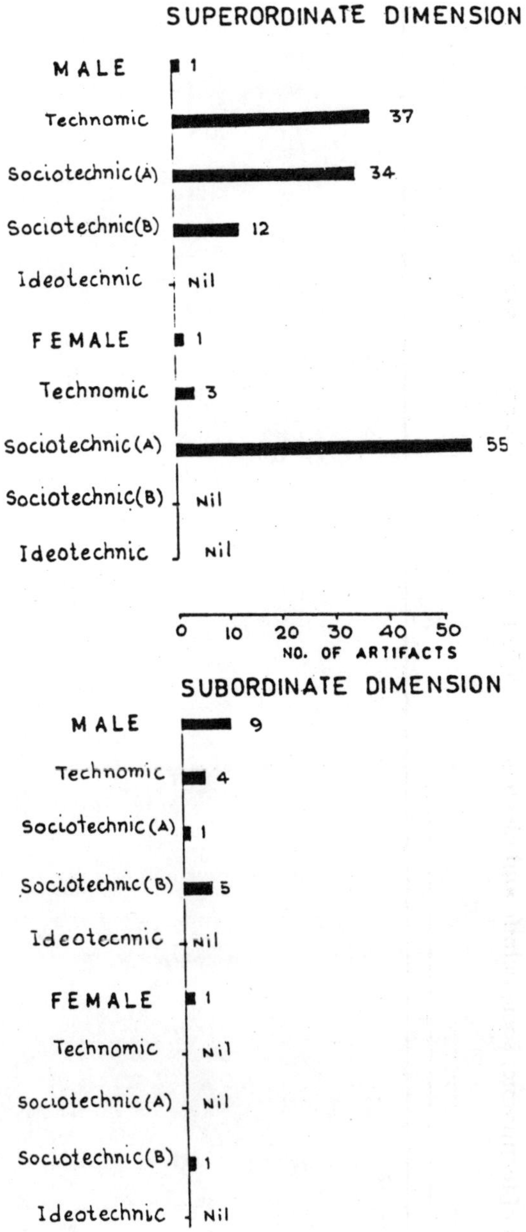

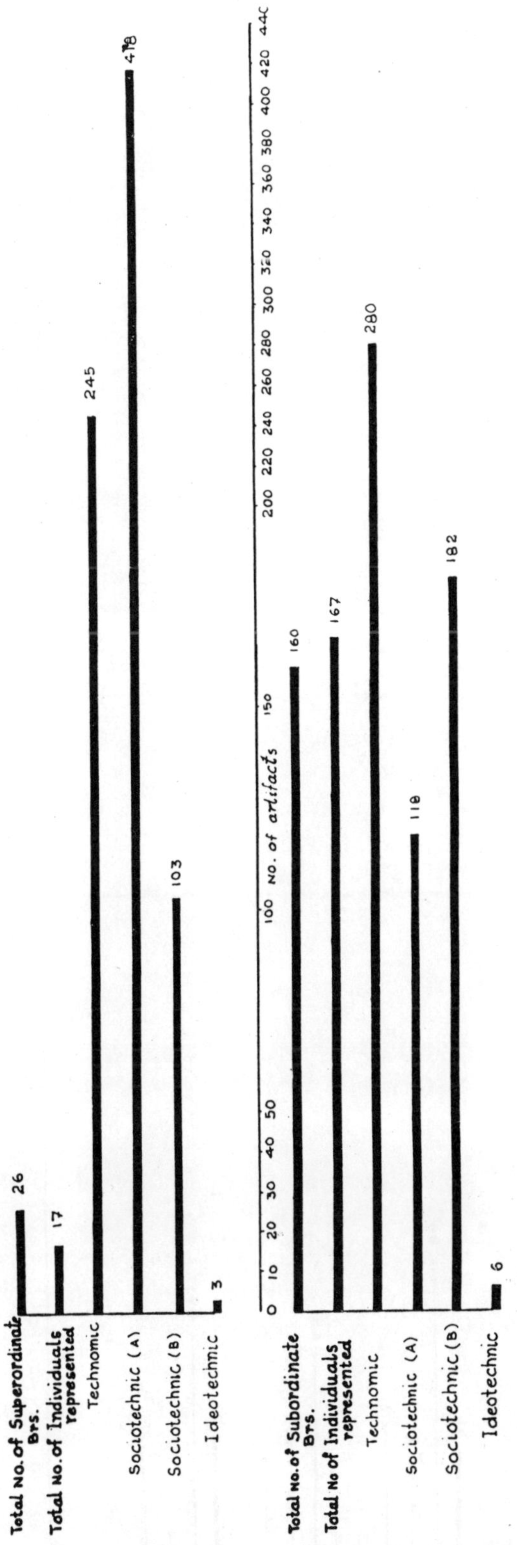

Fig. 14 Distribution of technomic, sociotechnic and ideo technic artifacts with respect to different burial categories and social dimensions

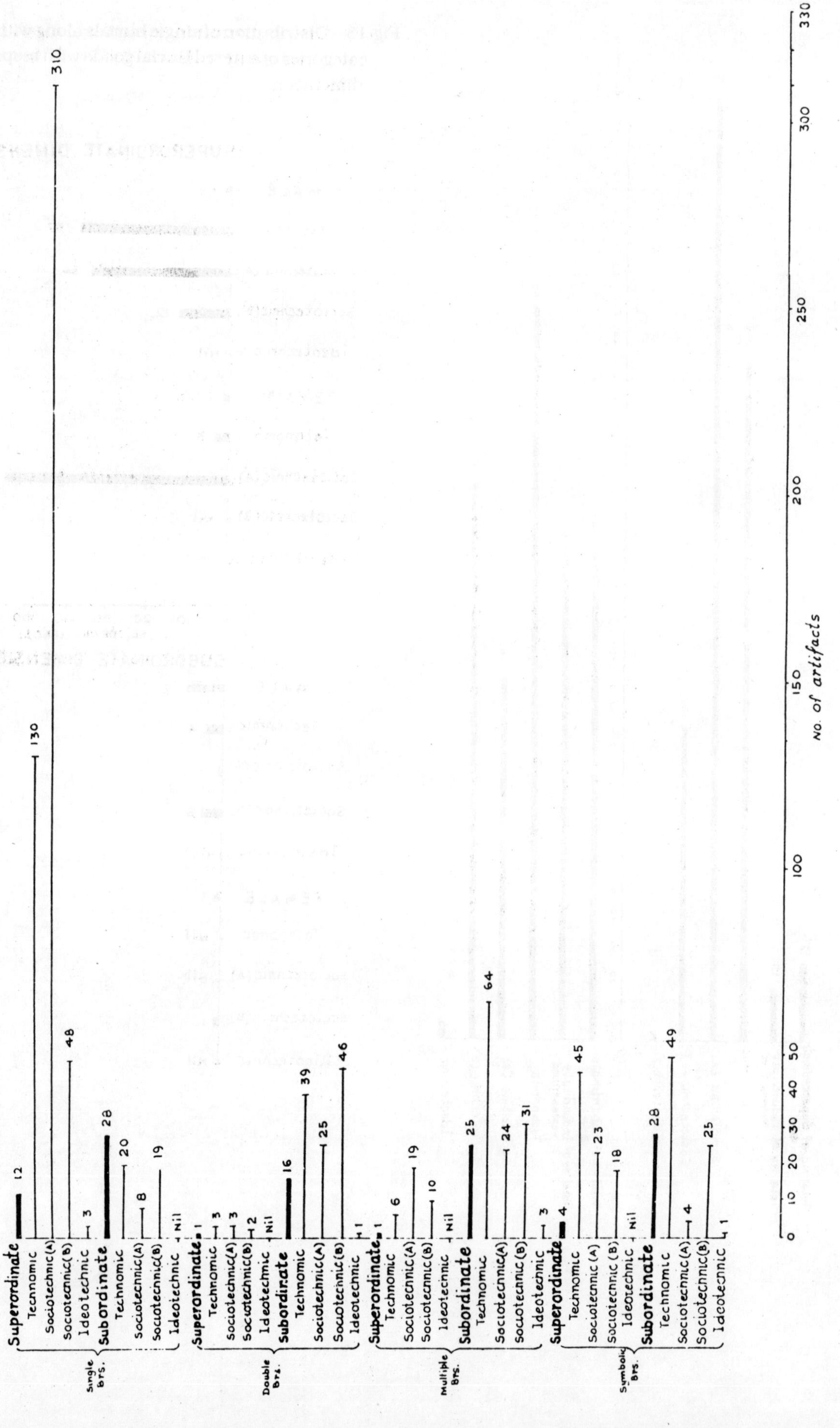

Distribution of technomic, sociotechnic and ideotechnic artifacts with respect to social dimension

DEOGARH ACHEULIAN ASSEMBLAGE : A PRELIMINARY REPORT

Makkhan Lal & Salahuddin*

The present paper deals with preliminary report of the acheulian assemblage collected from Deogarh, district Lalitpur during our exploration in the month of February 1989.

The first discovery of Prehistoric tools in Southern Uttar Pradesh is almost a century old. The credit for discovering stone Age tools in the region goes to Rivettcarnac (1832), Carlleyle (1883) and Cockburn (1888). They explored the districts of Banda, Hamirpur and Mirzapur and discovered a large number of Stone Age sites and rock- shelters. The most important discovery of the period was lower Palaeolithic tools from Singrauli basin in Mirzapur district (Cockburn, 1888). Though the region was very potential for Prehistoric research but was forgotten for about a century. This area again came into light with the discovery of Palaeoliths (Acheulian), by Zeuner and his colleague from Singrauli basin (Krishnaswami and Soundra Rajan, 1951). Since then the researches carried out in the area, covering districts of Varanasi, Mirzapur, Allahabad, Banda, Hamirpur, etc. has been proved to be one of the richest Prehistoric zones in the country (IAR 1959-60, 1961- 62; Pant, 1964 and 1982; Singh, 1965 and Sharma, at al., 1975, 1980)..

As far as the districts of Lalitpur and Jhansi are concerned, very little attention has been paid so far and very few sites of Stone Age culture have been discovered. A few of these are Lahchaura (Pant, 1964), Lalitpur (Singh, 1965), Deogarh and Moth (IAR, 1959-60, 1961-62). Taking the point into consideration we explored the districts Jhansi and Lalitpur for nearly two weeks and collected Acheulian artefacts from Deogarh and its vicinity. Though the Acheulian artefacts have been reported from Deogarh by M.C. Joshi (IAR, 1961-62: 104) but no detail reports are available. Therefore, this paper will contribute some information towards the understanding of the Prehistoric Culture in the area.

The Site

The village Deogarh, famous for its Dashavatar temple of Gupta period and some other temples of later period and Jain group of temples, lies between Lat. 24°15'N and Long. 78°15'E. It is 30 km. South West of Lalitpur and situated on the right bank of the river Betwa. The Palaeolithic site is located about 200 m. West of Jain group of temples which is 1 km. West of Deogarh village inside the fort of Karnali is on the sloping surface along the high cliff section of river Betwa. The artefacts, partly covered in reddish soil were scattered on the surface covering about 300 x 300 m. area. The area is covered with thick forest of dry tropical type.

A selective tool collection was made and it is expected that in the coming season we shall be able to explore a strech of 15 km. long and 8 km. broad forest to locate the sites and make systematic collection.

Assemblage

The assemblage from Deogarh comprising 88 artefacts (collected selectively) falls in shaped and simple artefacts.

Typologically the shaped artefact group consists of handaxes, cleavers, scrapers, discoids, pick and point. The brief description of each group is as follow:

1. *Hand-axes* (Fig. 1, Nos. : 1-3, Pl. 1, Nos. : 1-5)

This group has 25 specimens of different shapes and accordingly they have been divided as pear shaped (5), elongated (5), cordiform (4), Ovate (4), triangular (4), Lanceolate (1) and almond shaped (1). One piece is broken and can not be placed in any group. Most of the hand-axes (20) are made on heavy flakes. Only five are on thick stone blocks or cores. The specimens on flakes show wide angled prepared or simple striking platform. Except for a some all are bifacially flaked but the flake scars are very few. Because of that almost every piece has patches of cortex or natural surface. The hand-axes on cores are also bifacially trimmed but have cortexed butt end. In cross-section they are biconvex or lenticular.

Maxi. leng. 15.0 Cm. Maxi. Widh. 10.7 Cm.
Maxi. thick. 6.4 Cm
Mini. leng. 9.6 Cm. Mini. Widh. 6.2 Cm.
Mini. thick. 2.1 Cm
Aver. leng. 11.7 Cm. Aver. Widh. 8.2 Cm.
Aver. thick. 3.9 Cm

2. *Cleavers* (Fig.2, Nos.: 1-3 & Fig.3, Nos.: 1; Pl.2, Nos.: 1-4)

This category has 8 pieces and except two which are on indeterminate flakes, are fashioned on end flakes. The flakes are heavy with less secondary work

* Department of History, Aligarh Muslim University, Aligarh

on ventral, dorsal and butt end. Shape wise 7 specimens have U shaped butt with parallel sides and in one case butt is V shaped with divergent sides. As far as the cutting edge is concerned it is either straight (3) or oblique (1). Four pieces have damaged edge. In cross-section they represent parallelo gramatic profile.

Maxi.leng. 15.7 Cms. Maxi.Widh. 9.2 Cms.
Maxi.thick. 5.1 Cms.
Mini.leng. 7.0 Cms. Mini.Widh. 7.0 Cms.
Mini.thick. 3.7 Cms.
Aver.leng. 12.4 Cms. Aver.Widh. 8.2 Cms.
Aver.thick. 4.2 Cms.

3. *Scrapers* (Fig. 4, Nos.: 1-3, P1. 3, Nos. : 1-5

This category has 23 specimens. According to their working edge these are of several types, like side scrapers (concave 5, straight 10, convex 1), end scrapers 3, diverse 2, straight cum-concave 1, transverse 1. The scrapers are made on flakes which show plain as well as prepared striking platform. In most of the cases very less secondary work has been done on the dorsal and ventral sides. However, the working edges are well trimmed and retouched. In most of the cases the retouching is steep, but shallow types are also present.

Maxi.leng. 16.6 Cms. Maxi.Widh. 15.3 Cms.
Maxi.thick. 5.5 Cms.
Mini.leng. 8.9 Gms. Mini.Widh. 7.3 Cms.
Mini.thick. 2.1 Cms.
Aver.leng. 12.9 Cms. Aver.Widh. 4.5 Cms.
Aver.thick. 3.6 Cms.

4. *Point* (Fig. 5, No.: 1; P1. 3, No.: 6)

There is only one piece in this category and is made on indeterminate flake. The point is made by trimming the upper portion of both the sides of flake on one surface.

Length	12.5 Cms.
Width	8.0 Cms.
Thickness	3.6 Cms.

5. *Pick* (Fig. 3, No.: 2; P1. 2, No.: 5)

There is only one piece and is made on an elongated think flake. Dorsally it has three big flake scars. The picking edge, made by removal of three small flakes is like a inverted U shaped with sharp cutting edge. Butt is also U shaped.

Length	17.8 Cms.
Width	8.9 Cms.
Thickness	5.0 Cms.

6. *Discoid* (Fig. 3, No.: 3; P1. 5, Nos.: 1-3)

There are three specimens in this group. All are bifacially flaked. However, small patches of cortex is present in all the cases. The working edge is extending to the almost entire periphery.

Maxi.leng.11.0 Cms. Maxi. Widh 9.8 Cms.
Maxi. thick. 7.7 Cms.
Mini.leng. 9.1 Cms. Mini. Widh 8.1 Cms.
Mini. thick. 3.5 Cms.
Aver.leng. 9.9 Cms. Aver. Widh 8.9 Cms.
Aver. thick. 5.4 Cms.

The artefacts with no intentional secondary work has been grouped as simple artefacts and divided into flakes, cores and nodules.

1. *Flakes* (Fig. 5, No.: 2; Pl.4, Nos. : 1-4)

This group has 12 pieces of which 6 are indeterminate and 6 are end fakes. They have simple as well as prepared striking platform with less flake scars on the dorsal surface.

Maxi.leng. 15.7 Cms. Maxi Width 12.5 Cms.
Maxi.Thick.5.4 Cms.
Mini.leng. 10.6 Cms. Mini Width 6.9 Cms.
Mini.Thick.2.4 Cms.
Aver.leng. 12.4 Cms. Aver.Width 8.7 Cms.
Aver.Thick.3.5 Cms.

2. *Cores* (Fig. 5, No. 3; Pl.5, Nos.: 4-6) :

There are five specimens in this group. Shape-wise they are round, rectangular and triangular. Size-wise they are very small and fully exhausted with small, shallow and deep flake scars.

Maxi.leng.10.8 Cms. Maxi.Widh 9.2 Cms.
Maxi.thick. 6.7 Cms.
Mini.leng. 9.8 Cms. Mini.Widh 7.8 Cms.
Mini.thick. 6.0 Cms.
Aver.leng. 9.8 Cms. Aver.Widh 8.5 Cms.
Aver.thick. 6.3 Cms.

3. *Nodules*: This group has 7 pieces with one or two flake scars which may or may not be man made or might have been detached during the core preparation. These pieces can be treated as debetage :

Maxi.leng.13.1 Cms. Maxi.Widh 10.5 Cms.
Maxi thick. 7.0 Cms
Mini.leng. 9.1 Cms. Mini.Widh 5.1 Cms.
Mini thick. 4.0 Cms.
Aver.leng.10.6 Cms. Aver.Widh 8.7 Cms.
Aver thick. 5.4 Cms.

Discussion

The assemblage comprises of hand-axes cleavers, scrapers, point, pick, discoids, flakes, cores and nodules. Technologically the assemblage shows crudeness and assymetrical type of artefacts. The tools are fashioned on thick and heavy flakes. Few hand-axes are made on blocks or cores. In most of the cases they retain cortex on the dorsal side. Generally they have prominent bulb of percussion and deep flake scars. They also exhibit prepared as well as unprepared striking platform. As a whole the assemblage shows heavy hammer technique for detaching the flakes and secondary works. However, in some cases controlled technique has also been applied. Besides, block on block and direct percussion technique have also been used. As a whole the technique shows an inferior quality of workmanship.

The southern Uttar Pradesh has four sets of Acheulian assemblage :

Group 1: It has a considerable number of pebble, artefacts, sites are Gopipur and Nihi.

Group 2: It has very negligible or less number of pebble artefacts. Sites are Lalitpur, Parsidhia and Mahugarh.

Group 3 : Represents high frequency of hand-axes the sites are Nihi, Singrauli basin and Lalitpur.

Group 4 : In this group the sites are Gopipur, Mahugarh and represent more cleavers as compared to the hand axes. However, the region represents a complex type of Acheulian industry and does not show any uniformity (Pant, 1982). On the basis of typology the Deogarh assemblage is very much similar with Lalitpur, Singrauli and Nihi which have more hand-axes as compared to the cleavers.

Like Africa, India do not has any stratigraphical evidence of early and Late phases in Acheulian industry. On the basis of typology the Indian Acheulian assemblage has been divided into two phases. Early Acheulian and Late Acheulian (Misra 1975-76). The sites like Lalitpur, Adamgarh, Kulaina, Mahadeo Piparia, Chirki nevasa, Anangwadi and Hunsgi falls in the first group and Bhimbetka rockshetter III F-23 and F-24, cliff gravel at Mahadeo Piparia, etc. fall in the second group (Misra, 1975-76). This is also confirmed by the statistical measurements on the hand-axes of Chirki-Nevasa which show less refinement and crude nature of hand-axes as compared to the advanced Acheulian industry (Joshi, et al. 1976-77; Marathe, 1980).

Taking above characters into consideration the Deogarh assemblage can be grouped with early phase of Indian Acheulian tradition. Our this observation was confirmed by Prof. V.N. Misra and Prof. B.B. Lal who examined these tools when they visited Aligarh.

However, the assemblage is very small and no statistical work is possible, therefore, it will be premature to draw any concrete conclusion on such meagre data. Hopefully next year we shall return with a much bigger collection and report on it.

Description of Drawings

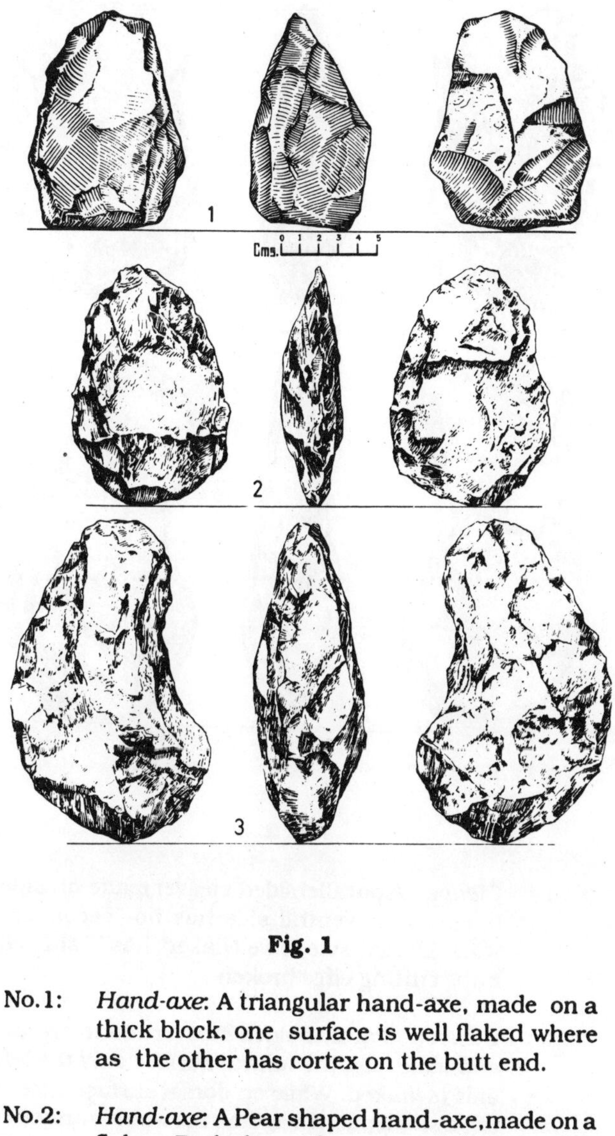

Fig. 1

No. 1: *Hand-axe*: A triangular hand-axe, made on a thick block, one surface is well flaked where as the other has cortex on the butt end.

No. 2: *Hand-axe*: A Pear shaped hand-axe, made on a flake. Both the surface are well flaked, scars are small and shallow.

No. 3: *Hand-axe*: A kidney shaped hand-axe, made on thick block. Except small patches of cortex, both surfaces are flaked, but scars are shallow, except a few which are deep.

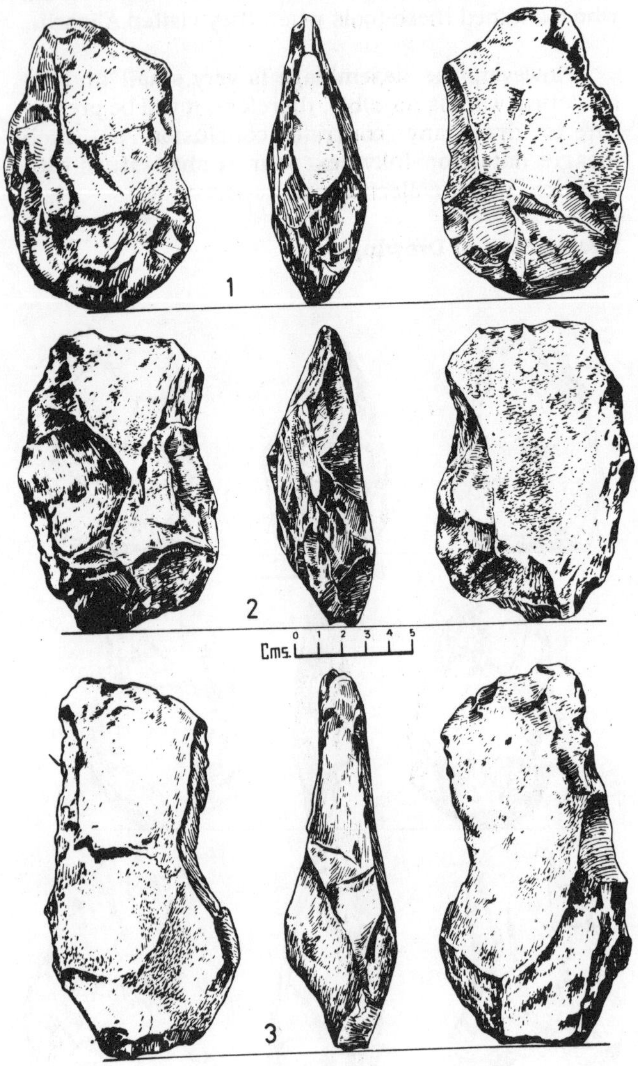

Fig. 2

No.1 : *Cleaver.* A parallel sided cleaver made on side flake. The ventral side has no secondary work. Dorsal side is well flaked, has U shaped butt, cutting edge broken.

No.2 : *Cleaver.* Parallel sided cleaver made on an end flake. On the ventral surface only the left side is flaked. While on dorsal surface except for a small patch of cortex the whole surface is flaked. It has straight cutting edge and U shaped butt and prepared striking platform.

No.3 : *Cleaver.* A parallel sided cleaver made on an indeterminate flake. One surface is unflaked where as other has few big scars. It has oblique cutting edge and U shaped butt.

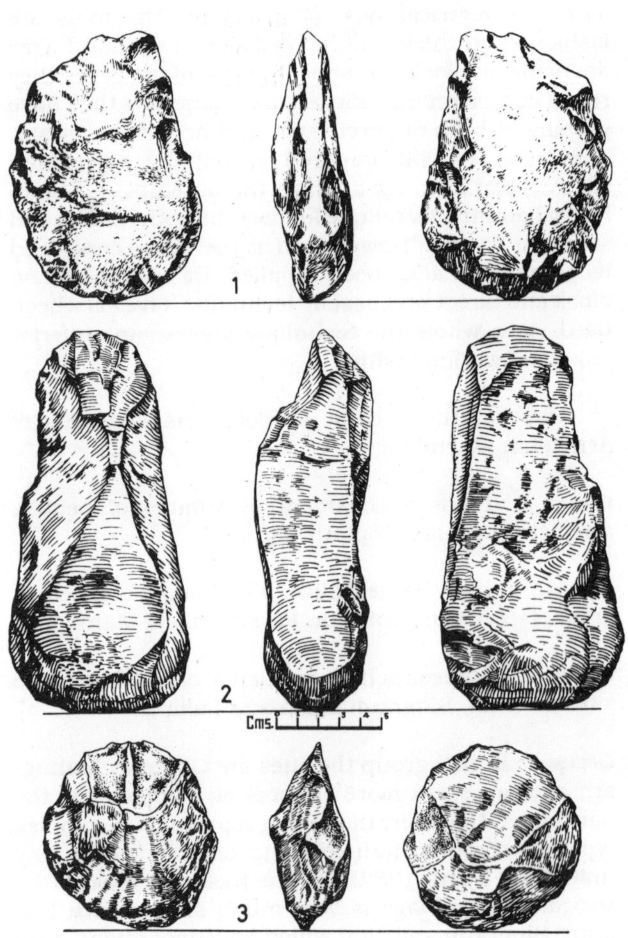

Fig. 3

No.1 : *Cleaver.* A parallel sided cleaver made on an end flake and has simple striking platform. Dorsally it is well flaked but ventrally only sides are flaked. The cutting edge is broken and butt is U shaped.

No.2 : *Pick.* It is made on an elongated thick core-like block. On one surface three big flake scars are present. Butt is broad and has cortex. The picking edge is very sharp and is made by removing small flakes.

No.3 : *Discoid:* It is more or less round. Except a small patch on one surface, both the surfaces are well flaked, prephery is very sharp.

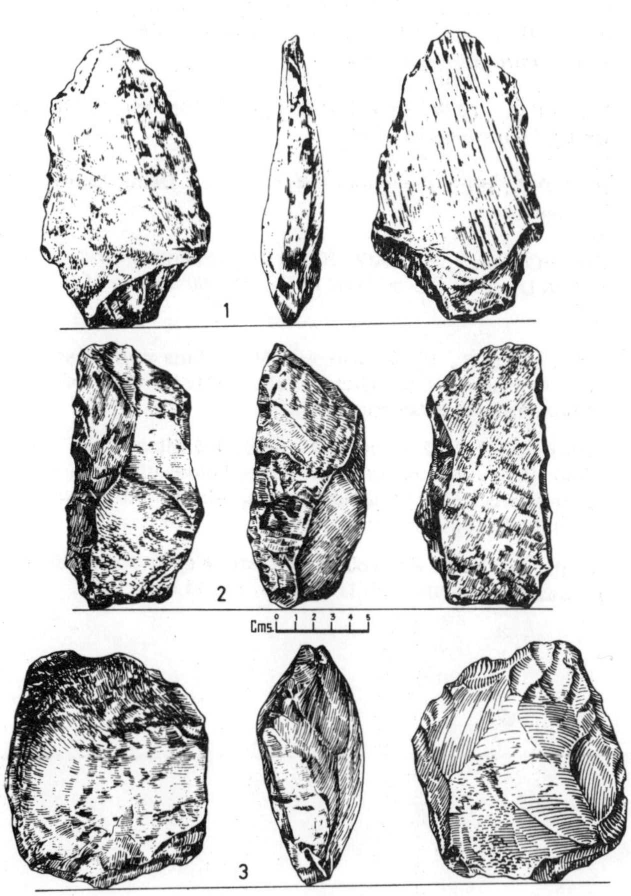

Fig. 4

No.1 : *Scraper*: A side scraper made on an end flake. The scraping edge is at left side on the ventral surface Dorsally it has natural surface; on ventral side, except the scraping edge there is no secondary work.

No.2 : *Scraper*: It is made on a rectangular thick block. The scraping edge is straight and steeply retouched. The opposite side of the scraping edge is thick and flaked for the hand hold.

No.3 : *Scraper*: It is made on a thick indeterminate flake. Both the surfaces have few flake scars. The scraping edges are present on two sides.

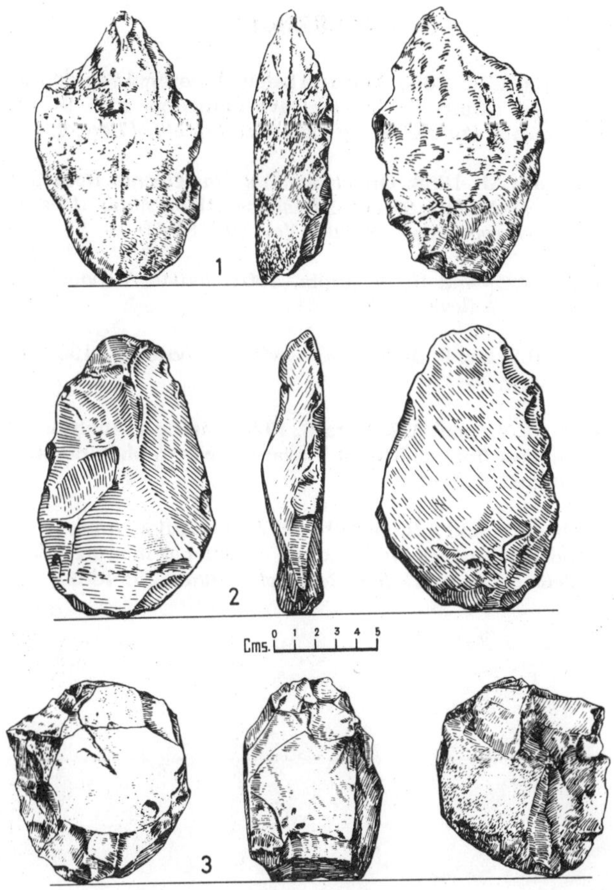

Fig. 5

No.1 : *Point*: Made on an indeterminate flake. One surface is more or less flat while other is ridged. The point is made by trimming the upper portion from both the side. patches of cortex are present.

No.2 : *Flake*: An end flake. Dorsal surface has flake scars but cortex is also present. Ventral surface has no secondary work. It has prepared striking platform.

No.3 : *Core*: It is a round shaped core. Small flake scars, deep as well as shallow are present; along with patches of cortex.

Acknowledgements

We acknowledge the assistance given by Sri Ghulam Mujtaba and Sri Anis Alvi for the preparation of Photographs and line drawings respectively in this paper.

REFERENCES

Carlleyle, A.C.L. 1883: Notes on Lately Discovered Sepulchral Mounds, Cairns, Caves, Cave-Paintings and Stone Implements. *Proceedings of the Asiatic Society of Bengal*, 49.

Cockburn, J. 1888: On Palaeolithic Implements from the Draft-gravels of the Singrauli Basin, South Mirzapur. *Journal of the Anthropological Institute*, Vol. XVII: 57-65.

Joshi, M.C. and R. Sengupta, 1964: *Indian Archaeology*, 1961-62 - A Review: 104.

Joshi, R.V. and R. Singh, 1960: *Indian Archaeology*, 1959-60 - A Review, 46-47.

Joshi, R.V. and A.R. Marath, 1976: Metrical Analysis of Hand-axes from Chirki on Pravara, Western Maharashtra, *Puratattva*, 8: 3-12.

Joshi, R.V. and A.R. Marath, 1977: Correlation Analysis of Hand-axes and cleavers and the Functional Interpretation. *Bulletin of Deccan College Research Institute*, 37: 48-60.

Krishnaswami, V.D. and K.V. Soundrarajan, 1951: The Lithic Tool-Industries of the Singrauli Basin, District Mirzapur. *Ancient India*, No.7: 40-65.

Marathe, A.R. 1980: Method for Discrimination of Hand-axe Assemblages. *Bulletin of Deccan College Research Institute*, 40: 112-116.

Misra, V.N. 1975-76: The Acheulian Industry from Rock-Shelter III F-23 at Bhimbetka, Central India: A Preliminary Study. *Puratattava* 8: 13-26.

Pant, P.C., 1964: Some Lithic tools Industries of Banda. *Bharati Supplements*, No.2.

Pant, P.C., 1982: *Prehistoric Uttar Pradesh*, Delhi: Agam Kala Prakashan.

Rivett-Carnac, H. 1832: Stone Implements found in the Banda District, *Proceedings of the Asiatic Society of Bengal:* 6-8.

Sharma, G.R., 1975: Seasonal Migrations and Mesolithic Lake Cultures of the Ganga Valley. *Presidential Address, Indian Prehistoric Society*, Delhi.

Sharma, G.R., V.D. Misra, D. Mandal, B.B. Misra and J.N. Pal, 1980: *Beginnings of Agriculture (Epi-Palaeolithic to Neolithic Excavations at Chopani-Mando, Mahadaha and Mahagara)*. Allahabad: Abinash Prakashan.

Singh, R., 1965: *Palaeolithic Industries of Northern Bundel Khand*. Unpublished Ph.D. Thesis, Poona University.

DHOLAVIRA: NEW HORIZONS OF THE INDUS CIVILIZATION

R.S. Bisht*

The ancient site at Dholavira in Kutch is one of the two largest known Indus settlements in India, the other being Rakhigarhi in Haryana, and may probably rank the fourth in the sub-continent, following Mohenjodaro in the Sind, Ganweriwala in Bahawalpur, and Harappa in the Punjab (all in Pakistan), in terms of area coverage, if not the status or hierarchy. Both the Indian sites are, however, notable for their planned lay-out also, albeit with a variance.

The ancient mounds of Dholavira, eversince their discovery in 1967-68 by Jagat Pati Joshi,[1] had aroused curiosity among archaeologists.[7] After a lapse of almost-two decades, the present author along with his team made a systematic survey and documentation of the visible structures and other features of the mounds and their environs. The results were much revealing[8]. The very first excavations conducted there for six months, since January 1990, by the team of Vadodara Excavation Branch of the Archaeological Survey of India have shown that there lies buried the spectacular remains of a Harappan city which are highlighted by enormous proportions, intricate planning delineated by an elaborate fortification consummate architecture, fine water structures and huge accumulation of successive settlements of over a millennium. The excavations have also provided ample proof that the Indus Civilisation had not only lived its mature phase at Dholavira but was also preceded by an antecedent culture and followed by impoverished culture-complex.

Location and Climate

Dholavira is today a modest village in the Bhachau taluka of Distt. Kutch in Gujarat. It is situated in the north-west corner of the Khadir which is a large island surrounded from all sides by the Great Rann of Kutch.

The mounds (lat.23°53'10"N, long.70°13'E), (two parts being locally known as 'Kotada' and 'Bazar'), located 1 km north-west of the village, are embraced by two seasonal torrents, namely, the Mansar and Manhar, which emanate from the hills in north-east and flow in their defined beds cut through the motley terrain of rocks and alluvia till they join each other just before running into the Great Rann. These are emphemeral streams which carry a heavy volume of water after downpours in the catchment area but dry up quickly within hours. There is, however, no available source of surface-water other than the artificial lakes and ponds which too are solely dependent on the monsoon. However, Dholavira in the entire Khadir is exceptionally blest with such good ground-water reserve in its soft sedimentary limestone deposits that they did not fail it even during the recent four years of the severest drought of the century that occurred in this region. The soil is, however, rich and fertile sandy loam but not available plentiful for cultivation as it is largely restricted to a narrow strip running alongthe Rann from north-west through south to south-east or to a few patches in an otherwise rocky terrain intersected by numerous torrents which radiate from the hills in the north. The Khadir is the second poorest in the Kutch in respect of the rainfall which averages out at more 262 mm per annum mostly received from the monsoon that remains active from June to August, sometimes extending to September. The Kharif is, therefore, the main crop. However, failure of the monsoon, sometimes for three to five years consecutively, is frequent and so are the famine. As a result, both surface and ground-water dry up causing large-scale migration of people along with their livestock from the hostile environment in which much of the wild life and vegetation perishes miserably. The forest cover in the hills is otherwise too sparse and is more so in the sloping landscape. Both flora and fauna are semi-arid in nature. Thus, the land has almost an incongenial environment for human occupation and the situation might not been much different in the past. In such circumstances, location of such a large city as Dholavira, indeed poses an enigma and as such a challenge to archaeologists for a satisfactory solution.

The Site

Joshi[10] found two mounds: one smaller but higher than the other and identified them as the 'citadel' and the 'lower town'. He also noticed remains of defense walls, bastions and gateways on the citadel mound in addition to the Harappan material scattered all over. He rightly declared the site to be the largest Indus settlement in India. The site was subsequently visited by Pandya[11] who further confirmed its archaeological potential besides making some modifications, even if incorrectly, in respect of the positioning of the mounds with reference to the directions. Our field-work, however, brought further precision in relation to the bearings although our earlier reporting of the dimensions worked out hurriedly by improvised measuring

* C/o Excavation Branch, Archaeological Survey of India, Baroda.

methods[12] have had to be corrected by more intensive survey conducted later.[13]

On first visit to the site, one is likely to be overwhelmed by the enormity of both size and deposit. Conspicuously, there are two mounds. The one in south is pre- eminently higher but smaller in extent, and the other in the north and north-east is twice as large but comparatively lower. Both are separated from each other apparently by a 45 m wide vacant area. These are the mounds which were examined and dealt with by the earlier explorers. We, however, brought to light a series of other small mounds as well as built-up areas or constructions visibile on the surface far and wide to west and north-west of the main site. Some of them are well within the city proper; some are within separate enclosures, at places, well integrated to the city walls; and others just lie today *disjecta membra*. They should be representatives of those suburban establishments which grew up in course of time bearing some relationship to the urban nucleus of the Harappans. Among these, those numerous circular stone-structures which can anywhere be seen containing the protohistoric material in and around are not included as they might not have been parts of the urban centre as a whole and were more than likely pasterior to the latter. They are found spread over an area upwards of 100 hectares.

The area or dimensions of the city or its components, in fat denote the extent to which the respective debris, in situ or fallen, is found spread over and should, therefore, not be taken at their face value.

a. General Conformation: The debris of the main fortified city covers about 800 m EW and 650 m NS. The line of the fortification is indicated by a linear elevation running straight and taking turns at right angles. The elevation shows up at several places mud-brick masonry and/or stone masonry walls. The stone-wall segments appear again and again, singly or in twos or threes which are usually found running parallel to each other. The elevation is fairly intact for full length in the west and north whereas in the south it is preserved for a length of 600 m starting from the south-western corner upto a few metres beyond the Mahar nallah, and in the east, it is nicely extant for a length of 210 m with faint traces, here and there, for another 200 m. Then comes the Manhar which traverses the city to cut out its south-eastern part, not wantonly indeed, but as per the planner's scheme of damming it, most probably for conserving the precious monsoon run-off in a large reservoir set within the city enclosure which is no more extent hereabouts now. The relics of the enclosing fortification so pertinently significant do not seem to have been spotted or looked for by the others obviously for three reasons. First, there was no precedent of such a provision of a common peripheral enclosure incorporating walled or unwalled parts of an Indus settlement elsewhere. Secondly, the vast vacant areas, themselves a hitherto unkown phenomenon in the Indus urban planning, were strong enough to hold back any unsuspecting explorer from further search. Thirdly, in the east, where the wall ran very close to the built-up area of the lower town, does not survive now.

Among other features of the planning, there is provision in the city of vast open areas as wide as from 70 m to 140 m or even more, albeit partitioned by several massive cross-walls tying together the outer and inner defensive walls specially at strategic points, turnings, or corners of the inner fortifications, or, near gateways. We have open spaces in all major divisions and the same wil be dealt with at respective places.

As far as the principal mounds are concerned, as already mentioned, there are apparently two mounds designated as the 'citadel' and the 'lower town' following the traditional nomenclature. However, a closer examination revealed[14] that there, existed three principal divisions two of which were strongly protected by rectangular fortifications faced with stone-masonry. Further, the citadel lay to the south of the second walled division, albeit separated by a 45 m wide open space, running from east to west all along the length of both. Besides, a third divisions, having no appertinent wall-enclosure, was laid out to the east of the second one. These three principal divisions, in view of their respective location and construction, have been christened as 'citadel' or 'acropolis', 'middle town' and 'lower town', borrowing from the *RGVEDA*[15] of three significant terms viz., *parama, madhyama* and *avama*. These terms are frequently used therein to denote three different orders or types of divine or mundane horizons, zones, assemblies or settlements, rather divisions. Importantly, the *ATHARVEDA*[16] mentions the occupants of these respective divisions as *paramesthin, madhyamesthin* and *avamesthin*. Hence, the above nomenclature in English. We shall use them frequently in this paper, even when we are aware of the inherent limitations and difficulties.

b. Acropolis: Commanding over the entire cityscape and its environs, the citadel or acropolis mound stands high in the south-western quarter of the general or outer enclosure. It was carefully insulated from all sides by wide open areas, duly enclosed and partitioned by broad walls. The mound today measures 300 m in length from east to west and 140 to 160 m from north to south. As already reported elsewhere,[17] the surface study made before the excavations had revealed that this mound consisted of two conjoined rectangles, both circumvallated, hence the steep slopes on all sides, more so pronounced on the eastern

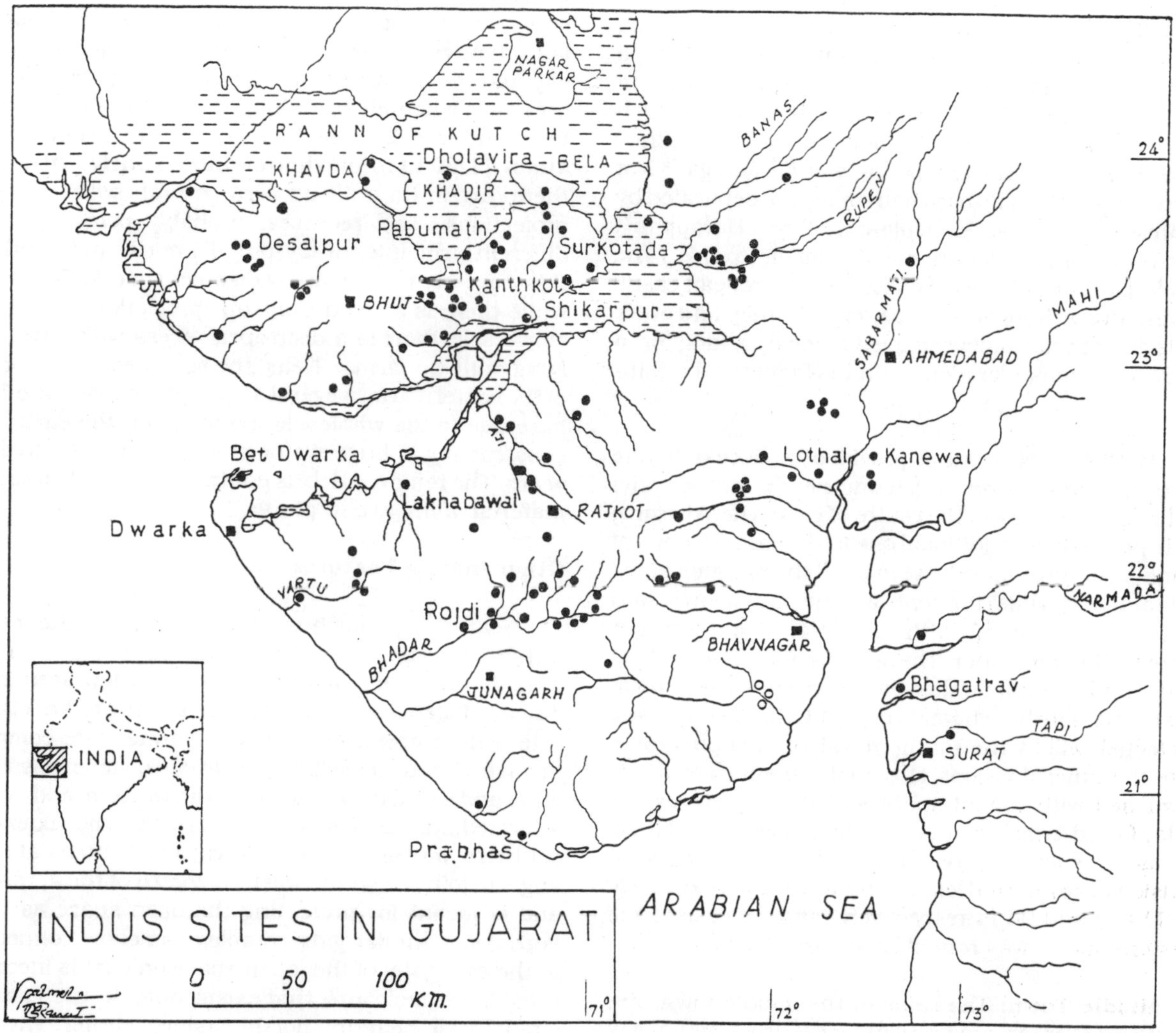

INDUS SITES IN GUJARAT

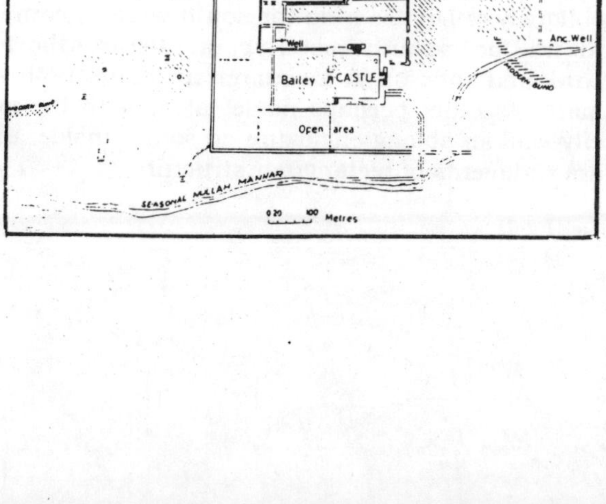

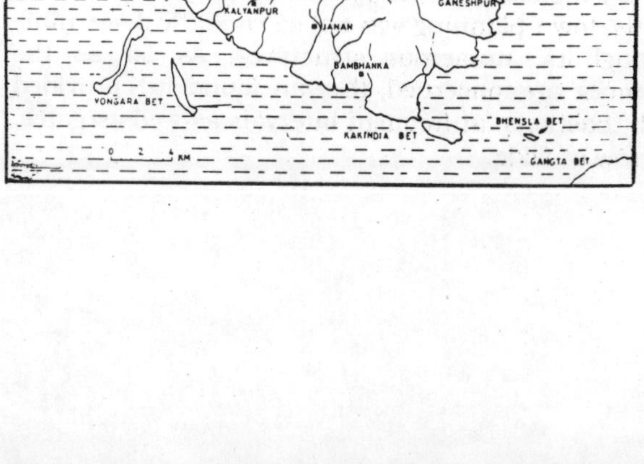

half which was most meticulously designed and strongly fortified and which rises twice as much of the western part. From the firm natural ground in south and west it registers a height of 15 m and 18 m respectively, while the other one does just half as much in either case. It reminds of a similar situation obtained at Surkotada[18] and also perhaps at Kalibanga.[19] Not surprising, if the southern half somewhat separated by depressed gulley at Mohenjo-daro[20] or Harappan[21] also conceals an evidence not dissimilar to this. The whole planning strikes likeness to a European castle having two well-fortified areas, called inner and outer baileys, both normally occupied alone by a king or a garrison commander along with his family and retainers.

At Dholavira, there is provided for access to the eastern sub-division, a gateway nearly, not exactly, rather staggerredly in the centre of each defensive arm with probably an additional one in the east. Stumps of stone-structures may be seen in all the margins along the ramparts while the central zone, much lower and flat, is today covered with a mantle of silt brought there by the rain-water. The western sub-division was also found carefully walled on three sides, viz. north, west and south, whereas on east, it is already protected will by the southern wall of the upper one. Like the other divisions of the city, the former too is furnished with vacant space and the structures are today found largely confined to the eastern half of it. As far as dimensions are concerned, the eastern subdivision gave internal length and width approximately as 114 m and 94 m respectively and in case of the western one, it was roughly a square of 123 m.

c. Middle Town: The ruins of the middle town are scattered over an area roughly measuring 360 m EW and 250 m NS with a maximum rise of 13.5 m. Like the citadel, it too, in its turn, is found fortified as well as separated from the outer wall by wide vacant areas on north and west and from the citadel by another space, as already stated, while it almost adjoins the lower town sprawling to east of it. This division runs parallel to the citadel and rather slightly outmeasures it in length both east and west. Within its walled area too, there are vacant spaces; a wide open area in west in addition to two open quadrangles each on north and south. From three sides, these quadrangular areas are closed in by built-up houses. Although a east-west thoroughfare running through the middle of the width and across the densely built-up area was surmised, yet a congnisant street-system so germane to the Indus town-planning was not so candidly discernible through its numerous structures. As far as the defences are concerned, they are found duly provided with bastions at frequent intervals as well as gates, narrow or wide.

d. Lower Town: The relics of the lower town today cover an area roughly making an square of 300 m lying between the eastern arms of the defences of the city and the middle town, whereas along north-south they approximately run along the width of the middle town and the intermediate space. In height, they attain 11.50 m in maximum. Interestingly, here too, there are in its built-up area several bold or mild projections and recesses, probably pointing to a different principle of lay-out. To north and south of this core-area there are wide open spaces. On north, while there is a bold built-up projection, on south, conversely, there is a deep open recess within two far-lying built-up arms. Near the south-eastern corner of the eastern arm, several Harappan houses are laid bare due to the wholesale removal of the earth for constructing a huge water-storage bund in recent years. The removed debris contains profuse Harappan material of the urban phase.

Other Inlying Features

Nearer the north-western corner of the outer fortification and internally attached to the northern wall, there is a small mound bearing a few seemingly damaged structures perhaps pertaining to an elaborate gatecomplex. Another elaborate gate-complex furnished with possible guardrooms, steps, passageways and a well may be seen at the western end of the intermediate open space. It is in the extended southern wall of the middle town, which turns at right angle to join the south-western corern of the acropolis and is meant for protecting the open space as well. Perhaps, a similar gate-complex somehow connected to the east gate of the open space on east is incorporated in an enclosure that exists outside the eastern citadel-wall near its north- eastern corner. There is one more built-up area that lies, quite interestingly, in a special walled enclosure to the south of the citadel. Densely built structures about the walls hereabouts and were possibly used by royal retainers.

From near the east gate of the citadel emanates a massive wall, which runs with obtuse-angle, turns towards east, south-east and south to joint the city-wall across which it reappears to pursue its southward course upto the river (Manhar) -bank where it now takes a westward course along the bank for an appreciable length before being washed away by floods. Most possibly, its counterpart on west obliquely originates from the south-western corner of the wall for its south-westerly course towards the river-bank and ends up at a square structure. Both segments together perhaps made along with the main city-wall an ablong enclosure on south. Inside, there are rudiments of rectangular structures.

Outlying Ancient Remains

To west and north-west and even across the Mansar, over an extensive area outlying the city-enclosure, there are five or six mounds of low to very low profile or, at places, almost level with the present ground level. They exhibit ruins of carefully constructed building foundations of stone or *disjecta* enclosure-walls with stone facings. They may very well repreent suburban establishments related in some way to the urban nucleus. Though a little confirmatory material is available on the surface as is not unusual there, there is strong evidentiary information to drive the point home. To cite an example, far-lying structure-bearing area of somewhat similar nature, visible on surface in south-west, when despoiled for earth to construct a water-collecting bund, has yielded several building rooms and walls associated with a Harappan storage jar *in situ* in addition to plethora of broken pottery and other items. Furthermore, three pockets in north-west, on both sides of the Mansar, are firmly integrated to the city-fortification by their respective enclosure walls one of which appears to have run across the stream, most probably to hold back or divert the monsoon-run-off into a water-structure. This wall although seems to be non- existent now on the other side but it probably enclosed an area which contains several building-foundations which, very significantly, are found bounded by an architecturally identical broad wall appearing in north as well north-west continuing right upto the rocky river bank downstream. Still more significantly, its counterpart makes its appearance on the other bank - possibly another evidence of damming the channel. Yet another low mound stands halfway down to south and in front of the western city wall. It appears to contain an important structure on account of its strategic location and its proximity to the city-wall.

The foregoing account makes it abundantly clear that Dholavira houses an extensive and planned city, of course, with a variance from other sites. Much of forethought must have had gone into its layout and execution. A fair visibility and a fine state of preservation of the ruins immensely helped to set objectives for the excavations.

Objectives and Strategy

The recent excavations aimed at confirming or otherwise the salient features of the broad outlines of the city in particular and its interior planning in general besides at obtaining a stratigraphical sequence.

The entire walled city was divided into square of 10 m each oriented 4 degree off the north in view of the average bearing of the visible structures. There cardinally located rows of squares running from wall to wall one laid out north-south, centrally across the upper acropolis and the middle town, and two, along east-west: one across the both subdivisions of the acropolis and the other across the middle town and the lower town: were selected for surface striping or shallow digging. The policy was to etch out extant structures to topmost working floor and to sink to the natural soil one square each at all the three principal divisions of the city for obvious reasons.

Excavation: Surface excavation was satisfying to a great extent though the objective could not be realised fully in view of unexpected increase in the quantum of work due to the monumental character of gateways as well as the defensive walls and huge pile of downwash over the penultimate working floor of the intermediate open space. As a result, western half of middle town and eastern half of lower town together with their open spaces could not be striped nor could be made deep-probing of sediments at these to areas. In the north- south trench, operation-area on south was shifted to west. For stratigraphical sequence at the higher subdivision of acropolis a broad and deep rain-gully cut through the deposit and the southern defensive wall near its south-western corner was chosen for speedy excavation down the virgin soil besides getting an opprotunity of understanding the growth of the fortification threat. Furthermore, another deep probing nearer the centre of acropolis did yield an enormous deposit, of 10.50 m, but failed in providing structural sequence because, as subsequently found, it fell in a large water reservoir. Further digging thereabouts was not possible as the operation area was reduced to a small pit.

A Brief of Findings

(i) a stratigraphical sequence both of the deposit and the wall of the higher part of acropolis was obtained;

(ii) almost all walls whether of the general, or divisional, or subdivisional fortifications, (excepting the eastern city wall because of its destruction by both man and nature and the northern wall of lower acropolis for want of time), were confirmed:

(iii) further at acropolis, the east gate partially, the north gate nearly fully and west gate marginally exposed and existence of a seemingly large rain-water reservoir along with its feeder channel was brought to light besides other structures;

(iv) a succession of meticulosuly laid floors on open space at depth of 2.30 to 2.40 m from the present level of the field was obtained;

(v) useful, albeit not full, information was gleaned with regard to the interior lay-out of each division or subdivision of the city; and,

(vi) last, although not the least, existence of a water-reservoir in the south-eastern quarter was established in a sporadic dig.

Results

A regular occupational deposit of over 12 m as ascertained in the aforesaid gully has provided valuable information. Evidence from other digs has further supplemented as well as complemented it. Study is still under way. The site, however, witnessed the pre-Indus early, mature, late mature and post-urban Indus periods or phases of culture.

The first occupation of the site (Pl. I), as on today, pertains to a non-Harappan or pre-Harappan culture represented by an accumulation of 60 to 70 cm that lies over sterile strata made of disintegrated rock loosely knit with sand, which may be an artificially raised deposit. Interestingly, the archaeological strata which are represented by four main layers from No. (7) to No. (10) precede the first known defensive wall. No enclosure-wall to the settlement is found hereabouts, but the layers tend to rise towards outside. An enclosure wall today concealed underneath the later one, cannot, therefore, be ruled out. Use of moulded bricks measuring 36 x 18 x 9 cm is attested to in a demolished debris forming layer (8). Most significantly, layer (10) as well as layer (7) have yielded evidence of copper working to which should relate a fireplace associated with a lot of ash and copper slag and tools. While the former has offered pieces of crucible (s) and two well chiselled stone-blocks, probably associated with metallurgical work or stone working, the latter presented bag fulls of burst globules of totally vitrif'ed clay.

The ceramic pieces, too meagre for a meaningful study, however, represented diverse fabrics with equally diverse surface treatment. The majority of the pottery is wheel-made red ware of lighter or pinkish tones treated with a variety of slip or application, or decorated with incised horizontal grooves on the body, or incised patterns executed including one example of incisions done in reserved slip technique. Of surface application, there are examples of pleasing red slip, casual smearing with dull brown pigment, thick-coated buff paste, deep black slip on leather-coloured ware, or thinly applied white paint. Noteworthy are two examples (Pl.II). A few light red ware sherds, probably of a medium-sized vessel, are treated with carelessly applied drab brown slip over which are executed black bands, or a series of strands arranged horizontally or vertically on specially white-painted areas. In another case, a deep dish is externally provided with a carination below the neck and internally first decorated with shallow wavy patterns and then treated with a white slip or paint all over. Yet another example of pottery, interesting both technically and typologically, is represented probably by upper body of a vessel of red ware treated with a smooth red slip on the outer surface as well as upto the throat internally and further decorated with a black line round the rim. It has a wide mouth with a flaring rim making a C-profile with the neck and the shoulder. Besides, the assemblage includes sherds of soapy, buff, coarse red and crude hand-made wares. Minor antiquities are rare. Copper tools and pieces are found in a good strength. Pending further study, it is premature to hazard a comparison with an assertion of certainty. The Indus elements in pottery as well as antiquities are conspicuous by their absence.

The following two layers, i.e. (6) and (5), which are contemporary of the first defensive wall, have produced very little material, ceramic or otherwise. Whatever collected is, at present, non-Harappan in character while the upper strate from layer (4) to layer (1) have provided engouh diagnostic items of the Harappan civilization in the form of terracotta triangular cakes, chert blades, steatite beads, perforated jars, a few other pottery forms of standard fabrics as well as surface decoration. It, however, remains still uncertain whether the Harappan themselves were the real authors of the first fortification or else they incidentally came there quick on the heels to be the real beneficiaries of that. Doubt is raised by its brick-masonry-work which is marked by poor workmanship as well as by use of hand-made bricks of irregular shape and size along side the use of a few moulded ones a feature quite unusual with the Harappan builders.

Having lived through quite some time, enough for an accumulation of about 1 m, Harappans added another wall, almost 5 m thick, to the anterior one and raised it at a stretch to a height of about 9 m. This wall too, in its turn, was pastered with white or pinkish earth. Unfortunately, a deposit of nearly 1.30 m contemporary to its early phase could not be examined as yet. It is, however, clear that it was much later revetted internally by a 1.90 m thick mud- brick wall raised on a thick stone base.

All through these constructions, the mature Harappans plausibly marched on from strength to strength as revealed by the huge collection of pottery and other antiquities collected from the contemporary deposit accounting for upwards of 10 m. This early mature deposit has yielded a large number of antiquities in the form of several seals, sealings, weights, a variety of beads, bangles and other ornament pieces of gold, silver, copper, lead, semi-precious stones, shell, or clay, and also different clay objects like 'cakes, balls, marbles, model caste-frames, stoppers etc., besides shell ladles, spoons, inlay pieces, bangles, rings and others - all essential cultural attributes of the Indus civilisation. However, terracotta figurines, human or animal, so profuse in the adjoining Sind and further north and north-east of the Indus cultural area are either absent or bafflingly rare.

Likewise, the ceramic reportoire is much more remarkable for its non conventional wares, particularly the course red ware in which many Indus forms are translated and surface decoration simulated although the standard Harappan wares are present, albeit with notable oscillation in its quantity through the strata. In addition, buff, white, cream and greenish weres are also availalbe. A large number of miniature forms generally fabricated with remarkable dexterity evoke great admiration. Indus paintings are sparsely noticeable.

This discernible shortfall in classical ceramics and in certain categories of antiquities are widely compensated by the excellent town-planning as well as monumental yet exquisite architecture, which will go a long way to understand the cultural spectrum of the Harappans and also to prompt for reassessing the town-planning of the known and excavated sites.

To carry forward the sequence, the upper levels have provided two more cultural phases of immense archaeological significance. First comes the late phase of the yet mature Indus culture largely indicated by the continuous use of all essential objects like beads, blades, bangles, metal tools, ceramic forms and ornament pieces, and most importantly by weights and seals. Seals, however, become simpler, smaller and usually devoid of animal figures although engraving of characters received all the more attention. That apart, there are as well crude terracotta seals or amulets bearing simple geometric motifs or bold and short strokes. In the ceramics, new variety of wares with surface decoration closely related to the Jhukar assemblage on one hand and to the black-and-red were tradition bringing along a different class of thin grey and black wares often burnished smooth on the other make their appearance. Of white painting, there is a solitary example and that too on a thin and burnished grey ware. This phase may somewhat compare with Surkotada IC, Desalpar IB, Nagwada and several sites in Saurashtra. Architecturally, it appears that they maintained for sometime the cityscape not unlikely in subdued or diminished form and even carried out repairs and even built-up of a few constructions, but they all loudly speak of falling standards. Hereabouts, something drastic occurred and the city lost its glory and grandeur and also its urban character. With the result, the city was rapidly abandoned by the administrative authority and the affluent people. Only, the poorer folk and artisans stayed on. These squatters raised their jerry-built constructions anywhere, preferably under the protective shelter of and right against the standing fort-walls, or on the gate-terraces. They even occupied the gate chambers for sundry use. Attractive and useful architectural members were removed and put to different uses as per need or fancy.

They were still living in and building rectangular houses. But those who succeded them, surely after some gap of time constructed circular structures of stones collected from the earlier houses. These circular structures, still in vogue in the kutch and locally called *Kuda* were copied from the wooden prototypes found at Zadada[22] in the Indus context itself. Culturally, they migh not be otherwise a different people as their pottery suggests. The firm layers caused by them have considerably suffered at the hands of nature. These people do not seem to have had a compact or permanent settlement. They may have been coming here periodically or seasonally. As such structures can be seen anywhere at the site of even in far-flung fields on any side After the post-urban nomadic phase, the site was never again occupied.

Fortification

a. General: The outer walls which are otherwise fairly well-preserved for long stretches were somehow found in most cases badly eroded or damaged or even missing in our trenches. Nevertheless, their existence but for that of the east city wall, was confirmed precisely at expected points.

On north, internally stone-faced rampart showing its brick masonry over a wide stretch was laid bare although the outer edge cold not yet be traced. Not unlikely that there was a bastion beside another one that is still visible on the surface to the west of it.

On south, the mud-plastered inner face of the brick rampart providing a width of 8.40 m inclusive of a thin stone-veneer on the outer face was determined with a possibility again of a bastion or else an outward shift of the entire-wall at such an vantage point where a broad tie-wall emanating from the juncture of the defensive walls of the upper and lower oblongs of acropolis joins the outer fortification.

On the west, the city-wall was ascertained at two points: one, in the southern EW trench, and, the other, in a rain-gulley close to its northern counterpart. In the first, the inner half was found completely eroded while the other half together with a bastion was exposed. The wall was rebuilt once. The other trench exhibited that the outer wall was initially around 3.60 m wide and subsequently widened internally by adding another construction of 1.20 m at a later date. Initially, there was no stone veneering as is evident in both the digs. It was perhaps a later innovation as evidence from elsewhere at the site, whatsoever meagre at present, tends to indicate. One thing is, however, certain that either side of the wall was successively floored for an easy walk of the petrolling guards round the fortification.

On the east, the city wall, as already said, was found worn down to the rock-bed which itself is much higher than the level on which lower town was raised.

b. Acropolis: The deep trenching in the gulley has evidenced that the Harappan occupation at least in eastern subdivision of acropolis started within a massive mud-brick fortification which was either built by themselves or their forerunners a short time ago. Subsequently, it was first widened, then further strengthened with a revetment, at both occassions from the inner side, and finally reconstructed substantially, this time around from the outer side, most plausibly, in consequence of a devastative natural calamity (Pl. III).

We have already stated about the large scale use of hand-made bricks of indifferent dimensions and of poor masonry of the first fortification wall. Its truncated top and chopped-off exterior do not today provide its full height and width. Whatever that remains now sufficiently demonstrates that its extant height of 6.30 m was raised at a stretch with a steep batter of 75°. Its maximum available width at a height of 4 m reads 2.65 m whereas outer face is not traceable there. In spite of that, given the same rate of batter for the outer face from that point downwards, its basal width should be more than 6 m a formidable thickness indeed. As regards the treatment of the face, it was plastered successively for eleven to thirteen times with aesthetically chosen clays which range from white to pink in colour with the exception of use of grey clay only once.

Probably after a century or so, the existing wall was internally widened to more than 5 m. This construction shows superb workmanship as well as use of standardised and moulded bricks made of good clays of different colours (suggestive of community contribution). Its total extant height of 9 m does not show any phase of raising, therefore, indicative of great concern for protection on the part of the Harappans. Its inner side registers a taper of 80°. It was carefully plastered over with white, buff, pink-coloured clays.Much later when there had already accumulated habitational debris of nearly 3 m, a 1.90 to 2 m broad revetment was added to it from inside. In this case, upon an 1.5 m thick rubble masonry, there is raised the brick work of more than 2.80 m. It remains to be seen whether it was indeed a revetment of a single make, or was a successively raised as fender-wall or a raised walk, or both denoting two or three phases.

Sometime during the early mature phase itself and surely subsequent to the first addition, the city was visited by a catastrophe, very possibly by a severe earthquake followed by heavy rains. With the result, a substantial portion of the defensive wall collapsed from outside. The parallel-running multiple cracks, wide fissures soon filled in with the slipped masonry as visible on the second wall and badly broken, tilted, or dislodged masonry of the first today stand mute witness to that great disaster. Naturally, a large-scale reconstruction was undertaken. The fallen debris was removed and badly affected portion of the walls was dressed up to receive the fresh masonry now made of the better quality bricks, neatly veneered with the hammer- dressed stone-blocks and rubble. The work was as broad as 6 to 6.50 m. Further, the added masonry was raised over a considerably thick rubble-base. Similar large-scale reconstruction appears to have been carried out extensively at the site, most particularly on the citadel which might had suffered the most due to its monumentality.

The lower end of the reconstruction still remains to be exposed. still, the present basal width of the combined walls excluding the revetment amounts to nearly 15.50 m, with a sure possibility of further increase downwards while at the middle height it is 13 m and on the eroded top it measures 11.50 m . Which may come down further on the horizontal plane at the extant top to 9.50 m given the rate of taper which approximates to 65° on average.

The exposed width at the eroded top varies considerably at other places. It measures 12.30 m at the east gate,. 11 to 11.20 m at the north one and 14.75 m near the west one, while the western wall of the outer bailey gives a reading from 6 to 6.60 m. Of the south wall of the last mentioned one, only a part of the south-eastern corner was uncovered. On all the exposed surface of the fortification the brick masonry show striking similarity to the ultimate phase of reconstruction as witnessed at the gulley, thereby indicating the scale of repairs as well as the damage by implication.

c. Middle Town: Of the middle town, all the four walls have been confirmed. While those on the east, north and west have displayed, more or less, similar architecture, but that on the south stands apart. While the others are basically mud- brick walls faced with stones, the south one consists of three thick stone-walls running close as well as parallel to each other with the interstices hearted with earth. Further, this wall is constructed on a thick Harappan deposit which, in its upper strata, contains the material of late phase. Besides, it unusually registers a shift of placement with a right angle turn somewhere halfway down. Apart that, it is the highest as ell as widest of all on middle town. It registers a width of 6.60 m while the west one which was found in a fine state of preservation is only 4.20 m broad. The other two have yet to show up their outer edges firmly. Of the south wall, it remains to be ascertained whether it is a late construction and as such cuts off from the middle town a 43 m built-up area that today lies to the south of it towards the open space. This cut off area in its turn, is delimited by a stone-wall which yet remains to be exposed fully across the width. Pending that, precise dimensions of the middle town should remain elusive particularly in respect of the breadth.

d. Emerging Dimensions: The above observation stands true to the city proper as well as its principal divisions. Pending further work, it too is hazardous to spell out precise dimensions. In this regard, it must be borne in mind (i) that the grid plan is oriented not accurately but on basis of average bearing of the structures, (ii) that exposure in a square of 5 or 10 m of a small segment of a considerably long wall is utterly too inadequate to firmly decide the orientation, and (iii) above all, that both the edges of most of the walls-segments whether pertaining to the outer or inner fortification system are not yet ascertained to full satisfaction. As such, approximate measurements can be indicated only and that is what is being done below.

The entire city inclusive of the wall and exclusive of the bastions should admeasure approximately to 772 m EW and 626 m NS ± 2-3 m in either case internally, the upper bailey of the citadel at the present top measures about 114 m EW and 94 NS and the lower one is about 123 m, whereas a statement about external dimensions should remain subject to more work. So far middle town is concerned, it is internally 333 m EW and 181 m (-200 m in the western half-) NS. If the built-up area outlying on south is also included the width from north to south will rise to 230 m.

Lower Town is around 300 m from east to west while the other side remains unprobed.

The open space between citadel and middle town stretches to nearly 55 m in width.

Gates

a. East Gate: Occupying the central location in the eastern arm of the towering castLe, the east gate was laid bare for half the width falling in the EW trench in south. It, as exposed, consists of a staircase, a sunken passageway, an elevated chamber and a high front terrace. The flight of 13 steps leads to a passageway running beside the chamber. All the three are provided in the thickness (12.30 m) of the defensive wall. The doorway which once opened on to the high terrace projecting from the defensive wall was blocked perhaps by the late Harappans during the period of decline. The lateral sides of the terrace are not yet exposed and as such any provision of descending, if provided, is not known. The walls of the chamber are exceedingly thick and made of stone blocks joined by mud-mortar.

Besides planning, the most important, rather unique feature, is aesthetic arrangement on the ege of chamber beside the passageway of nearly cut and highly polished limestone blocks at far ends, and of an equally polished and beautifully moulded pillar base into the shape of a bead or *damaru* placed on two polished stone blocks right in the centre of the length. The other polished slabs placed inbetween have since been robbed of. However, further interesting are two identical pillar elements similarly a polished found placed upon one another by the side of the *in situ* pillar base. Each of them is perfectly circular in cross section with a convex side and flattened top as well as bottom with a circular socket-hole in the centre. A similar hole is preent in the *damaru shaped* pillar base. It is a matter of conjecture as to how and where those large bead like members were placed in a composite pillar. A probable answer perhaps lies in a late Harappan lapidary's workshop near the west gate. There are found three pieces of a tapering piller-shaft along with an identical pillar base. Surely, they were removed from a monumental structure like a gate or a palace. As regards the stone-blocks, each contains two 31 cm long and 3 cm deep grooves for holding probably a square pilaster made of stone or wood. The following paragraphs will show as to how amply the evidence from the north gate has further supplemented as well as complemented the information bearing on designing and architectural embellishment of gate-complexes at Dholavira and how immensely the site holds promise of unveiling unknown aspects of regal architecture of the mighty Harappans.

b. North Gate: Located somewhat off the centre of the northern arm of the citadel wall, the north gate stands pre-eminently with its grandiose proportions and majestic apeparance highlighted by its lofty and projected terrace in front of a towering stone-made chamber pierced through with a broad and deep passageway once furnished with two doors now poorly envisaged by traces available at outer and inner thresholds. Behind that a high flight of steps fecilitated access to a corridor running between the rampart and the screenwall. Overall, the gate commanded over the long and wide open space which was so meticulously maintained level and floored over several centuries, obviously for special ceremonies presided over by the highest authority of the city.

Of different components, the chambers and the passageway are built in the thickness of the rampart which varies in width from 12 m at the level of the passageway to 11 m at the top-level of the corridor admitting a height of 4.50 m inbetween.

The staircase is designed like an 'L'. Descending from west through thirteen steps, the first flight terminates on a broad and wide landing provided in a chamber at the depth of 2.30 m from the top-stair. From the landing towards north another flight now of ten steps scaling a depth of 2 m or so ends upon the first threshold made of polished limestone slabs. The threshold is 3.50 m broad and 1.50 m deep. It supports today two seemigly free-standing columns of stone-masonry of unusually poor workmanship. Besides, they do not appear today to make a proepr bond with the nearby wall-ends which are neatly faced with well-chiselled or even moulded blocks. On closer examination, it appeared that these columns in fact were encased or panelled with wood and properly bonded with the main wall-faces. The other threshold of identical finish and size at the outer end of the passage is, through today bereft of the stone columns yet bears enough clue for their existence in addition to that it contains neatly cut rectangular holes for holding the surrounding wooden members. Furthermore, the earthen section still kept intact inbetween the aforesaid masonry columns has provided a highly valuable evidence of a fully decayed wooden jamb which divides the height of those columns into two halves. About its probable import we shall revert to shortly.

So far the length of the passageway between the thresholds is concerned, it measured around 7 m along which it runs between two elevated chambers, or, in other words, the passageway pierces through an oblong chamber whom it divides into two equal halves. The thresholds add up another 3 m or so to the run of the passageway. The working level of the chamber (s) is nearly 2 m higher than that of the passage. It is a considerable height to negotiate without any permanent or temporary device like steps or a ladder. So far no such evidence had come up. Besides, it is also noteworthy that the polished stone-blocks, slabs and the central pillar were found placed upon the side-wall of the passage, which incidentally make the open edge of the side chamber in the east gate. Exactly the same arrangement was followed here as well, although vandalism has displaced both the central pillars. Luckily, one pillar-base along with its supporting block were found lying in a spoil-pit at the self-same place in the eastern side wall. Similar spoil-pit present in the corresponding wall on west is not yet probed deeply. Two banded limetones blocks found lying in the debris on the front terrace should belong the central pillar on west. However, of the polished blocks but for the north-eastern one, the remaining three were found *in situ*.

All that said, it is significant to probe as to why the side chambers are so high and the elegant architectural members of specially high finish are placed on that height which was more than that of a tall person. Here, we wish to refer to the find of the faint traces of wooden jamb with entablalure observed on both faces of the section above the inner threshold. We believe tht the sunken passageway was once bridged by a wooden floor which might be either level with or extended over the floor of the flanking chambers. There might have been a separate and direct means of getting into the chamber nearabout the height of the landing. Not unlikely that the unprobed space interlying the chamber-wall and the EW staircase was then fecilitating a separate approach to get on to the wooden construction and get in through another doorway right above the lower one on the obtaining ground. And the decayed door-jamb belongs to that one standing on the ground. Given this postulation a credence, both the sidechambers joined together by a wooden floor bridging the deep passageway would make a wide chamber approximately measuring 7.20 m deep and 12.80 m broad. On that the supremo might had his seat with a large inscription hanging over his head. This may be a probable reason of that inscription of 9 letters lying on the floor of one (western) of these chambers.

The front terrace is 6 m high from the topmost working level of the open space. It projects 12 m while the exposed breadth along east-west is today confirmed for 19 m. As such the lateral sides are yet to be exposed and so is the provision for descending onto the lower level. There may be buried one or two staircases. At least, there is none in the centre, as is obvious.

Water Structure: Behind the north gate, in the central zone of the citadel there has been exposed a 12.80 m wide water reservoir furnished with a 24 m long and 70 m broad inlet channel for carrying the rain-water which is so precious in that semi-arid environment. Its length remains indeterminate at present. The exposed part is only 9 m. Quite likely, it claims a large area of the citadel at the prevailing landscape thereabout is any indication.

So far, other remains are concerned, they include parts of domestic structures, workshops of lapidaries and shell- workers, big drains, smaller house drains including a cut- stone one and so on so forth. All those can be dealth with separately.

Before concluding, we must write a few words about the inscription (Pl.IX). Each letter is about 37 cm in height and 25 to 27 cm in width. It is composed of carefully cut pieces of a crystalline material, may be a rock, mineral, or paste. Several pieces are arranged together to, make a single character. The faint traces that are available on the upper side of the inscription tend to suggest that these characteres were engraved on a wooden board. However, this is indeed 'the discovery of the decade' in the words of V.N. Misra.

REFERENCES

1. Indian Archaeology; A Review 1967-68. New Delhi pp. 14-17, fig. 4 & 5.

   The site is mentioned herein as Kotadi;

   Joshi, Jagat Pati, 1972. "Exploration in Kutch and Excavation at Surkotada and New light on Harappan Migration", *Journal of the Oriental Institute*, Baroda, Vol. XXXII, Nos. 1-2.

   Bisht, R.S. 1989, (a) A New Model of the Harappan Town Planning as Reveald at Dholavira in Kutch: A Suface Study of its Plan and Architecture. *History and Archaeology*, (ed.) Bhaskar Chatterjee, Delhi, pp. 397-408;

   Bisht, R.S. 1989, (b) The Harappan Colonization of the Kutch: An Ergonomic Study with Reference to Dholavira and Surkotada. *History and Art*, (eds) Krishna Deva and Lallanji Gopal, Delhi, pp. 267-272;

   Bisht, R.S. 1989 (c) Banawali and Dholavira: Two Different Models of Indus Town Planning. Paper presented at *conference of the Association of the South Asian Archaeologists* held at Paris on 5th July, 1989 (N.P.)

2. IAR, 1966-67, p. 11

   Suraj Bhan, 1975, *Excavations at Mitathal (1968) and other Explorations in the Sutlej-Yamuna Divide.* Kurukshetra.

   Shaffer, Jim G., 1986, "Cultural Development in the Eastern Punjab", *Studies in the Archaeology of Indian and Pakistan*, (ed) J. Jacobson, New Delhi, pp. 223-4: herein, the site is referred to as 'Rakhi Shahpur' while in fact it falls in the revenue jurisdiction of two villages namely Rakhi Khas and Rakhi Shahpur, both collectively called 'Rakhigarhi' (District Hissar) by the people. Besides, the area of 80 hectares as assigned to it is certainly on higher side although there are five contemporary mounds. They all together with due allowance for open areas should work out for about 50 hectares unless there was enormous open space in which case it may add up another 15 hectares or so.

3. Wheeler, REM 1953, *The Indus Civilization*, Cambridge, pp. 15-16.
   Possehl, G.L. 1982, "Harappan Civilization; A comparative perspective", *Harappan Civilization* (ed) G.L. Possehl, New Delhi, p. 19.

   Mughal, M.R. 1982. "Recent Archaeological Research in the Cholistan Desert", *Harappan Civilization* (ed) G.L. Possehl, New Delhi pp. 85-95.

   Tosi, Maurizio; Bondioli, L & Vidale, M, 1984, "Craft Activity Areas and Surface Surface Survey at Mohenjo Daro", *Interim Reports, Vol. I*, (eds) M. Jasen and G. Urban, New Delhi, p.15.

4. Mughal *op.cit.*

   Possehl, *op.cit.*

5. Vats, 1940, *Excavations at Harappa*, Vol. I Delhi, pp. 2-3; Wheeler, *op.cit.* pp.16-18.

6. Joshi, *op.cit.*

7. Chitalwala, Y.M., 1982, "Harappa Settlements in the Kutch Saurashtra Region. *Harappan Civilization* (ed) G.L.Possehl, p. 198-201.

   Pandya, Sumanben, 1982, Kotado - A major Urban settlement in Greater Raun of Kutch. *Indian Archaeology New Perspectives* (ed) R.K. Sharma, pp. 127-30.

   Mughal, M.R. 1990, "The Harappan 'Twin Capitals' and Reality" *Journal of Central Asia*, Vo. XIII, No.1, pp. 155-162.

8. Bisht, 1989 a,b,c, *op.cit.*

9. *Ibid.*

10. Joshi, *op.cit.*, IAR-67-68, *op.cit.*

11. Pandya, *Ibid.*

12. *IAR*, 1984-85, pp. 14-17.

13. Bisht, 1989 a,b,c, *Ibid.*

14. *Ibid.*

15. *Rqveda*, I.108.6; VI. 25.1; X.81.5

16. Elsewhere also, *Atharveda* makes similar references to them.

17. Bisht, a,b,c,. *op. cit.*

18. Joshi, Jagat Pati, 1979, "The Nature of Settlement at Surkotada." *Essays in Indian Protohistory*, (eds) D.P. Agrawal and D. Chakraborti, Delhi, pp. 59-64.

19. Lal B.B., 1979, "Kalibangan and the Indus Civilization." *Essays in Indian Protohistory*, (eds) D.P. Agrawal and D. Chakraborti, p. 76;

Thaper, B.K. 1979, B.K. 1979, "Kalibanga : A Harappan Metropolis beyond the Indus valley", *Ancient Indian cities of the Indus* (ed) G.L. Possehl, p. 199.

20. Wheeler, *op.cit* pp. 25-26.

21. *Ibid* pp. 18-19.

22. Mehta, R.N., 1982, "Some Rural Harappan Settlements in Gujarat". *Harappan Civilization* (ed) G.L. Possehl, pp. 170- 71; fig. 14.3.

THE CHALCOLITHIC CULTURE OF SOUTHERN BIHAR AS REVEALED BY THE EXPLORATION AND EXCAVATION IN DISTRICT ROHTAS

Birendra Pratap Singh*

The remains of the chalcolithic culture in Bihar is known mainly from the excavations of Chirand[1], Sonpur[2], Champa[3], Oriup[4], Taradih[5], Chechar-kutubpur[6] and Maner[7]. All these sites are located in north Bihar; in this context no satisfactory field-work has been done so far in southern Bihar. With a view to understand the details regarding the nature of chalcolithic settlements, distribution pattern of sites, etc., in southern Bihar, with particular reference to district Rohtas, was subjected to field-survery[8] by the author.

It brought to light a number of chalcolithic sites,important among them are those of Senuwar, Sakas, Daindih, Kushuridih, Raja Ki Ankori, Akorhi, Madhuri and Shaharidih. These settlements are found in two contexts:

i) Chalcolithic culture preceded by Neolithic culture and

ii) Chalcolithic culture being the earliest culture.

The settlements of the former kind clearly pre-supposes a selection on the part of the Neolithic communities high grounds of habitation, whereas the settlements of the latter category were usually located in the plains commanding fertile lands, much less vegetated area and away from the flood zone. Thus the first three sites come under category i) while the remaining ones belong to ii) category.

In both the cases the chalcolithic culture is succeeded by the NBPW deposit.

The site of Senuwar (lat. 24° 56'N, Long.83° 56'E) is located 7 km south of Sasaram in district Rohtas, Bihar. Excavations revealed a thick deposit of four cultural periods.[9] The two seasons' (1986-87, 89-90) work has now brought to light a continuous sequence of culture in the region from the neolithic to the chalcolithic period, down to the period when the NBP ware came into vogue. The excavations at Senuwar had a significant bearing on our knowledge of the Neolithic culture[10]; it was equally important for the chalcolithic culture of southern Bihar chiefly characterized by microliths, copper, ceramic industries of plain and painted variety and sometimes by neolithic artifacts.

Period II is represented by the chalcolithic culture of 2.30 m thick occupational deposit. Significantly, the lowermost deposit overlapped with the preceding neolithic sub-period IB and its uppermost deposit with the succeeding period (III) which is characterized by the introduction of iron and NBP Ware. Thus the chalcolithic culture on the one hand, is a gradually development of the neolithic culture, and on the other it paved way for the growth of the NBP Ware culture.

The evidence of successive occupational floors are encountered in the trenches. The thickness of floors ranges between 6 cm and 30 cm. These are made of rammed earth. A large number of burnt lumps of clay with reed or bamboo impression was obtained from the associated strata, indicating that the people lived in huts made of wattle and daub, plastered over with husk-mixed earth. Though no house-plan could be exposed fully, the available evidence suggests that some of the houses were circular. In this context, however, some remains of a circular mud structure with 4.26 m and 3.8m in diameter, inner and outer respectively need special mention. It is made of compact yellowish clay mixed with small pieces of *Kankar*. The height of the structure is 30 cm. Its thickness at the bottom and top is 30 cm and 16 cm, respectively. The floor encountered in the circular structure is made of rammed sticky yellowish clay mixed with kankar over which remains of two clay lined pits are found. It may also be noted that burnt patches are noted on this floor.

Associated with this phase are the remains of several other burnt clay lined pits, circular, oval or rectangular in shape. They first appeared in the neolithic-chalcolithic phase and are found continuing in the succeeding chalcolithic and the NBPW phases. The contents of these pits include ash, charcoal, potsherds, etc. Their specific use could not be ascertained.

The pottery of chalcolithic culture at Senuwar fell into several groups: (1) unslipped and slipped red ware (the latter being plain and painted both) ii) black-on-red ware, iii) black and-red ware (plain as well as

* Department of Ancient Indian History Culture and Archaeology Banaras Hindu University, Varanasi-221 005.

painted), iv) black slipped ware (plain as well as painted), v) burnished black ware (plain as well painted), vi) Cord impressed pottery and vi) rusticated pottery. The majority of the vessels are wheel-thrown, a very small percentage is represented by hand made specimens. Besides the continuation of pot forms of the preceding neolithic period, the pottery shows change in fabrics and shapes as well. Similarly, the painted pottery also reveal changes from the preceding culture in painting tradition. This change is noticed in the style of painting the mode of execution and in the use of pigments as well. Execution of painting in the form of rim band with red ochre in the post-firing stage is a feature of the neolithic culture. During the chalcolithic phase new motifs in painted design emerged which included lattice, group of parallel oblique or slanting lines, small vertical wavy lines in a row, short parallel slanting lines, etc. The paintings are executed in prefiring stage but specimens with postfiring painting in red ochre are also met with, suggesting continuation of tradition of the preceding neolithic culture. During this phase new pigments are introduced to decorate the surface, viz. white, cream and black. Besides painting, the pottery is found decorated with incised designs represented by criss-cross, finger-tip and cut-motifs etc., on the applique bands of clay (Fig. 4,6,7).

Red Ware

The study revealed the following two groups on the basis of fabric and surface treatment.

A) Unslipped red ware

B) Slipped red Ware.

A. The specimens belonging to this group are coarse and ranges in fabrics from medium to thick. The clay is highly tempered. The core is gritty, porous and generally complete black but in certain cases leaves a thin red zone on either side. The specimens belonging to this group are without any surface treatment. The common shapes met with included bowls and vases of varying profiles.

B. Next to the course red ware, the slipped red ware forms a significant group. It is plain as well as painted. The sherds belonging to this group is further divisible into two broad categories, one which is treated with a metallic bright red slip and highly burnished showing glossy surface. It is made of well levigated clay with less admixture of coarse material. This is possibly evolved from the burnished red ware of the preceding neolithic culture. The other category is characterized by thin drab red slip (with one exception where thick slip is applied) showing porous core. The slip shows two shades, viz., bright red and dark red. Burnishing is inferior in comparison to the former category.

Quite a few painted specimens in the above two categories of pottery are also recovered. The painting is done in post-firing stage showing small circles of miniature dots with creamish pigment, a tradition continuing from the neolithic-chalcolithic sub-period IB.

Black painted Red ware

The black painted red ware, commonly known as black-on-red ware, is a significant group of pottery of the period. It is introduced from the very beginning of the period II. The painting on the ware is shown in dull black pigment. The repertoire of painted motifs is extremely limited, represented by linear patterns alone. The paintings are to be seen mostly on the outer

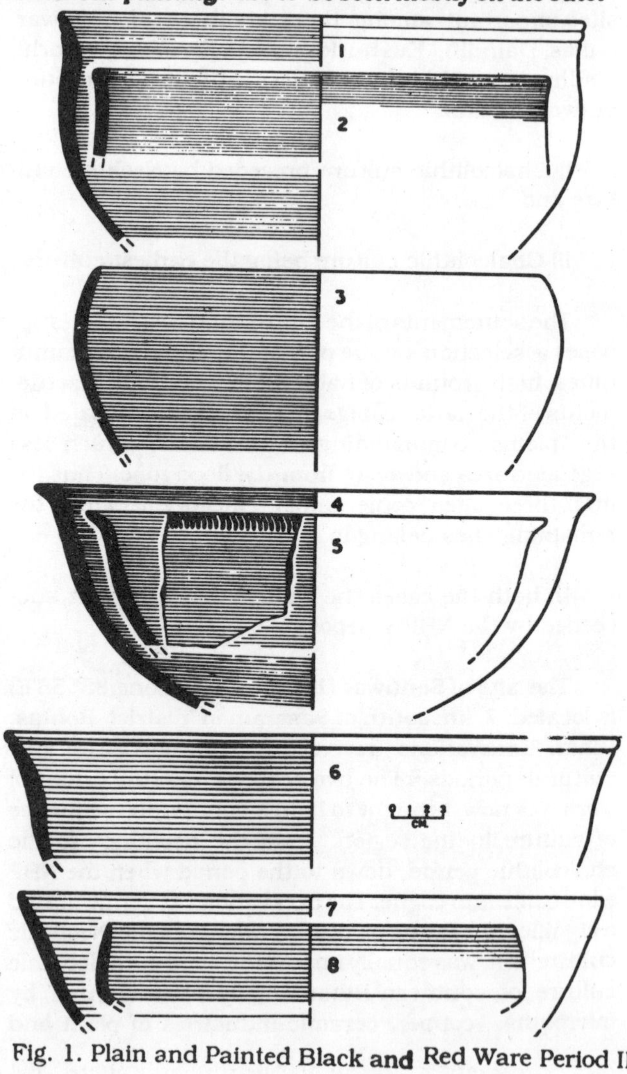

Fig. 1. Plain and Painted Black and Red Ware Period II.

surface while in a few cases they are also to be seen on both the sides (Fig. 5,13-18). The design element in most of the case is similar to that of the burnished black ware. The study of painted motifs clearly showed that the potter-artist by this time had become quite well versed in executing the painted designs as evidenced by the representation of thin lattice. The thin fine lines suggest full control over the brush.

The ware as a rule is treated with red or light brown slip and the surface is often burnished. The burnishing in some cases are of high order as evidenced by the glossy surface of the specimens. Leaving a few sherds which are slipped on both sides, the vessels in general are decorated like that externally. The pottery is of medium fabric, made of comparatively well levigated clay with usually compact core. Due to limited number of sherds, that too mostly shapeless, it is not possible to know much about the full form. However, among the recognized shape mention may be made of small sized vases and bowls.

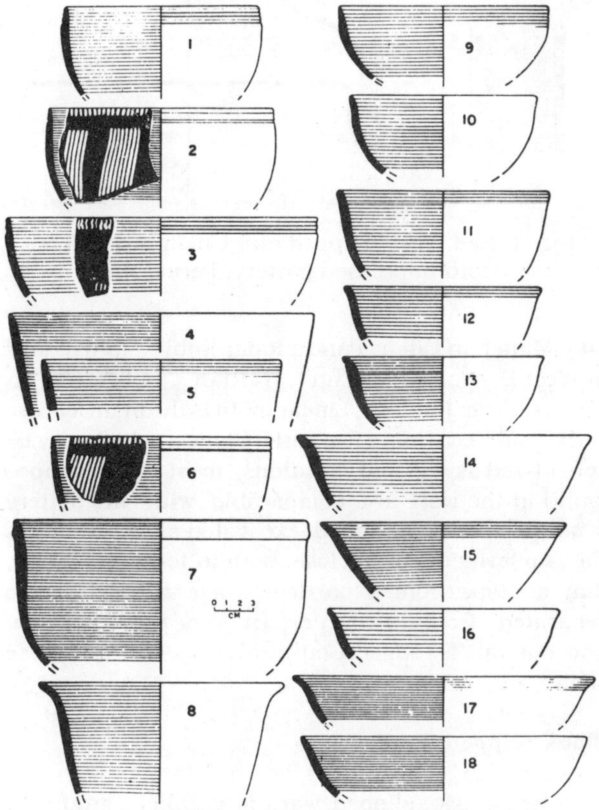

Fig. 2. Plain and Painted Black and Red Ware Period II.

The pottery forms and painted designs of the ware recall black-on-red ware of the Central Indian chalcolithic culture, for instance lattice motif, groups of parallel vertical wavy lines, bowls with straight or convex sides having featureless rim, etc. This may suggest some sort of contact between the two cultures which in any case not far removed from each other either in point of time or space. Here it may be mentioned that the occurrence of black painted red ware with linear designs is reported from chalcolithic phase of Koldihwa[11] and Sonpur also.

Black-and-Red Ware

The black-and-red ware forms another significant group of pottery. It is plain and painted both, the latter is however, meagre. The painting is done in white pigment. The motifs included groups of parallel slanting lines on the inner surface, small vertical wavy lines in a row at the rim on the inner surface, short oblique strokes near the base, and group of short parallel slanting lines (Fig. 1.5, Fig.2, 2, 3, 6, Fig. 3, 4). Occasionally, post-firing paintings in red ochre are seen. The study reached the following groups of the ware.

i) The black-and-red ware with slipped and burnished surface. The slip is applied on both the surfaces, though the external surface is treated with brighter red slip.

ii) The black-and-red ware with external dull surface. The red slip applied on the outer surface is thin while on the inner surface the black slip is comparatively thick. In comparison to the preceding group, the burnishing is also inferior.

iii) The black-and-red ware with an outer rusticated surface. Internal surface is also devoid of any surface treatment. The shapes are limited to vases and bowls. No complete shape is recovered, however, it appears that the vases are roughened from base to shoulder while in cases of bowls the roughening is done upto the rim. The coarse grained paste is prepared out of ground pot sherds, stone particles and sand.

It is applied by fingers as suggested by their marks. The fabric ranged from thin to medium, showing compact core. The clay employed is levigated. This group is represented by limited number of sherds.

iv) The black-and-red ware represented by sherds of thin section having compact core. The clay is better levigated which provides in some examples metallic sound. The majority of the sherds show burnished external and internal surfaces.

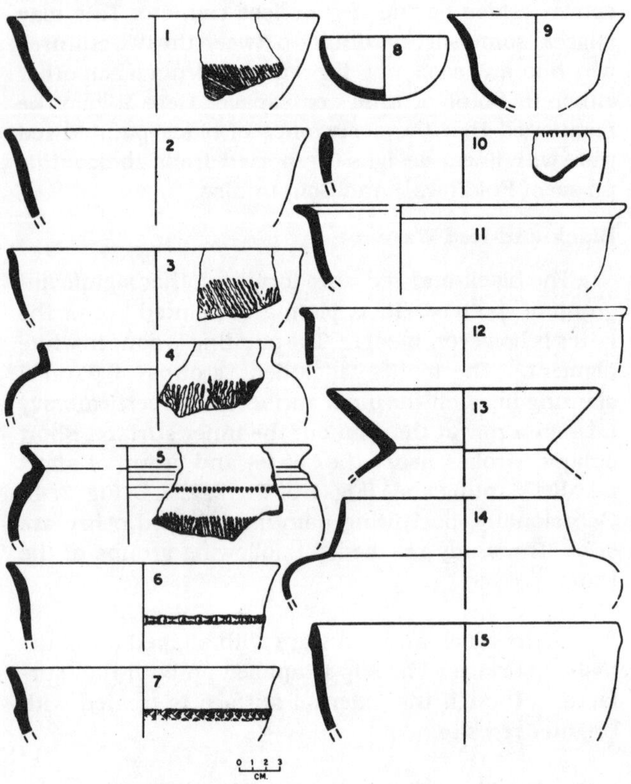

Fig. 3. Plain and Painted Black and Red ware Period II.

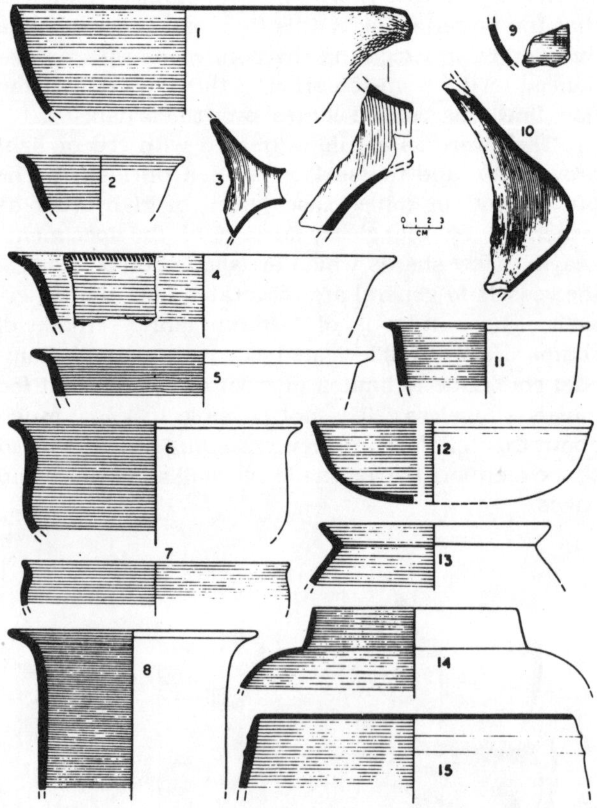

Fig. 4. Red Ware; Slipped and Unslipped 1, 3-5 Cord impressed pattery, Period II.

The pottery belonging to the groups i) and ii) ranged in fabric from medium to thick. The clay used in the manufacture of these groups contains husk, straw, etc. The core is gritty and porous. In majority of examples, it is either complete black or it leaves a thin red zone. The noteworthy shapes include: 1) narrow channeled bowls, 2) broadened channeled bowls, 3) long widely channeled deep bowls, 4) bowls with straight or convex sides, 5) bowls with blunt carination, 6) pots with vertical sides having an out-curved rim, 7) dishes, 8) vases with flared rim, 9) dishes-on-stand, 10) basins, 11) vases with straight sided featureless rim with rounded body, 120 shallow bowls, etc. (figs. 1,2 and 3).

The black-and-red ware, plain as well as painted, is reported from corresponding strata from sites like Oriup, Champa, Chechar-Kutubpur, Taradih, Chirand and Maner in Bihar; Pandu Rajardhibi[12] Mahishdal[13] in West Bengal; Khairadih[14], Narhan[15], Sohgaura[16] in eastern Uttar Pradesh. Linear motif is the main feature of the ware. Leaving a few pottery types, which may be considered as regional variations, most of the shapes found in the ware are comparable with the pottery from the above mentioned excavated sites. At times, the similarity being so close, both in form and fabric, that a type from a particular site can hardly be separated from its counterpart from the other site. These parallels suggest cultural links between these sites.

Black Slipped Ware

The black slipped ware is another group of pottery associated with the chalcolithic phase. It is plain and painted both, the latter being only a few in

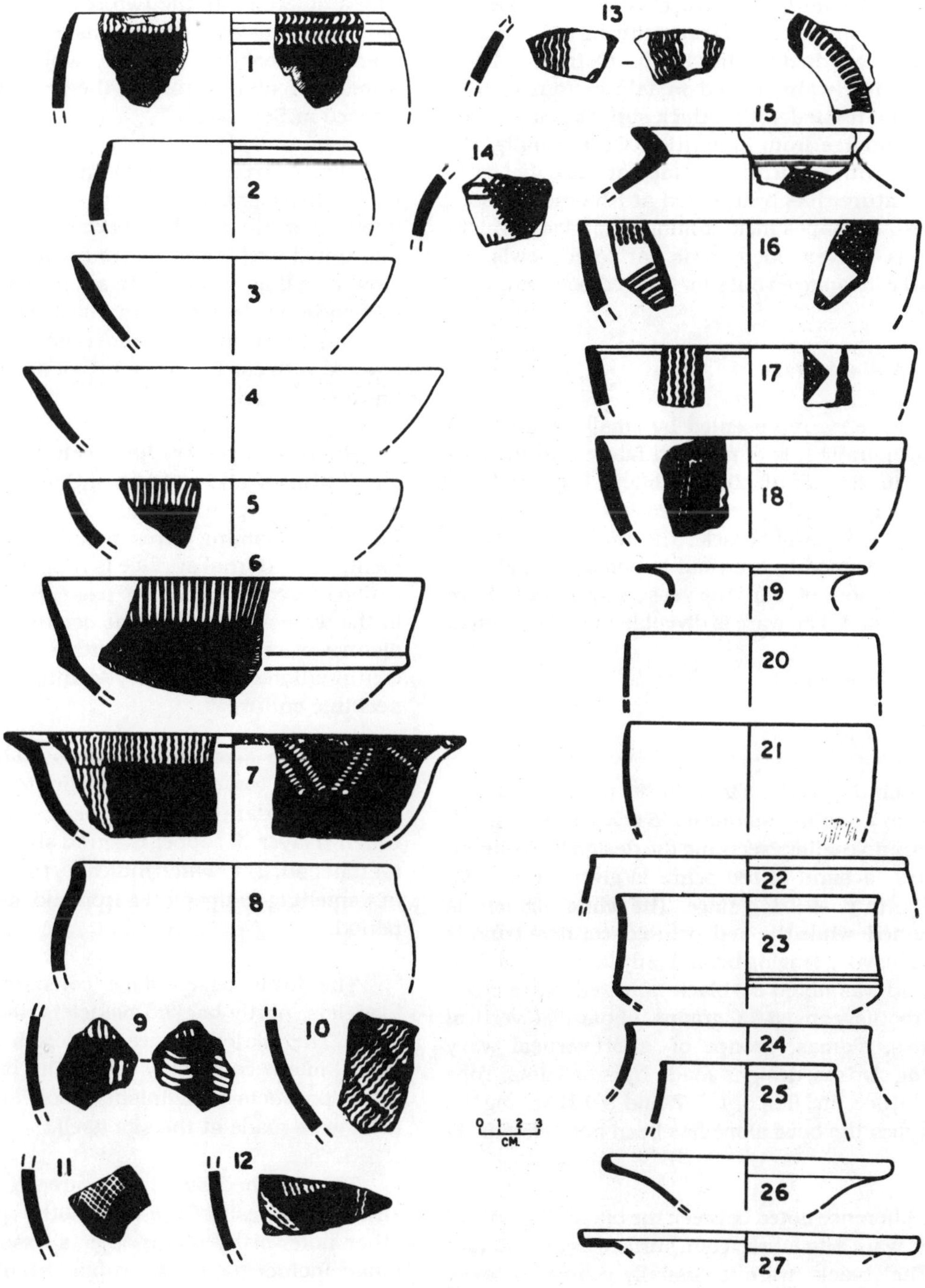

Fig. 5. 1-12 Burnished Black Ware, 13-18 Black and Red Ware, 19-27 Black Slipped Ware, Period II.

number. The painting is in white, showing groups of verticals, criss-crosses, etc., comparable with those recovered from Khairadih, Sohgaura, Koldihwa, Chirand and Oriup. It is important to note that sherds with identical paintings have also been found at Gulrihvaghat and Lohra Dewa during the recent exploration conducted in Basti district, Uttar Pradesh.[17] The ware ranged in fabric from thin to medium and treated with a thick slip. The clay is well levigated and free from impurities. Occasionally, the specimens with rusticated surface are also met with. Similar feature has been noted at Khairadih also.[18] The important shapes include miniature vase, straight sided bowls, convex sided bowls, carinated bowls, lid-cum-bowl with splayed out rim, flanged bowl, etc. (Fig. 5,19-27).

Burnished Black Ware

The ware is represented by small number of sherds. Generally it is of medium fabric and the clay employed in the manufacture is highly tempered and not well levigated. The core varies from grey to black while the slip is bright black. The surface of the pots in general are smooth, even and in some cases glossy. After application of slip the vessels apeears to have been burnished. The ware is divisible into two groups:

i) Painted black ware

ii) Plain black ware

The painting is done in white in pre-firing stage, however, in a solitary instance red ochre is also used. In this example after executing the design in white on both sides a band of red ochre is given at the rim externally in post-firing stage. The white pigment is fully retained while the red ochre decorative band is mostly removed, leaving behind only faint traces. Red ochre band was noted in black- and-red ware also. Painted motifs consist of groups of parallel vertical wavy lines, sigmas, groups of short vertical wavy or slanting strokes, designs made by small dots, rope pattern, lattice, etc. (Fig.5, 1, 5-7 and 9-12) Among the pottery types the bowl alone has been noted (Fg. 5, 1-8).

The difference noted between the black slipped and the black ware is in fabric, core, surface treatment and forms. The black ware is usually coarse, heavily tempered with gritty porous core while the black slipped ware is made of well levigated clay with less admixture of tempering materials, well fired, exhibiting compact core. The bright black glossy appearance also distinguishes it from the black slipped ware. Even the pots with dull appearance show difference on account of its fabric. Among other noteworthy points which differentiate the two is that the black ware is possibly evolved from burnished grey ware of the preceding neolithic culture while the black slipped ware is a new entrant in the chalcolithic pottery as evinced at Senuwar.

The occurrence of cord impressed and rusticated pottery has also been noted in small number. The cord impression are found in various patterns in bold relief and noted exclusively on red ware bowls and small sized pots (Fig. 4.1, 3-5). In such examples the upper half portion is treated with thick red slip to cover the rough surface and the remaining lower portion is covered with cord strokes. It is of medium section and has a coarse fabric.

Rusticated pottery has been noted mainly in red and the black and-red wares. Occasionally it is found in the black slipped ware also. This has been separated from the remaining wares mainly by its surface treatment. The external surface is roughened by the application of a coarse grained paste. Shapes represented in the ware are limited. The occurrnce of these two distinct wares in the chalcolithic phase may indicate continuation of the pottery tradition of the preceding neolithic culture.

The use of copper is witnessed by the presence of bangle, a tool of an indeterminate use, pin (?), ear-ring (?), pendant (?), copper pieces and a pot-sherd in which a layer of copper is found still adhered all along its inner surface which indicates that it was a pot used in smelting copper ore. Iron did not occur in this period.

The lithic assemblage consisted of retouched bladelets, partly backed bladelets, flakes, blades and cores. The materials are chalcedony and chert, the latter more commonly used. The preponderance of waste products over finished tools suggests that the tools were made at the site itself.

The polished stone axes are recovered from the stratified deposit of the chalcolithic period. Amongst other noteworthy stone objects associated with this phase include hammers, rubber stones, pestles, sling balls, sharpeners, discs and *ukhali*. Most of these continued from the preceding neolithic culture.

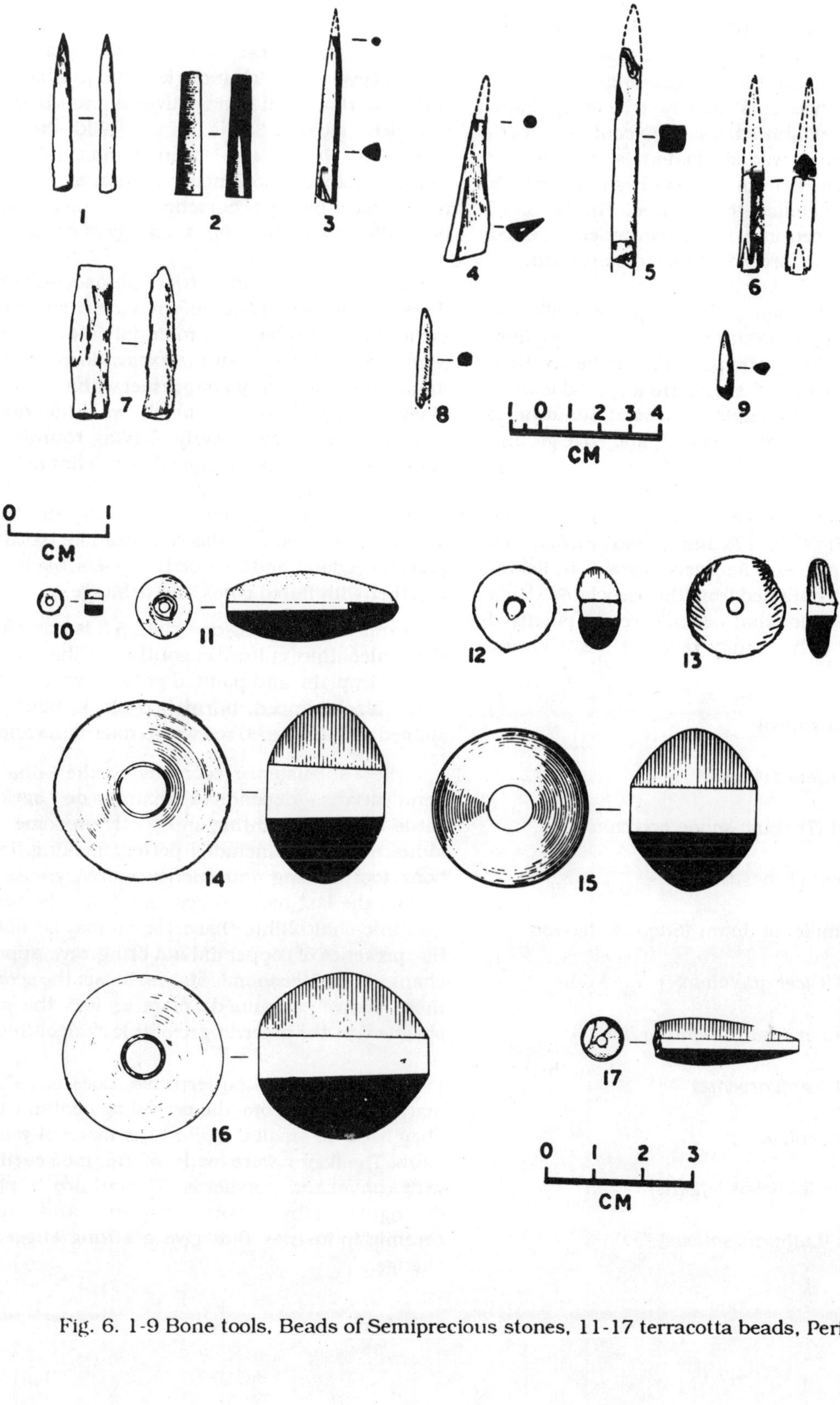

Fig. 6. 1-9 Bone tools, Beads of Semiprecious stones, 11-17 terracotta beads, Period II

Bangles of bone, beads of agate, chalcedony (Fig. 6.10) and faience formed objects of personal adornment. It may be mentioned here that the overlapping phase between sub-period IB (neolithic-chalcolithic) and Period II (chalcolithic) yielded an important discovery of faience slage strewn in an area measuring 2.45 m E-W and 1.60 m N-S. suggesting evidence of an industry of faience. This appears to be the first site in this region to exhibit such a signifcant evidence. Chalcedony and agate were the materials employed for manufacturing beads from the very beginning which continued in the chalcolithic period. The beads of faience are introduced in IB which continued in Period II. The shapes of the preceding period continued.

The bone tools include borer, point,needle (?), chisel and arrow-head, both socketed and tanged (Fig. 6,1-9). The last make their appearance for the first time in this period. Objects of shell form a special feature of neolithic and chalcolithic phases at Senuwar. It comprised of pendant and shell cut and edge ground to a triangular shape.

Among objects of terracotta mention may be made of beads. (Fig. 6.11-17), animal and bird figurine, hop-scotch, stopper, etc. Recovery of grains by floatation method was obtained from the associated strata of the period indicating that agriculture was practised on large scale.[19] The study revealed the following crops:

1. Rice (*Oryza sativa*)
2. Barley (*Hordeum vulgare*)
3. Darf-wheat (*Triticum sphaerococcum*)
4. Bread Wheat (*T. aestivum*)
5. Sorghum-millet or Jowar (*Sorghum bicolor*)
6. Chick-pea (*Cicer arietinum*)
7. Green gram or mung (*Vigna radiata*)
8. Field-pea (*Pisum arvense*)
9. Lentil (*Lens culinaris*)
10. Horse-gram (*Dolichos biflorus*)
11. Grass-pea (*Lathyrus sativus*)
12. Oil seeds belonging to sesame or til (*Sesamum indicum*)
13. Linseed (*Linum usitatissimum*)

Apart from these weed and wild taxa have also been recovered which included wild jujube (Ziziphus nummularia), vetch (vicia sativa), a grass belonging to Cenchrus ciliaris. Seeds of a Wild shrub Perilla Ocimoides have also been found.Cattle-breeding formed another important occupation of the people as is suggested by the occurrence of a large number of domesticated animal bones, mainly of cattle.

The field survey in district Rohtas resulted in the discovery of several sites referred to earlier, where the same class of pottery and material culture have been found as recovered from the excavations of Senuwar. Among the noteworthy shapes met within the red ware, black-and-red ware and black ware incuded bowls with globular or ovoid body having rounded base, perforated footed-bowl, lipped or channeled bowl, ovoid bowls with an out-curved rim, vases with sharp carinated neck and flared rim, basins, etc. The tools are made on locally available rocks like basalt, chert and chalcedony, and included bladelets, blades, flakes, together with fluted cores and debitage.

From the foregoing description it is now clear that the chalcolithic culture of southern Bihar is characterised by plain and painted pottery, viz., black-and-red, black slipped, burnished black, black-on-red, slipped and unslipped red wares,microliths and coppr.

The subsistence economy of the chalcolithic Senuwarians, dependend mainly on agriculture, cattle-breeding, hunting and partly on some cottage industries which included pottery making, lapidary, bone tool making and faience industry. As noted earlier, the last had its beginning in the preceding neolithic-chalcolithic phase. Here it may be noted that the presence of copper did not bring any appreciable change in their economic status. In fact the economy of these people remained more or less the same as observed in the preceding neolithic chalcolithic phase.

The settlement pattern, too, does not show any marked change from the preceding neolithic culture. They lived in small circular huts made of wattle and daub. The floors were made of rammed earth mixed with *kankar* and potsherds. The culture is primarily distinguished by various painted and unpainted ceramic industries that give a strong suggestion of change.

A close examination of the material culture recovered from the excavations of Senuwar leads to infer that the Chalcolithic Culture in southern Bihar gradually evolved from the preceding neolithic culture. The occurrence of burnished black ware and burnished red ware (in the slipped red ware group) is indicative of the fact that the former evolved from the burnished grey ware and latter from the burnished red ware of the elderly neolithic culture. Similalry, the use of thick slip and burnishig arc among the important neolithic pottery traits which found their way in the chalcolithic period. Cord impressed pottery, rusticated ware, post-firing painting in red ochre and in cream colour pigment, incised and applique modes of decoration may be treated as continuation of the tradition of the preceding neolithic culture. Besides, the continuation of several pottery shapes of neolithic period some of the pot-forms get modified. Vases with carinated neck and flaring rims, bowls of varying profiles continued in modified form. Similarly, the channeled bowls have certainly emerged out of the preceding neolithic culture mainly in the black-and-red ware and occsionally in the red ware. Spouted vessels of the preceding period are conspicuous by their absence in the chalcolithic phase. Among other neolithic objects which continued in the same or slightly modified form are polished axes of basalt, stone hammers, rubbers, pestle sling balls, sharpeners and shell tools of an indeterminate use. Beads of semiprecious stone exhibit an evolution from the preceding neolithic culture. To recapitulate, the evidence is in favour of an evolution of neolithic culture into the chalcolithic culture. It is interesting to note that similar development from the neolithic to the chalcolithic is evinced at Koldihwa also.[19]

From a comparative study of the different ceramic industries and pottery types recovered from Senuwar and other excavated sites in the regions under review family-likeness is indicated, linking one regional industry with the other suggesting thereby one integral culture. Correspondence in shape between Senuwar pot forms and Khairadih, Narhan, Chirand, Taradih and Koldihwa pot forms is amply attested. Particular mention in this regard may be made of dish-on- stand, lipped or channeled bowl, bowl with globular or ovoid body, vases with carination at the neck and flared rim, perforated footed bowl, basins with splayed out rim, etc., in the red and black-and-red wares and straight sided bowls, convex sided bowls, carinated bowls and lid-cum-bowls in the black slipped ware. The occurrence of identical painted sherds and specimens with rusticated exterior surface in the black slipped ware and incised criss-cross design on the slipped red ware sherds are noteworthy evidence which indicate links between Senuwar and Khairadih. Here in this context the presence of black-on-red ware, is especially interesting, since the ware is found in Central Indian Chalcolithic culture. The similarity in form and painted designs in pottery suggest Central Indian contracts or influences.

The objects used by these people are limited in each region and include beads of semiprecious stones, steatite, terracotta, querns, pestles of stone, bone tools which comprised of points, tanged as well as socketed arrow-heads, chisels, etc., and very small number of copper objects. In view of the entire evidence there appearas to be basic uniformity in the cultures represented in the regions under study. The village character of the culture is reflected in each region.

Among the points of difference noted, particularly at the excavated sites of eastern U.P. is the complete absence of lithic tools which is an essential chalcolithic appellation. But the presence of copper, ceramic industries (with a few local variations) pottery shapes and material culture exhibiting striking similarities testify to the existence of a comparable chalcolithic phase at the sites of eastern U.P.[20]

On the basis of above evidence it is also inferred that there is a regular chalcolithic settlement spread in eastern U.P., Bihar and parts of Vindhyan area. That the duration of this phase is fairly long as at most of the sites the occupation thickness is over 2 m.

The NBP ware culture is preceded by the chalcolithic culture in southern Bihar and eastern U.P. but no such evidence is found so far in the Vindhyan plateau.[21] The NBP ware culture shows a gradual development from previously existing chalcolithic culture in southern Bihar and eastern U.P. as evinced by the excavations of Senuwar and Khairadih. At both the places there is an overlap between the chalcolithic and NBP ware deposit.

REFERENCES

1. *IAR* 1971-72, p.6, Verma, B.S., 'Black-and-Red Ware in Bihar' *Potterels in Ancient India*, pp. 102-110, Patna (1969); also in Srivastava, K.M., *Community Movements in Proto-Historic India*, pp. 97-98, figs. 47-50.

2. Sinha, B.P., and Verma, B.S., *Sonpur Excavations*, pp. 20- 21, Patna, (1977). From the report it is not clear whether the painted black-and-red ware is found from sub-period IA and IB or not. B.S. Verma is of the view that it is absent at Sonpur. He, however, mentions the occurrence of painted black slipped ware (*Potteries in Ancient India*, pp. 102-110), Elsewhere (*IAR* 1970-71, pp. 5-6) it is reported that a solitary sherd of black and red ware with linear paintings in white is found from Period I at Sonpur. See also Srivastava, K.M., *op. cit.*, pp. 99-100.

3. *IAR* 1974-75, p.8. Black and Red is similar to the chalcolithic black-and-red ware from Sonpur and Chirand.

4. *IAR* 66-67, p.6, pl. IIIA. Period I is mainly represented by black-and-red ware, both plain and painted, black slipped and red wares. Other associated objects included bone points, beads of agate and carnelian, terracotta female figurine, copper bangles and microlithic carnelain, terracotta female figurine, copper bangles and microlithic core.

5. *IAR* 1981-82, pp. 10-11, 1983-84, pp. 12-13. On the basis of two seasons (81-82, 83-84) work period I at the site is chalcolithic. It is characterized by the occurrence of black-and-red. Quite a few sherds of these wares have linear white paintings. Main pottery types include dish-on stand, bowl with pedestal base, bowl with globular or ovoid body, perforated bowl, dish, jar with sharp carination at the neck, flared out rim etc. Among other objects associated with the culture are a neolithic celt, carnelian blade, quern, pestle and hammer of stone, points, chesels, tanged as well as socketed arrow heads of bone, copper fish-hook, etc. In the subsequent season's work (*IAR* 1984-85, pp. 9-10) a separate neolithic horizon has been identified by the excavators and as such Periods I and II are neolithic and chalcolithic respectively.

6. *IAR* 1977-78, pp. 17-19.

7. *IAR* 1984-85, pp. 11-12.

The earliest Period I is chalcolithic in cultural content. The pottery recovered during the period included black-and- red and some pieces of black ware. The shapes in black-and- red ware comprised bowl, dishes and dish-on-stand.

8. The exploration was conducted by the author during the season 1985-86.

9. The two seasons (1986-87 and 89-90) work conducted by the author, brought to light deposits of four cultural priods. The earliest Period is neolithic. It is divisible into two sub-periods IA and IB. IA is devoid of metal and it can be regarded as pure neolithic, while IB is marked by the presence of copper and thus has been regarded as neolithic- chalcolithic. Both sub periods IA and IB, however, showed cultural continuity. Period II, is chalcolithic in Character. There is evidence of an overlap with the preceding sub-period IB. Period III is characterized by the introduction of iron and NBP. It also overlapped with the preceding chalcolithic culture. The excavation revealed that only the early phase of NBP is represented while its late phase is conspicuous by its absence. Period IV, is ascribable to the Kushan times. There was an appreciable time-gap between the end of Period III and the beginning of Period IV.

10. For details about neolithic culture see, Singh, B. P. "Early Farming communities of Kaimur Foot-Hills", *Puratattva*, No.19, pp. 6-18.

11. Pal, J.N., *Archaeology of Southern Uttar Pradeh: Ceramic Industries of Northern Vindhyas* (1986), p. 137, Allahabad.

12. *IAR* 1962-63, pp. 43-46, also Srivastava K.M., *op cit.*, pp. 101-102.

13. *IAR* 1963-64, p. 59. Period I is charactrized by black-and-red ware (plain as well as painted), black painted red ware, red and black ware, sometimes with incised and pin-hole decoration. Painted design included linear motifs. Among other objects included microliths, a flat copper celt, beads of semiprecius stone and steatite.

14. *IAR* 1980-81, pp. 69-70, 81-82, 82-83, pp. 92-94, pp. 86- 87. For details about the chalcolithic phase of Khairadih, see, Singh, B.P., 'Khairadih-A chalcolithic Settlement', *Puratattva*, No.18, pp. 28-34.

15. Singh, P., and Lal, M., "Narhan 1983-85: Preliminary Report" *Bharati*, New Series, No.3, pp. 120 ff.

16. *IAR* 61-62, p. 56, 74-75, pp. 46-47. Period II at Sohgaura is characterized by plain and painted black slipped ware, black-and-red ware, red ware and coarse grey ware. The painted designs consisted of linear patterns. The other finds include beads of jasper, agate and steatite and bone stylus.

17. The explorations in the districts Basti and Sidharthanagar in Eastern U.P. were conducted by the author during the season 1989-90. The two important sites, viz., Gulrihvaghat and Lohra Dewa are characterized by the black- and-red (plain as well as painted), black slipped (plain as well as painted), burnished black, and red wares. The noteworthy shapes include pedestalled bowl, dish-on-stand, vases with flaring rim, deep bowls with externally thickened rim, perforated footed bowl and basins in red and black-and- red wares and straight sided bowls, flat based bowls, convex sided and corrugated bowls and dishes in the black slipped ware.

18. Singh, Birendra Pratap, *op.cit.*, p. 30.

19. Pal, J., N., *op. cit.*, pp. 164-165. The author is grateful to the Director BSIP for deputing Dr. K.S. Saraswat, Assistant Director to the site to collect and study the botanical remains from excavation. The author also acknowledges thanks to Dr.K.S. Saraswat for providing preliminary details of botanical remains obtained from the excavation of Senuwar during the session 1989-90.

20. In the absence of lithic tools, the use of the term 'chalcolithic' for the sites present in eastern U.P. may be disputed by some scholars. However, since the assemblage of eastern U.P. sites have many identical features noted at other sites like Senuwar, Chirand, Taradih, Koldihwa etc., where microliths are present, the term is being retained to convery the status of the assemblage. See Sankalia, H.D., in Deo, S.B. (ed.), *Archaeological Congress and Seminar papers*, Nagpur (1972), pp. 157 ff.

21. Pal, J.N., *op. cit.*, p. 169. "No such site has been located on Vindhyan plateau so far at which NBP succeeds the chalcolithic in cultural sequence as in the middle Ganga Valley".

ARCHAEOLOGY OF THE WARDHA WAINGANGA DIVIDE

Amarendra Nath*

Like other major river systems of India, the Wardha-Waingana contributed significantly to the growth of culture. In recent years some important explorations and excavations were carried out in the cradle of these two rivers, the vidarbha region. (fig.1). Leaving aside the three stages of development of the Palaeolithic industry of the Pleistocene vidarbha noticed at Papamian-Tekdi[1], District Chandrapur, the protohistoric chronology in the region, before the mid-eighties, was known to have started with the emergence of iron. However, in the mid-eighties, a site at Tuljapur Garhi on the Purna river, a tributary of Tapti yielded some important clues to the existence of a chalcolithic settlement.[2]

The recent excavations at Adam (21°00'N 79°27'E), Taluk Kuhi, District Nagpur[3], have however, brought to light a five fold sequence of cultures starting from the aceramic microlithic deposit and passing, through the chalcolithic and early historical cultures. The mound from outside appears to be early historical in nature, showing the features of an earthen rampart and a moat, the latter encircling the former (fig. 2 & Pl.I).

Deposits

Period I is represented by fifty cm thick deposit, lateritic (secondary) in origin, composed of reddish brown compact earth mixed with grit and rarely with charcoal-bits and bone. It yielded, in the lowest pre-defence levels microlithic deposit free from pottery. The artefacts recovered include parallel sided blades lunates points flake blades and scrapers made of chert chalcedony agate and quartz. Tentatively, the period has been dated to circa third to second millennium B.C.

Period II has been termed as 'Vidarbha-Chalcolithic' as the ceramic industry does not correspond either in form or in description with any of the contemporary chalcolithic cultures of the regions adjoining Vidarbha. The deposit approximately a metre in thickness, altogether different in character from that of the preceding period, belonged to one compositional class of clayey earth, varying in colour from dark-brown to pale-brown with an admixture of grit and charcoal bits. There are six pottery types of medium to coarse fabric invariably of inadequate firing. The types include (i) red ware with a chocolate slip and painted in white, (ii) red ware with a red slip and painted in white,(iii) red ware with a red slip and painted in black (iv) unslipped red ware with painting in black, (v)unslipped red ware with painting in white and (vi) black and red ware with paintings on the outside in black. The design-elements occurring on them were limited to (i) hatched diamonds, (ii) combed pattern, (iii) series of short horizontal wavy strokes ('z' pattern) and (iv) groups of vertical strokes of varying number, occurring both externally and internally on the rim (fig.3). Among the plain pottery an average of about 64 per cent constituted the red ware while 26 per cent formed the black slipped ware and 10 per cent black and red ware.

Evidence of structures in the form of post holes and mud floors was noticed, but due to space limitation no complete house plan could be ascertained completely. However, a portion of circular house plan recorded in S5/1 had post holes spaced at regular intervals of fifty cm. along the perimetre of the rammed-mud floor. In B1/2 a floor with post-holes was recorded but it did not form a pattern; a whet-stone was also noticed on this floor. Slightly above this floor was exposed a burnt clay floor patch over which was noticed a polished celt like object of shale stone, perhaps used as a scraper[4];the microlithic industry of the preceding period however, continued, in use. Other finds of the period include a copper, ring circular in section; a crucible, bone stylus of cylindrical shape with an oblique cut end and an engraver with finely finished pointed end. The period has roughly been dated to the first quarter of the second millennium B.C.

Period III is characterised by the introduction of iron, although the cultural items of the preceding period continued to occur. The layers yielded ash-deposits, occasionally mixed with soft clayey earth and charcoal-bits. The painted pottery of the earlier period, with slight increase in the frequency continued with an addition of few new design elements. A notable introduction noticed was that of a coarse micaceous red ware painted with thick brush over a chocolate slipped base (fig.4). The other new design-elements include (i) chequer-board pattern, (ii) series of horizontally, occasionally obliquely inclined, coma-like strokes or dots arranged vertically. The horizontally or obliquely inclined coma-like strokes have been noticed on red ware, at times painted in white and occasionally in black; sometimes the strokes painted in black occur on the inner base of some table wares like dish or bowl. Towards the later phase of this period the frequency of white painted pottery got reduced as compared to black on red ware. Some of the black and red ware of this period bore graffiti marks,

* Archaeological Survey of India, Old High Court Building, Nagpur.

comparable to those found in the chalcolithic context. In the lower phase, the percentage of plain pottery noted were: red ware 59 per cent, black slipped ware 32 per cent and black and red ware 9 per cent. Towards the upper phase, the red ware continued to dominate with 64 per cent while black and red ware showed a marked increase of 23 per cent and black slipped ware declined to 13 per cent.

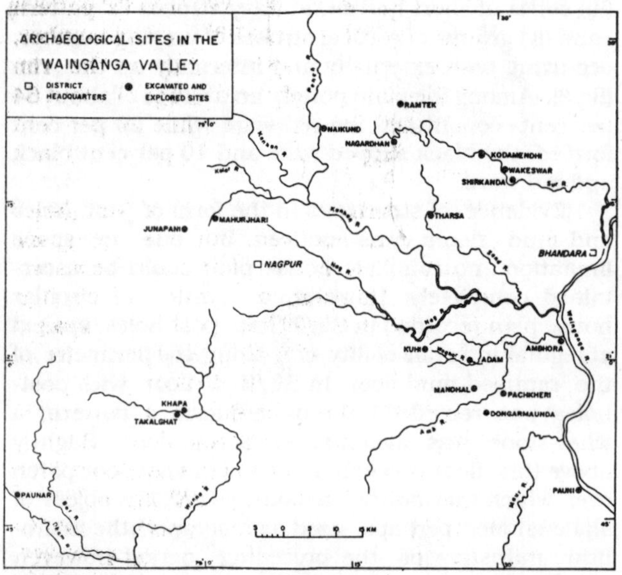

Fig.1

Traces of structure in the form of post-holes and semi-circular mud-floor were noticed. A pot-burial, in upright position, of secondary inhumation, was noticed in the habitation area. The medium sized vase of red ware contained a deep bowl of black and red ware filled with soiled charcoal and earth.

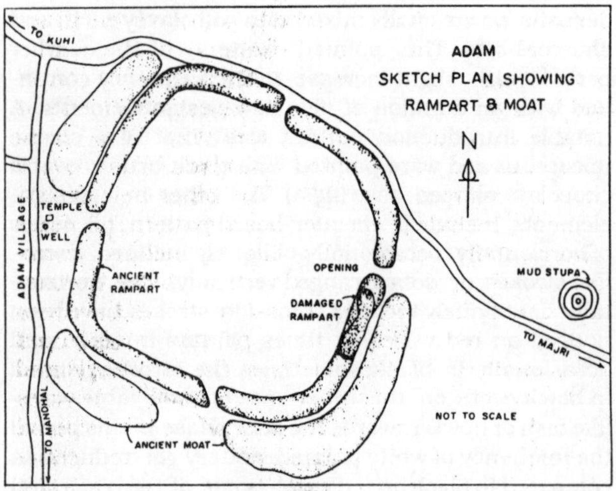

Fig.2

Introduction of iron technology made copper a subordinate metal at Adam. The artefacts of iron include, besides indeterminate and rusted pieces, a tanged point and nail fragments. Other important antiquities reported from this period are copper ring, short barrel- shaped carnelian bead etched with dots, annular terracotta beads, hopscotches dressed in pottery and stone, terracotta head of a bird and oblong shaped spool, bone points and stylus and a shell bangle fragment. Tentatively, the period has been assigned to *circa* 1000 B.C. to 500 B.C.

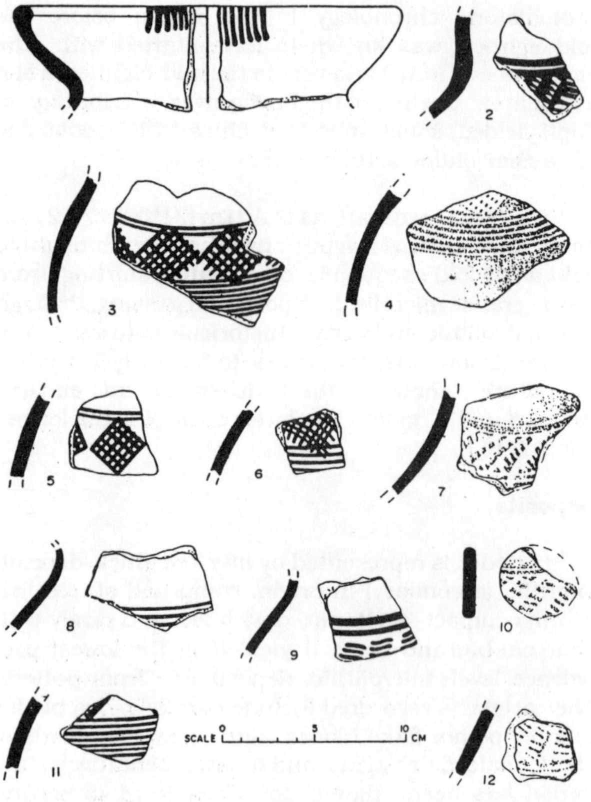

Fig.3 : Adam: Black-on-Red Ware and White-on-Red Ware pottery types, Period II.

Period IV, termed as pre-Mauryan and Mauryan, witnessed some fundamental change in the cultural content, perhaps due to the developed iron technology. An abrupt transformation in the total outlay of the house plan from circular or oval to square or rectangular and use of stone, brick and tile as building materials indicated a departure from the rural to urban settlement pattern. The deposit consisted of light brown earth of medium compactness, occasionally ash mixed with streaks of murrum. The ceramic industry was represented by the micaceous red ware and the black and red ware of medium to coarse fabric, generally associated with the NBP ware. Only one NBP sherd was reported from this horizon. The micaceous red ware was painted with linear bands of varying thickness below the neck. The types met with were vases, jars and bowls. The black and red ware bowl with a featureless rim, occasionally out-turned and slightly expanding sides, carinated to flattish base was an important type. The frequency of red ware (73 per cent) was more than of the black and red ware (27 per cent). No complete house plan could be exposed; however, in one of the cuttings (B1) a undressed shale stone wall, running east west (8 x 0.80 m.), was noticed with a right angle north turn (2 x 0.50) m.). It had mud flooring. In the stone-mud-masonry was noticed, occasionally, fragments of brick-bats and tiles which suggest existence of brick structure and manufacture of tile for roofing. The other structure (Q5) noticed was in the form of a fine murrum floor rectangular in shape, with post holes of 15 cm in diameter. The available extent of the floor was 3.85 x 2.25 m.

The outstanding discovery of this period was the fragmentary legged querns and mullers of sand stone with typical Mauryan polish. Two of the legged querns were engraved towards the shorter axis with auspicious symbols like *swastika*, *nandipada* (taurine) and *mina* (fish). However, these have been reported from the rampart cutting. Other antiquities of this period include beads of crystal, agate, carnelian and terracotta; amulet and ring of copper; arrow head of iron; and engravers both of bone and antler. Terracotta fragments of hand modelled female figures of 'ageless' mother goddess type with wide open legs shown without toe details were also reported from this period. The period has been dated to *circa* 500 B.C. to 150 B.C.

Period V has been attributed to the Bhadras, Mitras, Satavahanas and Maharathi rulers on the basis of numismatic and epigraphical evidences. The deposit belonged to one compositional class of clay of medium to hard in compactness and dark brown to black in colour. with some exceptions of grey and kaolin wares, the ceramic industry predominantly remained confined to red ware of medium to coarse fabric. Shapes included almost all types and variants of bowls, basins. dishes, jars, vases. lids and lid-cum-bowls. Devoid of paintings the red ware was occasionally slipped in red externally, and at times jars and basins were either treated externally with mica dust or it formed part of clay paste. Decoration on the pottery was introduced in this period for which various techniques were adopted like stamping incision pinch cording and appliqué. Of all the decorative elements *triratna* of different types, rosettes *swastika* birds hollow roundles and herring-bone pattern were common in occurrence. Spouts of plain and decorated varieties were also encountered. Both shale stone and brick structures were known to the people but due to local quarry the former was preferred over the latter. The only burnt brick structure (2.75 m.) worth mentioning was three coursed wall, running north-south with a door opening (80 cm) and post holes (dia.35 and 25 cm.) cut in the wall. It is too early to suggest that the brick structure was reinforced with wooden post or the post independently supported the tiled roof. The stone structure, complete on plan, was in the form of a compound wall of elliptical shape, with an entrance towards east encircling four circular structures perhaps memorial or votive in nature. Both the compound wall and the circular structures were laid after cutting the required foundation trench. Of the circular structure, seven courses were noticed in the foundation whereas above the stone paved floor there were three courses. A major portion towards north-west side of the structure got robbed due to later pit activity; however, the distribution pattern of circular structures suggests that there were originally more than four such structures within the compound wall. Outside this complex, specially towards east, several remains of burials, purely of secondary inhumation, were noticed.

Out of three broadly classified varieties viz. (i) pot burial, (ii) terracotta ring burial and (iii) pit burial there were noticed number of sub types in them. In case of pit burial, pits of oval and circular shapes of varying depths, occasionally stone lined, were noticed filled with bowls, basins and vases of medium size, invariably battered without following any uniform pattern.

In case of pot-burial bowls and vases were laid independently to form the burial chamber inside a pit of required shape and size. The bowls of red ware with featureless rim, oblique sides and string cut base were used frequently, at times placed upside down with stone lining, sometimes one covering the other, or one above the other in inverted position. Another variant noticed was that of vases of varying shapes and sizes (Pl.II). A wide mouthed vase with out-turned rim and slight carination was noticed laid in a circular pit in upright position; it was covered with a chambered base of micaceous red ware, thin in section. The pot contained soiled charcoal bits mixed in earth with fragments of bone. A hopscotch as grave goods was found from the pot-chamber. Another medium sized vase, complete, exterior stamped with *triratna* motif was laid in the chambered base of a thick micaceous red ware jar; the collared rim of the same formed a ring around the said pot- chamber which contained charcoal bits mixed in soiled earth (Pl III). Out of five terracotta-ring burials excavated at the site two were cut across to study the contents of the burial. One of them contained, in the centre, a red ware vase of medium size completely battered, perhaps for

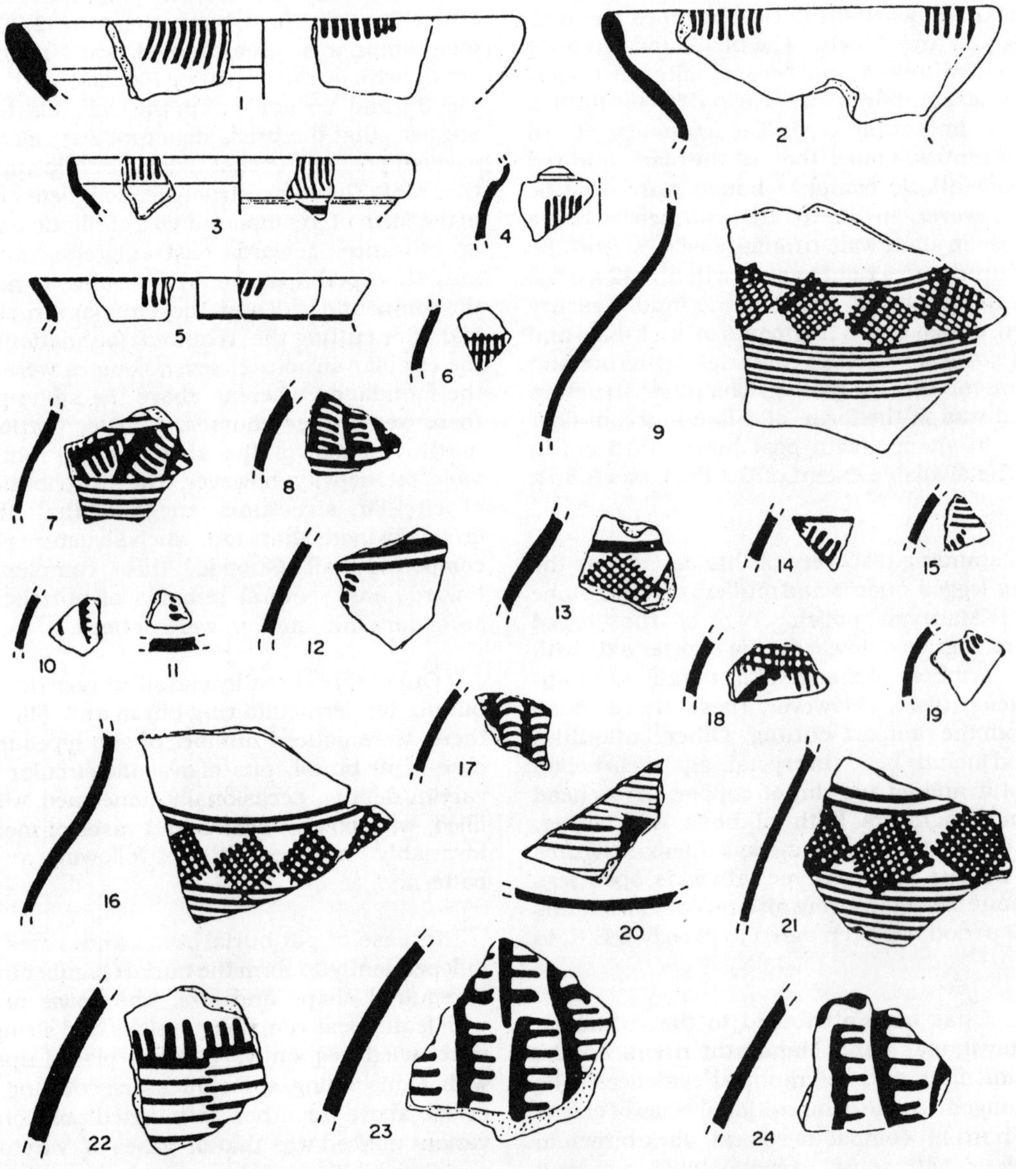

Fig.4 : Adam: Black-on-Red Ware pottery types Period III.

ritualistic reasons. Hopscotch as grave gods was noticed invariably in all the types of burials.

Of all the antiquities, the most outstanding discovery was that of sealing bearing the legend of *Asaka Janapada*[5]. The other was that of an etched carnelian bead depicting the most popular motif where bull is shown before a tree in railing. In all, two hundred and sixty three coins were recovered from the site. Of these twelve are silver based punch marked coins: one hundred sixty seven are of copper, eighty three are of lead and one is of brass. Amongst the inscribed coins, significant discoveries were of Bhadra, Mitra, Maharathi and Satavahana coins from the stratified deposit. The lead portrait coins of the later Satavahana rulers were unique.[6] Both handmade and moulded terracotta were recovered from the site and are classified under (i) human figurines, (ii) animal figurines, (iii) votive tanks, (iv) spindles and wheels and (v) crucibles. Besides four decorated ivory pendants, four hundred and eight-six beads in terracotta, glass, bone ivory, copper, agate, carnelian, chert, chalcedony, etc. were recorded. Two multigrooved sandstone slab fragments of bead polishers were also encountered from the site. Among metals, besides lead spools and copper pendants and implements, a good number of iron implements were recovered from the site which included ploughshares, chisels knives arrow-heads etc besides an intact shear to cut or clip the hair, fleece or wool. The period has been dated to circa 150 B.C. to 200 A.D.

The cutting (Q5 to Z5) laid across the rampart and moat revealed some interesting features, besides predefence deposits (Pl. I). Tentatively, it is believed that the iron using people raised a low rampart and dug a small moat around their settlement; it was subsequently reinforced by a stone battlement, perhaps coated with mud plaster. As per the requirements of defence, the rampart was raised in subsequent periods and so also the size of the moat expanded. In this process the earth and murrum dumps of the rampart went on encroaching upon the habitational area within. Towards the counterscarp of the moat cutting a V-shaped ditch was cut in the bedrock which either served as silting channel or defensive trap for the intruder.

Stupa

ADM-2, locally known as *Devi hudki*, contained the remains of a stupa (Pl I). The trenches were laid on the southern half of the stupa. It was ascertained from the cutting that the earthen stupa was built over made up earth with two distinct phases of construction. Circular on plan, the stupa consisted of medhi (radius 17.30 m) and *anda* (radius 10.30 m) which atops the basal remains of a square *harmika* (3.50 m) built out of random rubble; in the centre of it was noticed a ring-stone once supporting the *yesti* of a *chhatravali*. A shaft was cut in the centre of *harmika* which however, did not yield the expected relic casket, but the nature and formation of the stupa could be studied. After a more or less uniform basal treatment of clayey soil, the earth of habitational deposit, murrum, rubble, stone chips, sand, etc. were heaped up without following any uniform pattern of dumping. After the formation of circular *medhi* in stepped fashion, the core of *anda* was reinforced with heavy duty rubble which was ultimately covered by earth and murrum to form a hemispherical dome. The surface of the stupa was treated with rammed murrum in order to defuse the periodical erosion. Assigned to two phases of period V the stupa of earlier phase was built over layer (5) whereas towards the later phase the restoration took place on the top of layer(4). In earlier phase a L-shaped pathway (9.80 x 0.40 m.) leading to the stupa was demarcated with a single coursed shale stone wall whereas in the later phase the same was indicated by a brick wall (22.20 x 1.20 m.); mud as mortar remained common to both the phases. The inner width of the pathway was 4.90 m.

The stupa site brought to light punch-marked and inscribed and uninscribed cast coins assigned to the later Satavahana rulers. Hence it is assigned to circa first century A.D.

Excavations at Tharsa

Besides Adam, the other important sites excavated recently in the Wardha-Wainganga valley is Tharsa (Lat.21°13'N, Long, 79°25'E), Taluk Ramtek, District Nagpur[7]. It is about forty kilometres east of Nagar, lying on the left bank of sand, a tributary of Kanhan. The limited excavations conducted on the Western slope of the mound revealed a number of painted pot sherds strewn over successive floors with traces of conflagration. The pottery types compares well with that of Period II and III at Adam. However, neither post- holes nor any house plan could be ascertained in the lower horizon. The urn burials reported from the excavations had pot-chamber of red ware with flared rim, wide mouth and globular body, and were buried in the ovalshaped pits cut into the natural soil. The urns contained badly damaged post excarnated skeletal remains of an infant. In one of the pot- chambers, the corporal remains were kept in a black and red ware bowl wherein a thin copper ring was also found as grave goods. It is interesting to note that both the urns were battered and coated with soot externally upto the rim, and internally restricted to the base of the pot, In the upper horizon a few circular bin-platforms were also noticed. Further field work (1989-90) at Tharsa brought to light a neolithic celt comparable to the one found at Adam, and a ring stone as surface collection. Unfortunately not a single stone tool has so far been reported from the painted pottery horizon at Tharsa. However, the site is quite potential which needs further field work to establish the horizon as 'Vidarbha Chalcolithic'.

Shirkanda

Another site of interest is Shirkanda (Lat.21°17"N, Long.79°31'E), taluk Ramtek, District Nagpur. It lies on the left bank of Sur, a tributary of Wainganga[8]. The elliptical- shaped mound of about 200 x 150 m, rising over two metres from the surrounding plains, lies to the south- east of the present habitation. The mound yielded protohistoric and early historic remains comparable to those reported at Adam. The ceramic industry of the protohistoric period included, besides the black slipped ware, the plain and painted varieties of red ware and black and red ware (Pl IV). The design elements frequented both in white and black on these sherds are (i) hatched diamonds (ii) combed pattern and (iii) groups of vertical strokes of varying numbers occurring both externally and internally on the rim; and example of the strokes painted in black also occur on the base of a bowl of red ware. Some of these pot sherds bear typical graffiti marks. The other associated type was micaceous red ware. The types met with were of vases, bowl, dish, lid, plater etc. Some of the red wares of early historical period bear series of oblique knotches appearing over an applique band, it occurs on rim and at the junction of neck and shoulder. Besides an iron point, the site has yielded a good number of hopscotches dressed on pottery and stone, muller of dumb-well type, whet stone, etc. Microliths made on chert, chalcedony and quartz were also picked up from the site; types included crescents blades scrapers etc. (Pl V). The site appears to be quite potential, and there is all possibility of reascertaining the 'Vidarbha-Chalcolithic' horizon as noted at Adam.

Conclusions

The foregoing discussion brings home that the Wardha- Wainganga Valley also had a chalcolithic phase followed by the usual iron using culture. An over-lap was noticed in the heterogeneous ceramic industry of these two periods at Adam; whereas at no stage of development or interaction, it ever imbibed the fabric and typical pottery shapes common to the Chalcolithic-Malwa and Jorwe, incidentally, certain design elements like hetched diamonds, stylised fronds or comb and series of coma-like strokes appear to have had common origin. The occurrence of black on red ware is quite common to the chalcolithic India, however, white paintings on black, black and red, and red wares is something unique to 'vidarbha chalcolithic' noticed at Adam. White paintings on red ware was known to the pre- Harappan, whereas on black and black and red wares it was reported from several chalcolithic sites in eastern Rajasthan, central and eastern India, northern Maharashtra and peninsular India.[9] Though there are evidence from the surface of ground stone celts and ring stone from Adam and Tharsa, their cultural horizon could not be established from the regular excavations. Instead, microliths have been reported sufficiently from the copper and painted pottery horizon at Adam to justify the deposit being called as Chalcolithic. Shirkanda appears to be another site of 'Vidarbha Chalcolithic' from where in the course of exploration, typical painted pottery and microliths of Adam type were picked up.

The study of iron or the Megalithic occupation in vidarbha was made earlier by S.B.Deo[10], still Adam has something new to contribute to the understanding this phase in terms pot-burials from period III. Likewsie, the pot burial of Tharsa may also fall in the same category.

While period IV at Adam besides silver PMC yielded a few NBP ware sherds and typical Mauryan polished stone fragments, period V brought to light many other coins. It would significantly contribute to the history of Pre- Satavahana but later Satavahana rulers of Vidarbha, about which not much is known either from the traditional sources or from the stratified cuttings.

REFERENCES

1. *Indian Archaeology 1960-61 A Review*, pp.22-25.
2. *Indian Archaeology 1984-85-A Review*, pp.48-50.
3. *Indian Archaeology 1975-76-A Review*, p.36
4. *Ibid*
5. Nath, Amarendra, "Toponymy of Asaka and Asika", *Indica*, vol.51, 1990, pp.87-94.
6. Nath, Amarendra, "The first ever reported Lead portrait coins of the Satavahanas", *Nidhi*, The Journal of the Indian coin society, Nagpur, 1990, vol.I, pp.25-30.
7. *Indian Archaeology 1985-86-A Review*, (under publication).
8. *Indian Archaeology 1988-89-A Review* (under publication).
9. Allchin, Bridget and Raymond, *The Rise of Civilization in India and Pakistan*, New Delhi, 1983.
10. Deo, S.B. *Excavation at Takalghat and Khapa*, Nagpur, 1970, *Mahurjhari Excavation*, 1970-72, Nagpur.

THE KSETRAPALA SHRINE AT KANDHAR

M.K.Dhavalikar & A.P.Jamkhedker*

Kandhar (18°50'N 10°E), the taluka headquarters of the same name,is located 50 Km south-west of Nanded city (District Nanded, Maharashtra). The present town stands on the left bank of river Manyaa, a tributary of the Manjira which forms part of the Godavari system.[1] Kandhar has been identified as one of the capitals of the Rashtrakutas who styled themselves as *Kandhar-purva-var-adhisvara,* meaning the 'lords of the city of Kandhar'. Although an insignificant town now, Kandhar must have been a very important city in the ancient past. It appear to have been much larger than the present one for the simple reason that the ruins have spread far beyond the present township into the villages of Bahadarpura and Manaspur. The name Kandhar is said to have been derived from Krishna(III), the rashtrakuta king (Krishna - Kanha - Kanhara - Kandhara). However, it is likely that the name is derived from sanskrit *Kandhavara* Which means 'royal encampment'.

Kandhar is presently known for a very fine land fort which is located in the heart of the town. The gazetteer ascribes the fort to a certain king Someshwar and it is also suggested that Krishna III, a Rashtrakuta monarch, may have built it.[2] However, from the plan of the fort, the style of its bastions and its architectural details it is doubtful whether it can be assigned to the Rashtrakuta period. There should be little doubt that the fort belongs to the medieval period.

The fort is in a good state of preservation inspite of the fact that there is a vast growth of wild vegetation inside and even outside. The fort surrounded by a ditch which is 27.4 meters wide and 4.57 meters deep. It is filled with water which is supplied probably by natural springs in the ditch. However, it is also likely that water may have been supplied by the tank which is located nearby and which was built by Krishnā II as is testified by the inscription which has been found in the town.

Kandhar is also traditionally known as panchalpuri which is supposed to be the place of Draupadi's marriage with the Pandavas. The valley which is in close proximity of the town is known as Pandavdara and lends strength to the legend.

A fragmentary stone inscription was found at Kandhar in 1959 near an old well known as the 'Khas Bag' in the village of Bahadarpur which is about 1.5 Km from Kandhar.[3] The inscribed stone was actually lying in the well, but in the summer of 1957 the well dried up and the stone was noticed. It was then brought up and kept near the well. It was later removed by Sri Keshavrao Dhondge, a local leader and MLA, to his house and has been fixed in the Tulsi vrindavan.

The record is extremely important inasmuch as it gives us a detailed description of the building in the capital city and the munificent activities probably of Krishna III of the Rashtrakuta dynasty. However, the donor of the record is one Kalamegha. Among the deeds of king were the construction of a mandapa named Sarva-lokasraya near the temple of the well known god Ksetrapala. He also established five centers for distribution of water (prapa) at the following palaces :

1. *New makara-torana* in the royal palace.

2. Near *Yaksa-davara* which was adorned with *mandala-siddhi* Vinayaka.

3. In front of the temple of Kamadeva close to the house of the royal courtean (*pradhana-raja-Vilasini-pataka).*

4. In the courtyard of the 'temple of Kalapriya'.

5. In the pavilion named *Sarva-lokasraya.*

The king had constructed fire places at five places for poor people for protecting themselves during the cold season. They were located at the following places:

1. Sarvalokasraya pavilion in the courtyard of Mandalasiddhi Vinayakā worshiped at the *Yaksa-dvara.*

2 & 3. Near the Kalapriyanatha temple.

4. In front of the Sagareshwar temple.

5. In the vicinity of Bankeshwar temple situated to the north of the Sagareshwar temple.

In addition, the king built two water tanks (*Jala-dronyo*) and established five centres for supplying fodder to cattle (*go-grasah*) which were located as follows :

1. In the Market of the people from Gujarat (*Gurjara-apana*).

* Department of Archaeology and Museums, Govt. of Maharashtra, Bombay.

2, 3 & 4. Near the temples of Viranarayana, Srikrishneshwar and Ksetrapala.

5. At the much frequented market place (*Ksunnahattika*).

For this, the king had made a provision of 50 *drammas* a day.

Among other meritorious deeds of the king, the inscription mentions that he had made a provision of 500 *drammas* a month for supplying *pancha-amrit* and for *pancha- upachara* as also for curds, milk and flowers for the gods in Bankeshwar, Chhalleshwar, Gojjiga-somanatha, Tumbeshwara and Tudigeshwara temples in the town. Provision was made for sugar and sandal too. It also mentions the provision of two *prasthas* of oil and one *prastha* of salt daily to the college (vidya-sthana) situated on the banks of Nandi in the Godavari valley (*Godavari-tat-adhyasini Nanditate*) and belonging to the *brahmanas* engaged in studies. Arrangements were made for this purpose for storing nine *khandikas* of oil and four and half *khandikas* of salt by purchasing them from the *gramakatakas*. For the bulk purchase of articles, arrangements were made for the daily payment, in a lump sum of the price of oil and salt required per day.

The inscription is important because it helps us in identifying satisfactorily the ancient city of Kandharapura with the present town of Kandhar. The Rashtrakuta monarch Krishna III has been described as *Kandharapurvara-adhisvara* in some epigraphs[4]. He was also referred to as Krishna- Kandhara and Krishna-Kandhara with the title *Kandharapuravar-adhisvara* that is "the supreme Lord of Kandharapura, the best of towns". The town could not therefore be identified earlier, but the Kandhar inscription helps us in identifying it with the present town of the same name.

This, however, led to the problem of the identification of king Kandhara (Krishna). In this connection, it should be stated that there is a tradition according to which Kandhar was built by and named after a king[5] called Kandhar. As late D.C. Sircar has rightly concluded, the name of the king and the absence of pre-Rashtrakuta antiquities at Kandhar suggest that this Kandhar was a Rashtrakuta king[6]. Furthermore, this king was none else than Krishan III because most of the names of the temples in the ancient city were the titles of Krishna III [7]. It is however, quite likely that the town may have been built by and named after an earlier Krishna of the Rashtrakuta family.

The town of Kandhar and its environs are littered with the ruins of ancient structures. Some of these buildings were ancient temples as is evident from fragmentary sculptures and carvings scattered here and there. Some of them were converted into mosques by Muslim invaders in the medieval period. They are mostly located on the banks of the ancient tank in the town. Recently, several sculptures were brought to light in the precincts of the Shivaji College which is located on the eastern bank of the tank.

As already stated, the ancient ruins are also seen scattered in the neighbouring villages of Manaspuri and Bahadarpura. But the most noteworthy among these were those at Manaspuri because of their massive proportions. Among these could be recognised the fragments of gigantic sculptures of a male and female. These were found in a field (Survey no.279) at Manaspuri. From time to time these fragments were discovered and brought for safe custody to the medieval fort at Kandhar, which is a protected monument of the state Government of Maharashtra. Shobhana Gokhale visited the site in 1979 and identified many of the buildings described in the epigraph.[8] This led us to select the site for excavations.

Site

The ancient site where the fragments of huge sculptures were found is actually a cultivated field (S.No.279) owned by Sri Narayana Vithoba Manaspure. It is located about 2 km east of the town of Kandhar. The site resembles a small mound about 2 m in height and spread over an area of about 100 x 100 m. Since all the large sculptue fragments came from this site, this area was selected for excavation.

Excavations

A horizontal grid of squares, measuring 10 x 10 m. was laid in the east-west orientation. The trenches D3, D4, D5 and C4-C5, which were located in the central part, were selected for excavations first. We encountered an enigmatic stone structure at a depth of 10 cm below surface. It was constructed of dressed stones, set with mud mortar; in between was packed stone rubble and murrum. A round copper coin, considerably worn but showing traces of Persian legend, a few nails of iron, some coarse red ware sherds, and a few fragments of polychrome glass bangles all belonging to the medieval period were the other finds.

The plan of the structure (Pl. I) resembles an anthropomorph with a circular head portion in the northwest and the lower extremities in the southeast. The head is built of roughly dressed slabs around the margin, the portion in between being filled with stone rubble. The circular part measures 6.35 m in length and 4.85 m in width. Here the dressed slabs now survive only in the right half but their counterparts on the left are missing. Around the periphery of this roundish part is a patch of rubble masonry which on an average is 1.20 m wide. It looks like a buttress wall, but at the same time the possibility of its being the circumambulatory path (*pradaksina-patha*) cannot be ruled out since this path runs almost all around the structure.

The structure has two arms which have a facing of large dressed slabs and the portion in between is filled with stone rubble in mud masonry. The left arm of the structure is 10 m long and at its lower end, which is tapering, it is 1.05 m broad. Near the shoulder it is broader and measures 2.05 m. The right arm is 2.05 m broad in the uppermost part from where it starts; it also tapers down and is 9.95 m long. In its lower end it is 87 cm broad. Some of the stones of both the arms in their upper parts are missing.

The portion in between the two arms which resembles a human body has a maximum width of 4.65 m. The body, which is wide in the middle, narrows down in the southeastern direction and ends in what look like the lower extremities or the legs. The total length of the right leg alongwith the body portion is 15.35 m and its width in the lower end is 72 cm. Similarly, the left part of the body alongwith the left leg is 13.75 m long but it must have been equal to that of right side which is 15.35 m. But since the slabs in its upper part are missing, it is shorter. In the lower end it is wide.

Sculpture

The site was selected for excavations because fragments of a colossal image were found here. We, therefore, made an attempt to find out whether this sculpture could be fitted into the structure, if 'yes', the structure was a shrine. The face of the sculpture which is in two parts, measures from the top of the head to the nose is 1.57 m in height; the width across from eye to eye and upto the left ear is 2.48 m (Pl. II). The face appears to have been carved in two separate slabs which join at the eye level because the edges of both the slabs at this point are smoothened. The left part of the forehead is slightly broken. The ears too appear to have been carved separately. The left ear (Pl.III), which has been found, is 1.60 m long; it has an elongated ear-lobe (*pralamba-karna-pasa*) in which is adorned a heavy disc (*tatanka-chakra*). In the upper part of the ear-lobe are two rings containing three pearls each; they are clearly of the *bali* or *balika* variety. The slabs of the face are at best only 23 cm thick. The sculpture was not finished at the back since it was hardly intended to be seen from that side.

Of the body portion only a small fragment of the belly has been recovered. There are two pieces of hands which are broken at the wrist. The left hand (Pl. V) holds a citrus fruit (*bija-puraka*) whereas the object in the right hand (Pl. V), being broken, can hardly be identified. The left hand is 77 cm broad and the right hand is 1.15m broad. The height of the latter is 1.08 m. The hands were carved separately as the squarish projection below the wrist of the right hand indicates. Both the hands have heavy bracelets on them.

There are two leg fragments. They are broken at the level of ankles. The left leg is 1.75 m long, and is 55 cm broad at the back, near the ankle (Pl.VI). On the leg are two anklets and there are rings on all the toes. A most remarkable feature of the right leg, which we could examine from all sides, is that even its sole is finished properly and so also is the lower side of the toes. In the case of such a massive sculpture, if it was intended to be installed in a standing, position, there was no need to finish the under side of the feet, much less that of the toes. This would suggest that the image probably was intended to be kept in a reclining posture. This surmise gains strength from the squarish tenon which has been provided at the back of the ankle; it was obviously meant for fitting into the mortice hole in the floor. This then would be the *sayana* class of Siva images which are extremely rare or almost absent in the entire range of Indian art. The only parallel that can be cited is the painted representation of Vasuki-sayana Siva in the Vatakkunatha temple at Trichur in Kerala which belongs to 16th century.[9]

But how the image was fitted in the temple proper? The sculpture fragments are huge and are unlikely to have been moved much from their original location. We made enquiries with the owner of the field, Sri Narayanrao Manaspure, and others as also with the employees of the State Department of Archaeology who had shifted the fragments to the fort. They reveal that the two slabs of the face and the ear were found in the circular part of the shrine; these were slightly removed from each other. The two hands were somewhere near the arm-like projections of the structure whereas the two legs were found at the lower extremities of the structure.

The total height of the images can be estimated on the basis of the size of the face and also that of the foot. The extant length of the face from nose to forehead is 1.57 m and the total length of the face from the top of the head to the chin would be about 2.25 m. If we accept that the height of a person is generally seven times that of the face, then the total height of the image would be around 16 m.This is commensurate with the dimensions of the structure and as such the image can be easily accommodated in the shrine in the reclining posture.

Besides the fragments of the gigantic sculpture described above there are some more which do not belong to it. There are two pairs of hands (Pl. VII) and one pair of legs. They probably belong to other images, probably to the Siva *dvarpalas*.

It appears that the gigantic sculpture was carved out on the small hillock which is situated very close to the site, about 100 m to the east. A massive dyke of dolerite runs north-south through this hillock from which stone was quarried for the sculpture. The top surface and the slopes of the hillock are full of chips of stone, a fact which suggests, that the different parts of the image were fashioned here. Besides, it was easier to haul them the slope of the hill to the site of the shrine over.

Ksetrapala

It has been suggested that this gigantic image is propably of the god Kalapriya whose temple, as the stone inscription records, existed in the ancient capital.[10] This is, however doubtful because the image is that of Siva as the presence of the third eye clearly shows. Moreover, Mirashi has convincingly shown that Kalapriya, is one of the names of Surya.[11] It is, therefore, clear that here there existed a sun temple.

The image appears to be the Bhairava form of Siva. It was appropriate that the temple of Bhairava, who was also worshipped as Ksetrapala, whould have been built on the outskirts of the capital town, in the fields. In this connection, it must be mentioned that the inscription refers, among the many meritorius deeds of the king, to the construction of a mandapa (*pavilion*) named sarvalok-asraya near the temple of the well known god ksetrapala.[12] It further records that fire-places (*agni-sthitika*) were constructed at five places for saving the poor from cold during winter, and one of these places was the pavilion called sarvalok-asraya in the courtyard of the Mandalasiddhi which was probably the same as the Mandalasiddhi Vinayaka worshipped at the *Yaksa-dvara.*[13] It may be stated in this connection that very close to the temple of Ksetrapala exposed in the course of excavations, in the adjoining field on the south, was found an image of Ganesa which, in all probability, is the image of the Mandalsiddhi Vinayaka referred to in the epigraph. the *Yaksa-dvara*, that is a gateway adorned with a *Yaksa* figure, was perhaps one of the gateways for entering into the city, and was therefore located on the outskirts of the ancient capital. A similar gateway adorned with the image of a goddess is referred to in another Rashtrakuta inscription.[14]

The giant image can be identified as that of Ksetrapala Bhairava which has been referred to in the inscription.[15] However, the cult of Ksetrapala was not very popular in Maharashtra as it was in the south in the early medieval period. The Saivites in the south worshipped Ksetrapala usually in the form of Bhairava. The cult was very widespread in south India for long for the god was the protector of earth and was sometimes called 'the son of Siva' (*Sambhutanaya*). His main function was to protect the cultivated fields, hence his popularity.

The iconography of the god has been described in the *Vishnudharmottara Purana* according to which he should have three eyes which are large, round and protruding. His long hair are straight and project upwards. The god wears serpant jewels, *naga-vajnopavita*, a girdle of small bells and a necklace of skulls[16]. His form should be somewhat gruesome with fierce fangs and should be awe-inspiring. He is shown with two, four, or six hands though our image may have had only four arms. This form, according to texts, is the *satvika* form of god[17]. He holds a *khadga* (back right) and a bell (ghanta) or a *sula* (lance) in his back left hand; the two front hands, are in the *varada* and *abhaya mudra*. The Kandhar image may therefore, have been of the *satvika* form of Bhairava *Ksetrapala.*[18]

The shrine was possibly built by Krishna III as a result of his south Indian conquests, including Kanchi and Tanjore by 950 A.D.; he was occupying Tondaimandalam.[19] He may have been inspired by the South Indian examples.

According to *Amsumadbhedagama*, the shrine of the *Ksetrapala* should be built in the north-east corner of the city but the *Mayamata* prescribes that it should be in the north.[20]

Ganesa (Pl.VIII)

This is a pot-bellied image, about 55 cm high and 40 cm wide. The god is seated and two armed; the left hand holds a bowl of sweets (*modakas*) being eating with trunk. The right hand is broken from the elbow. The image however,is much weathered and has lost most of its features in relief. Stylistically, it may be dated to the 10th century.

Nandi-mandapa

In front of the shrine structure, there was a small circular pit, 1.90 m in diameter and 35 cm in depth. Perhaps it marks the spot of the *nandi-mandapa*.

Prakara

The human-shaped shrine structure had an enclosure wall (*prakara*) around it. It was built of roughly dressed stones set in mud mortar. It is 36 m long (north-east- south-west) and 33 m wide Southeast-northwest). there is some evidence to show that there was a double enclosure wall. The inner wall is also built of roughly hewn stones, which, however, are smaller than those of the other wall. It was observed that the outer wall was considerably destroyed at places whereas the inner wall is much intact; particularly, in its lower courses. The outer wall is built of large dressed stones with ledges along their edges, obviously for fitting the upper courses. The upper courses of both the walls have been destroyed by ploughing operations and vandalism.

Of the two enclosure walls, the outer one appears to be earlier in date. The relative age of the walls could be established in Sq. C5 in its western section where it was observed that outer wall, built of larger stones, rests over the natural or the virgin black soil. The stratigraphy observed was as follows :

1) surface humus,

2) slightly loose brownish clay

3) compact brownish clay mixed with murrum at places

4) Virgin soil- black-cotton soil.

The outer wall was sealed was sealed by layer (3) whereas the inner one was sealed by layer (1) and is thus later. The foundation trench of the latter has been dug into layers (2), (3) and partly (4). This stratigraphical evidence clearly establishes the relative age of both the walls.

Both the walls were partly destroyed, in some places either of them is completely absent because the dressed stones were removed by the owner himself. In the eastern part the nature of both the walls is entirely different and both of them often get mixed up to our eyes. Here we see a double line of very large, dressed stone blocks with ledges for supporting the upper blocks and the space in between is filled with stone rubble set in mud mortar. To the west of this and almost adjoining it is yet another wall built of small roughly dressed stone blocks, which is clearly a part of the later wall, but it is very badly destroyed and is seen only at places. In fact the only point at which it is clearly distinguished is in the north-west where four of its courses set in mud mortar have still survived. The later wall was perhaps destroyed in the medieval period.

The other wall at the front, consisting of two rows of large dressed stones and averaging 1.25 m in width, is extremely important and also equally enigmatic. In he first place its nature is entirely different from the earlier and the later walls which are exposed in the southern boundary of the shrine. Secondly, it is considrably preserved but is partly destroyed in the north-eastern part. This would suggest that either this wall is removed from the other two described above in point of time or that it is contemporary with the structure but was constructed elaborately as it constitutes the front wall. But there is no evidence to establish its relative chronological position vis-a-vis the other two walls. Being the front wall of the shrine it was in all liklihood built alongwith the shrine itself.

In the middle of the front wall was provided the entrance to the shrine (Pl.IX). It consists of a few steps of which two have survived. It is built of exquisitely dressed large stone blocks and the portion in between is filled with stone rubble. Of the two steps, the lower one is 27 cm broad and 2.26 m long. The lower step is equally long but is 30 cm broad. The entrance proper is in the form of a projection which is 2.26 m wide and 2.70 m deep. Only the periphery is built of dressed stones and the portion in between is filled with stone rubble. The entrance is not located exactly in the centre of the front wall because it is 16.30 m from the southeastern corner and 15.50 m from the north west corner. Moreover, it is also not exactly in the centre of the anthropomorphic shrine structure; one would normally expect it to be exactly in the centre of the two legs of the structure. In fact, it is slightly to the left of the shrine and it, therefore, appears that there was some other architectural feature to the left of the shrine. We had also encountered a patch of ground paved with stone rubble in mud masonry near the left arm of the shrine structure. It is 10.10 m long and 3.75 wide and just to the west of it are two rows of dressed-stone slabs which appear to have an arched top. Unfortunately, only the base of arched top is now seen on the left, the remaining parts being completely destroyed. If complete, this stone bedding with an arched top would have been 16.70 m long and 3.75 wide. There is, however, no such corresponding architectural feature on the left side of the shrine structure. This rubble bedding on the left of the main shrine may have been a sort of platform for yet another image, perhaps Parvati. It may be recalled that besides the two big hands of Siva now housed in the fort in the town, there are four smaller hands also which were found at the site of excavations (Pl.VII). Of these, one holds a bijapuraka, the fruit of plenty, an iconographical attribute of Parvati. If this surmise is correct then one can aver with certainty that the entrance to the shrine was located in the centre of both the images.

To the east of the right leg of shrine structure was found a circular cluster of stones, 1.9 m in diameter, at a distance of 1.60 m. The stones were lying loose in a circular pit which was about 35 cm deep. It also contained a few blocks of dressed stones. It appears that there was a circular platform here for keeping some loose image.

In Sq.F4 was noticed a small circle of stones, 1.30 m in diameter. There was only a single course of stone rubble which is located to the east of the enclosure wall. There is yet another stone circle in Sq. E6 which is located to the east of the main enclosure wall and is similar to the above one. It also consists of a single course of stone rubble. The circle on the left in Sq.E6 is 8.80 m from the main entrance whereas the other on the right in Sq. F4 is 9.30 m from the main entrance. It is quite likely that these were tree-rounds.

It has been observed that there are two circular patches rammed with rubble on either side of the entrance but at its back, almost on the inner (later) wall. It was perhaps inteneded for Siva *dvarapalas*.

Human skeleton (Pl.X)

In the south-eastern quadrant of Sq.E5, slightly to the left of the main entrance, was encountered a human skeleton overlying the outer enclosure wall. The skeleton was that of an adult which was in an extremely bad state of preservation as much of it including the skull was completely crushed below the heap of rubble and earth overlying it. Of the remaining parts of the body only a few fragments of hands, legs and ribs have survived[21]. The other parts have completely pulverised and become one with the black clay. The skeleton lay in the north-south orientation with head towards north and the legs towards the south. No pit for the skeleton could be discerned and it, therefore, appears that the skeleton was placed over the outer wall and rubble was overlying it.

If it was a case of human sacrifice, the skeleton should have been in the foundation, below the wall. But on the other hand it was found overlying the wall, suggesting that long after the shrine fell into disuse, the dead-body was buried here. A pit was dug into the ground which had more rubble than earth. When the wall was encountered, no further digging was possible and hence the body was placed there and the pit was filled with rubble and earth[22].This may have happened sometime in the late medieval period in the 17th cetury at the time of Mughal invasions, a period of considerable instability, or even recent past.

Vastu-purusa

The structure exposed in the course of our excavation at the site is no doubt extremely interesting as it is unique not only in the country but even beyond and is without parallel. But it is also equally enigmatic because of its unique plan. It can at best be described as a vastu in the form of *purusa.* Is it then the concrete expression of the concept of *Vastu-purusa?*

The concept of *Vastu-purusa* has so far proved to be a puzzle and has therefore remained a myth. Various scholars have tried to explain its significance and visualise it, but there is as yet no stisfactory explanation. It is generally supposed that the concept of *Vastu-purusa* has its origin in the Vedic Srauta tradition of fire sacrifice.[23] It has been suggested that god and his temple correspond to soul and human body. What is more, the temple building ceremonies are rituals which are akin to our *Jataka-samskaras.* The Vastu- silpa texts describe the *Vastu-purusa* as follows :

"Finally the presiding deity of the site (*Vastu-purusa*) who is described as hump backed and of crooked shape, is said to occupy the habited area (*vastu*) in such a manner that his limbs cover the several squares or groups of squares which, as set forth in the former part of the chapter, are assigned to and named after various deities. As he is supposed to lie down with his face turned downwards, his head being in the central square on the east side (assigned to Surya), his right and left hands must be in the partitions of Agni (south-east) and Isana (north east) respectively; and his right and left feet on those of Nairrita (south-west) and Vayu (north-west), respectively. The middle part of the body occupies the central portion of the plot which, as we saw, is assigned to Brahma"[25].

The description of the *Vastu-purusa* given in the *Agni Purana* is quite different. It describes the door of the temple as its mouth, the platform terminating the trunk of the superstructure as the *Skandha* (shoulders) of the *Purusa*, the *bhadra* or the projections as the arms, and the *jangha* and the lower-most moulding as the feet (*padukas*). The analogy of the human body is considerably followed on the structural plan of the temple and although it is not to be taken literally, its importance is not minimal. Later texts follow this image and in many we find reference to the worship of *prasada* (the temple) as *purusa.* It appears from various descriptions that purusa refers to the ground-plan but he is also the vertical man, with his head being the sky (the *amalaka*); his *nabhi* (naval), the *garbha-griha*; and the lower mouldings the feet (*pada*).

The *Vastu-Vidhana* of Narada (VII, 26-32) pertinently points out that the *Vastu-purusa-mandala* is the diagram (*yantra*) and the form (*rupa*) of the *Vastu-purusa* who, like his counterpart, the Vedic and Upanisidic *purusa* is beyond form. The *Vastu-purusa-mandala* is his body (*sarira*), the prinicple device (*sarira-yantra*) for building a temple.

According to Stella Kramrisch, Indian *Vastu-silpa*, the *Vastu-purusa-mandala*, represents a sacrificial body of the fallen asura and is analogous to the ritual body which the sacrificer builds for himself when piling up the Vedic altar. It is called *Yajna-tanu* (*Taittiriya-Samhita* IV, 4, 9). The sacrificial body of the *Visva-purusa* is the dwelling of gods.[26]

It will be clear from the discussion above the concept of *Vastu-purusa*, which become very complex and abstract later, was quite different originally. It appears from later Vedic literature that it simply represented the fallen body of an *asura*. If we accept this, then we will not be far off the mark if we identify the human shaped structure(shrine) exposed in the course of excavations at Kandhar as a concrete example of the concept of *Vastu-purusa*. The structure is gigantic, masive, built of dressed stones, and cetainly resembles the body of a fallen *asura*.

The next problem that then arises is whether any sacrifice was performed at the site before the shrine was built? it is likely since the Rashtrakuta king Krishna III, whose capital was located at Kandhar, was a great conquerer.[27] He carried arms far and wide, and his conquest of south India is well recorded.[28] His empire was spreading over Karnataka, Andhra and Tamilnadu besides Maharashtra. The fact that so many epigraphical records from the territories usually governed by the Cholas and the pallavas are dated in Krishna's reign shows that the whole of Tondai-mandalam was directly administered by Krishna III throughout the major part of his reign.[29] Hence the A.S.Altekar is justified in observing that, "Krishna III was the last able monarch in the Rashtrakuta dynasty. None of his predecessors had so completely dominated the Peninsula as he could do. Even Govinda III could not bring under his direct administration territories of the Pallava king... What he lost in the north was more than compensated by his solid gains in the south. He must have been an able ruler, and a skilful general, otherwise his achievements would not have been possible."[30]

Acknowledgements

The excavations at Kandhar were jointly carried out by Deccan College Postgraduate and Research Institute, Pune and the Department of Archaeology, Maharashtra State, Bombay, under the direction of the authors. They were assisted by Drs.Vasant Shinde and Shubhngana Atre, Sri Y.S. Rasar and Sri V.G.Vishwasrao of Deccan College and Sarvashri Ashok Joshi and Jagdish Bansod of the State Department of Archaeology. The drawings have been prepared by Sri Y.S. Rasar, and the photographs by Sri Vasant Nagpure and Sri Sunil Jadhav of Deccan College.

REFERENCES

1. It has been suggested that in ancient times the river was known as Nandi. See D.C.Sircar, "Fragmentary Rastrakuta inscription from Kandhar", *Epigraphia Indica*, Vol.XXXV (1964-65) , P.111.
2. *Ibid.*, p.566.
3. *Ibid.*
4. D.C. Sircar, *op.cit.*, p. 108
5. *Ibid*, p.109
6. *Ibid.*
7. *Ibid.*
8. "Kandhar through Epigraphy and Archaeology", *Jr. of the Epigraphical Society of India*, Vol.VII (1980), pp.22-24.
9. V.S.Nayar, "Vasuki-Sayana : A rare motif", *Jr. of Kerala Studies*, Vol. IV (1977), pp.517-524.
10. Shobana Gokhale, "Kandhar through Epigraphy and Archaelogy", *Jr. of the Epigraphical Society of India*, Vol. VII (1980), p.22.
11. Mirashi, V.V., "Identification of Kalapriyanatha", *Studies in Indology*, Vol.I (Nagpur, 1968), pp.37-44.
12. Sircar, *op.cit.*, p.107.
13. *Ibid*, pp.107-108.
14. Cf. Chinchani Plates of the time of Kaska III, EI, XXXII, p.56.
15. Sircar, *op. cit.*, p.107
16. See T.A. Gopinatha Rao, *Elements of Hindu Iconogaphy* (Madras, 1916), Vol.II, Pt.2, p.495-98.
17. *bid.*

18. *Ibid.*

19. A.S. Altekar, *Rashtrakutas and their Times*, (Poona, 1967, 2nd ed.), pp.116-117.

20. K.K. Ramamurthy, "Ksetrapala concept and Cult Images from South India" in Amita Ray, H. Sanyal and S.C. Ray (ed.), *Indian Studies*, Prof. N. R. Ray Volume (Delhi), p. 123

21. These too were removed by Sri Keshavrao Dhondge, the local leader, to the Shivaji College, Kandhar.

22. When the skeleton was discovered, Sri Keshavrao Dhondge, the local MLA, made much of it, writing in his weekly which he publishes from Kandhar, that was a case of human sacrifice and that the dead-body was that of a poor man belonging to the scheduled caste. No amount of explanation was of any use, since it served his political ends and he would exploit the situation to his advantage.

23. P.P.Apte and S.G.Supekar, "*Vastu-puruskara-samhita* and *Brihat-samhita : A Comparative Study*", BDCRI Vol.;42 (1983), pp.5-17.

24. D.N. Shukla, *Vastu-sastra*, Vol.I, *Hindu Science of Architecture*, (Lucknow, 1960), p.403.

25. P.K. Acharya, *Hindu Architecture in India and Abroad*, Series, Vol.VI (London, Oxford Univ. Press), pp.101-102.

26. Stella Kramrisch, *The Hindu Temple*, Vol.I (Calcutta, 1946), p.95.

27. A.S.Altekar, *The Rashtrakutas and Their Times* (Poona, 1967, second ed.) pp.115 ff.

28. *Ibid.*

29. *Ibid.*

30. *Ibid.* p.123.

AN EARLY TEMPLE IN GUJARAT—EXCAVATIONS AT GORAJ (MAHADEOPURA)

B.M. Pande* & Narayan Vyas

In December 1982, Dr. Umakant P.Shah informed us about some sculptures which he had seen in an ashram, a few kilometers away from Vadodara. These sculptures, in Dr.Shah's view, were fairly early, identical in style, execution and date with those found at Shamlaji, Devenimori and other Kshatrapa and Maitrake sites, particularly in north Gujarat. Based on this information we examined the sculptures and also visited the area with Dr. Shah from where these sculptures were reported to have been collected. The site was Sandhyapura—now renamed Mahadeopura—and village Goraj.

A visit to Goraj and Sandhyapura—hereafter referred to as Mahadeopura—on 22 December, 1982, was most rewarding. It not only suggested to us the need for excavating the site but also indicated that Goraj was an ancient village. [1]

Goraj is 30 kilometers to the east of Vadodara and 10 kms to the east of Vaghodia in Taluka Vaghodia of District Vadodara, Gujarat. It is situated on the left bank of the Deo river (also known as the Dhadhar). It is a sprawling though sparsely populated village mainly inhabited by tribals of the Naika community.

The mound is located about a kilometer to the west Goraj village and forms part of the village Mahadeopura.[2] The mound is distinguished by the presence of an eighteenth- nineteenth century structure in the centre enshrining a *Siva-linga* and three bull figures, one of them being of an exquisite from.[3] There were several loose sculptures on the low mound and in the neighbouring area some of which were shifted to the Archaeological Survey of India office in Vadodara.

The eighteen-nineteenth century Ramesvara Mahadeva temple stands on an unobtrusively low mound which merges almost imperceptibly with the landscape. The area adjoining the mound, particularly to its east and south, which is under cultivation, also contains ancient remains now represented in the form of potsherds and brickbats. The road in the middle of Goraj village leading to Mahadeopura one could see in the exposed sections deposits containing ash, pottery and other vestiges of ancient habitations. In the centre of the Goraj village, in a modern temple dedicated to Varahi, is kept a soft stone plaque depicting standing Vishnu which seems to be fairly early in date like the other sculptural pieces. To the south of the village there exists the door-sill of a temple now covered and shaped in the form of a mound. This temple, in all likelihood, is slightly later than the majority of the sculptures and may be dated to a period some-time between the ninth and eleventh centuries A.D. In fact, several specimens of sculptures and architectural fragments in Goraj would belong to this period.

Of particular importance was a seated Jaina *tirthankara* figure with its head missing, which could perhaps be dated to about the fourteenth century A.D. This not only substituted the presence of medieval remains but also provided significant evidence about the existence of Jaina Shrines in the area.

Finally, we may mention that there also exist fairly large-size mound at the entry of the village to the east and opposite across the modern road leading to Rustampura. As a matter of fact, we could say with fair amount of certainty that this high mound across the road represents some ancient temple of sufficiently large dimensions. Close by, on the almost flat ground below this high mound near Jhaverpur across the road, one could notice large quantity of iron slag and haemetitic stones lying scattered over a fairly extensive area. This suggests the existence of iron-working in the area. How early these are in terms of time is not possible to say at present; this point requires to be examined and studied in greater detail. However, the very presence of such a large quantity of iron slag and haemetitic stones in the area is important for, as far as our present knowledge goes, the nearest source of iron ore is the Jambhughoda area, near Pavagath,[4] not very far from Goraj.

All the above-cited evidence, though sketchy, naturally suggested that Goraj was not only an ancient village but was a large-size settlement of sufficient importance.[5] That this was so is also amply corroborated by inscriptional evidence as available in the Sarsavni (Sarsavani) plates of Buddharaja of Katachchuri (or early Kalachuri) dynasty.[6] These copper plates are of the year 361 corresponding to either A.D. 609 or 610. The fact that Goraj is referred to in the inscription as a *bhoga* forming part of Bharukachchha *vishaya* makes it clear that Goraj was an important administrative unit [7] in the seventh century. It is also not unlikely that Goraj may have been important even earlier than the seventh century in the Kshatrapa times and the

* Institute of Archaeology, 24 Tilak Marg, New Delhi - 110001

period following it as was evident from the antiquarian remains in and around Goraj.

Accordingly, excavations were under taken at the Mahadeopura (20° 15'N lat.; 73° 25'E long.) mound in the year 1982-83 and was continued in the years 1983-84, 1984-85 and 1985-86.[8] Simultaneously, trial trenching was also done in the area near the Jhaverpura mound where large quantity of iron slag and haemetitic stones are strewn. Exploration were also carried out along the Deo river which resulted in the discovery of a variety of remains ranging in time not only from the early centuries of the Christian era to the medieval times but also those belonging to the stone ages.

The most remarkable, of course, is the unearthing of the remains of the plinth of brick temple (Plates I and II) in Mahadeopura mound. That these remains represent vestiges of a fairly large-size brick temple was evident from the fact that the platform or the plinth measures 35 meters from east to west and 24 metres from north to south and is on an average between 1.45 and 1.50 metres in height. No evidence or trace was found of the superstructure of the temple of the plinth, 29 courses were exposed. Simultaneously, a brick wall, enclosing the temple was also excavated on three sides-north, south and the west.

The plinth of the temple is built of plain and moulded bricks (Plate III), some of which are decorated. Except for the north-eastern corner, where the plinth was found damaged, it was almost intact. On the western side, patches of lime plaster were also noticed. The plinth rested over a foundation varying in depth between 40 and 60 cms.

As already stated above, the plinth which was fully exposed is oriented east-west and north-south; the larger east-west axis is 35 metres with the entrance towards the east. The plinth is *triratha* on plan, the central *ratha* being shorter than the other two on the sides. On the eastern side was exposed the *chandrasila* (Plate IV) with one step each made of single stone. Both plain and decorated bricks had been used in the making of the plinth. The upper two courses had decorated bricks of triangular form, below which are plain courses followed by mouldings comprising *kalasa, antarapatta, kumbhaka* and *khura.* The *antarapatta* is half octagonal in shape and decorated with floral motifs. A number of open stone channels (*pranals*) were also found placed on the upper part of the plinth near its edge on the sides; on the north-western side some of them were to be found covered with bricks. One of the *pranala* was longer than the rest and was in three parts. The *pranala* was oriented north-south; it discharged into a brick-built *kunda* (Plate V) having 36 brick courses. This *pranala* was evidently meant for the discharge of the *abhisheka* water from the temple which was dedicated to Siva.

On the northern side, where the big *pranala* was exposed, an additional brick-paved floor or platform was also noticed, perhaps to provide for the *kunda.* The damaged portion near the *kunda* was also excavated and the original plinth having mouldings was exposed.

The plinth and the platform was build by making square hallow blocks in rows filled with murum and black clay and paved with bricks all around forming *triratha* plan. The bricks used in construction generally measure 44 x 25 x 7; 43 x 26 x 7; 41 x 26 x 7 and 41 x 26 x 6 cm.

The bricks were laid in fine courses using mud mortar. As already mentioned above, patches of lime plaster were noticed on the western side. It is thus likely that the entire plinth was originally covered with lime plaster.

The entire plinth was enclosed within a compound wall made of bricks which was traced on the, west and south sides. In contrast to the plinth of the main temples, the compound wall in a rather bad state of preservation. On the basis of the presence of post-holes, several iron nails measuring between 15 and 20 cm. in length, we may assume that the plinth in all likelihood had wooden superstructure.

This structure appears to have been built sometime during the period of Kshatrapa rule (*circa* first to fourth century A.D.). It seems to have been in use and was rebuilt during the time of the Gupta followed by the Maitrakas. This is evident from different stages of repair to the plinth and with which have been found associated a signet ring carrying the inscription "Om Jagesara" (Plate VI) in Brahmi characters of second-third century A.D., a silver coin of Kumaragupta (A.D. 414-455) and Maitraka sculptures. After it fell into disuse, on the same site was built the Ramesvara Mahadeva temple, by the Scindias of Gwalior sometime in the eighteenth-nineteenth century.

As already stated above, the area in and around Goraj and Mahadeopura had a good number of sculptures and architectural fragments. While a detailed analysis of these is under way, it is necessary to mention in particular a four-armed standing Vishnu in the sculpture of Mahishasuramardini (Plate VIII), Gajalakshmi, several image of Nandi, a miniature Vishnu, Surya (Plate IX), Sivaganas, Chaturmukha Siva-*linga*, Siva in the form of Andhakasurasamhar, dancing Siva, Brahma with consort,

Ganesa (Plate X) and Jain tirthankara (Plate XI). The beautiful life-size stone sculpture of Nandi is indeed a fine specimen of Maitraka sculpture and if it lent its name to the village Sandhyapura it is not surprising; it is a pity though that the inhabitants of the Sandhyapura village preferred to rename the village as Mahadeopura for whatever may have been the reason.

Not much pottery was found in our excavations at Goraj; however, the few that were found include some Red Polished Ware sherds.

The discovery of the plinth of a large brick temple at Mahadeopura assumes further importance if we try to understand the evidence in the light of the remains of bricks structures at Devinimori[9] on the one hand and Kayavarohana[10] on the other. In our view Goraj, Mahadeopura and the area in its close vicinity was an important Saiva centre connected in all likelihood, with the Lakulisa Pasupata cult[11] and was no less if not important than Kayavarohana which is known as a centre of the Lakulisa cult.

REFERENCES

1. The site was inspected (by BMP) on 22 December, 1982 in the company of DR. U.P. Shah. At the time of our visit it was quite obvious to us that the site adjoining the village Sandhyapura contains remains of some ancient temple which, if excavated, would bring to light important evidence about the Saiva-Sakti cult in Gujrat in sixth-seventh century A.D. It was also clear that the village Goraj and the adjoining area was a religious centre circa sixth-seventh century.

2. In the Survey of India sheets the village is mentioned as Mahadeopura while in revenue record as Sandhyapura. In our paper the excavated site is being mentioned as Goraj (Mahadeopura).

3. Some of the Nandi and other sculptures perhaps seem to have been taken away from the site as was evident from the collection seen by us in the Muni Seva Ashram near Goraj. Of the three Nandi figures, two were subsequently shifted and kept on the platform in front of the Ramesvara Mahadeva temple at the Mahadeopura mound.

4. This however needs confirmation.

5. During the course of digging by the Irrigation Department of the Government of Gujarat, in 1986, below the village towards the north along the bank of the river Dhadhar or Deo, trace of brick walls (fortification ?) were noticed, suggesting thereby that the village Goraj was perhaps fortified. This was also suggested by Dr. Umakant P. Shah in the course of our discussion with him.

6. Sarisavani is a village about seven km. to the south of Pardra. These copper plates were issued by Katachchuri ruler Buddharaja, the son of Sankaragana, from the victorious camp at Anandapura. The inscription records the grant of the village Kumarivadao situated near Brihannarika in the Gorajja-*bhoga* which was included in the Bharukachcha *vishaya*, to the Brahmana Bappasvamin, an inhabitant of Debhaka. Kielhorn, who originally edited the inscription, had suggested the identification of Gorajja with Goraj and Kumarivadao with Kawarwara, 'about 11 km west- north-west from Goraj '. He identified Debhaka with Dabka, 'a village in the Baroda State, about 8 miles west of Padra and 40 miles north of Broach'. Keilhorn also cited the following note of Dr. Fleet, which was sent by him at his request after his research of sheets No. 22 S.E. (1883) and No. 36 S.W. (1897) of the *Indian Atlas* : - "The Gorajja of this grant must be the 'Goraj' of sheet No. 36 in lat. 22°20', long. 73°32', in the Halol subdivision of the Panch Mahals; it is shown as a town or large village 11 miles on the south of Halol, and is about 54 miles towards the north- east-north from Broach. Kumarivadao must be the 'Kawarwara' of sheet No. 22, about 11 miles towards west-south-west from 'Goraj' and about east- south-east from Baroda; it is about 24 miles almost due the same sheet 4-1/2 miles on the south of 'Kawarwara'. We have quoted Kielhorn and Fleet in extense since it has not been possible for us to give exact reference to the Survey of India Sheet showing location of Goraj. See, F. Kielhorn. 'Sarsavni' plates of Buddharaja; (Kalachuri) samvat 361', *Epigraphia Indica*, Vol.VI, pp. 294-300. V.V. Mirashi, who subsequently edited the inscription identified 'Brihannarika (the larger Narika) with Naria, 7 miles south of Kawarwara'. See V.V.Mirashi, 'Sarsavni plates of Buddaraja: (Kalachuri) year 361', *Inscriptions of the Kalchuri-Chedi Era, Corpus Inscriptionum Indicarum*, Vol.IV, part I, Ootacmund, 1955, pp.51-56, pl.IX.

   The relevant portion of the inscription, translated by V.V.Miraśhi, is as follows: (line 19) 'Be it known to you. For the increase of religious merit of (*our*) mother and father and of ourself, we have granted with a libation of water this village (*viz) Kumarivadao (situated)* near Brihannarika (the larger Narika) in the Gorajja bhoga included in the Bharukachchha vishaya together with udranga and uparikara, inclusive of all receipts and exempt from all gifts, forced labour and special rights, which is not to be entered by *chatas* and *bhatas*, according to the maxim of waste land, (*which is*) to be enjoyed by a succession of sons and sons'sons as long as the moon, the sun, the ocean and the earth will endure—to the Brahana Bappasvamin, the son of Bhattu of the Parasara gotra who is a student of the Vajasaneya Kanva (*şakha*) and resident of Debhaka, for the maintenance of *bali, charu, vaisvadeva*, and other (*religious*) rites.'

7. Line 18 of this inscription, there is also mention of *bhogika* alongwith *vishayapati* and other officials, which suggests that *bhoga* was an administrative unit of which *bhogika* was the administrative head. In the inscription, Gorajja is referred to as *bhoga* included within Bharukachcha- *vishaya*. According to R.S. Sharma, *bhoga* and *bhogapatika* was the title of officers who were 'assigned offices not so much for exercising royal authority over the subjects and working for their welfare as for enjoying the revenues'

(p.15). He further refers to *bhogikaplaka* occurring in the early Kalachuri inscriptions who, in this view 'may have acted as superintendent over the *bhogikas*' (p.16) According to him 'such terms as *bhogika, bhogapatika* and *bhogikapalaka* smack of feudal relations'. He further states (p.18) that in Kalachuri inscrptions 'the term *bhoga* indicates a somewhat smaller revenue area placed under the charge of a *bhogika*'. See, Ram Sharan Sharma, *Indian Feudalism : c.300-1200*, University of Calcutta, 1965, pp.15 ff. These bhogikas or *bhogapatis* who were hereditary administrators, according to Sharma, were 'officers in charge of *bhuktis* or *talukas*' (95). Sharma has considered *bhukti* with *bhoga* as a term of similar import; the former, in his view, was a territorial unit 'meant for the enjoyment of the governor under whose charge it was placed' (p.17).

D.C. Sircar also refers to *bhoga* as a territorial unit which, according to him, is identical to and has the same meaning as *bhukti*, literally meaning enjoyment that is jagir. Among other instances of the occurrence of the word bhoga, where it is referred to as a subdivision of district, D.C. Sircar has especially referred to the Gorajja-*bhoga* in Bharukachchha-*vishaya* in the Sarsavni plates of Buddharaja. According to him, the term here may be *abhoga* (p.382). In his view again, 'the word *bhoga*, as also bhukti, came to be used in the sense of 'the property under one's position' (p.383). He further states that, the use of *bhoga* and *bhukti* in the sense of a territorial unit seems to be due to a further expansion of this meaning of the words (p.383). In this inscription the word bhoga has not been used in the sense of periodical offering which is also one of the meanings of the word *bhoga* as it referred to in several copper plate grants, nor has it been used in the sense of impost or enjoyment.

In the Sarsavni plates there is also the expression '*rajasmantabhogikavishayapati*'. Now, *bhogika* is also a term connoting an official to whom a charter has been communicated. In fact a *bhogika* is considered by D.C. Sircar as a *jagirdar* (p.371). See D.C. Sircar, *Indian Epigraphy*, Motilal Banarsidas, Delhi-Varanasi-Patna, 1965, pp. 363-64, 368-371, 382-383. We are grateful to Dr. S.P. Shukla for drawing our attention to these references.

8. See *Indian Archaeology 1982-83-A-Review* (hereafter *IAR* followed by the year under references), p. 31, pl.16; *IAR 1983-84* pp.23-24, pls. 18 and 19; *IAR 1984-85*, pp.19-20, pl.9; *IAR 1985-86* in press.

9. *IAR 1959-60*, PP.19-21, PLS. XXI-XXIV; *IAR 1960-61*, pp. 9- 11, pls. VIII-XII; *IAR 1961-62*, pp.12-13pls XXX-XXXI; *IAR 1962-63* p.8, pls. XVIII-XIX. R.N. Mehta and S.N.Chowdary, *Excavation at Devanimori (A Report of the Excavation conducted from 1960 to 1963)*, Department of Archaeology and Ancient History, M.S. University of Baroda, Baroda, 1966.

10. *IAR 1974-75*, pp.15-16, pls. XVI-XVIII; *IAR 1975-76*, P.15, PLS. XIV-XVII; *IAR 1976-77*, p.18, pls X-XI; *IAR 1977- 78*, pp.23-23,pls. XV-XVIII. It has not been possible for us to refer to the articles on Kayavarohana excavations other than the above cited reports in the IAR.

11. We may refer to the paper U.P. Shah, 'Lakulisa: Saivite saint', in Micheal W. Meister (Edited) *Discourses on Siva Proceedings of a Symposium on the Nature of Religious Imagery*, Vakils, Feffeer & Simons Ltd., Bombay, 1984, pp.92- 102

IRON AND GEMSTONE INDUSTRIES AS REVEALED FROM KODUMANAL EXCAVATIONS

K. Rajan*

The habitation-cum-burial site of Kodumanal lies on the left bank of the river Noyyal in Perundurai Taluk of Periyar Dt., Tamil Nadu (fig.1). The excavations conducted in three seasons during the years 1985, 1986 and 1989 by the department of Epigraphy and Archaeology in association with the department of Ancient History and Archaeology, Madras University and the State Archaeology Department exposed 2m cultural deposit datable to the time-bracket between 3rd century BC and 3rd century AD. The trenches laid in the settlement area and 10 burials opened in the megalithic burial complex revealed two prominent industrial activities, namely, iron and steel making and gemstone cutting, beside spinning and weaving, shellbangle manufacturing, etc.

Raw material

The magnetite iron ore used extensively for iron smelting at this site is found in and around Chennimalai hill, the offshoot of Salem ranges, which lies about 15 km east of Kodumanal.

The area is known for its semi-precious stones. Even today the gemstone cutting survives as a cottage industry in the nearby towns of Tiruppur and Kangayam situated respectively about 15 km and 25 km east and west of this site. A good number of semi-precious polished stones are being sent to Gujarat and Rajasthan. The semi-precious stones like beryl are still being collected now and then from the surface. The famous beryl mine at Padiyur lies 10 km south of this site. The hillocks Sivanmalai and Perumalmalai, which were yielding sapphire until some time back, lie 15 km south-east of this site. Besides these two stones, crystal is found in abundance in this region. The quarrying of quartz by the Tamil Nadu State Mineral Department is still in progress near the village Arasampalayam and Vengamedu, about 5 km respectively north and south of Kodumanal.

Gemstone Industry

Both the habitation cuttings and the megaliths yielded beads made of semi-precious stones. Beads of sapphire, beryl, agate, carnelian, amethyst, lapis lazuli, jasper, garnet, soapstone and quartz were collected from the habitation whereas beads of carnelian and agate were restricted to burials.

Carnelian beads, mostly of etched variety, were found in large number in megaliths (Pl. I). Fo· instance, Meg.II yielded 80 beads, Meg.V, about 2220 and Meg.X, about 1000. The occurence of 2220 carnelian beads in a single burial may be the first instance of its kind in India.

Broken pieces of rock crystal occurred in the habitation trenches throughout the deposit. Quite a variety of quartz objects has been noticed: finished as well as semi-finished beads (Pl. II), roughly shaped balls, cylindrical discs, rings, truncated cones, blades, etc.; strangely, all these were found only in the habitation area and none from the megaliths. This may perhaps show that the people attached some ritualistic or spiritual faith to the carnelian beads.

The absence of the raw material like carnelian and lapis lazuli in this region suggests that thses have been brought from Gujarat and Afghanistan or Baluchistan respectively; through trade.

The limited area of excavations restricted to 29 trenches in the 50 acre habitation mound could not locate the actual manufacturing centre. However, one trench (A1), placed in the central part of the mound, yielded two interesting circular pits dug into the natural soil and filled with sand (Pl.III). Quite near to this another pit yielded a heap of rock-crystal chips.

The beads in different manufacturing stages, finished and semi-finished, drilled and undrilled, polished and unpolished, occuring along with the raw material and discarded chips, clearly demonstrate that these were manufactured locally at Kodumanal.

Even to this day, the rock crystal beads are bored by using simple instruments like steel needle fixed with diamond point (borer) and bow drill. The bead to be drilled is fixed on the wax, and, while boring, water kept in a coconut shell is made to drip on the bead to keep it cool. The Kodumanal beads were bored from either side to make a single hole of hour-glass section. The same technique is still followed in the bead-making centres of Tiruppur, Kangayam and Trichirapalli. The use of simple instruments and the long survival of this tradition in the vicinity of Kodumanal recalls the technology adopted in ancient days.

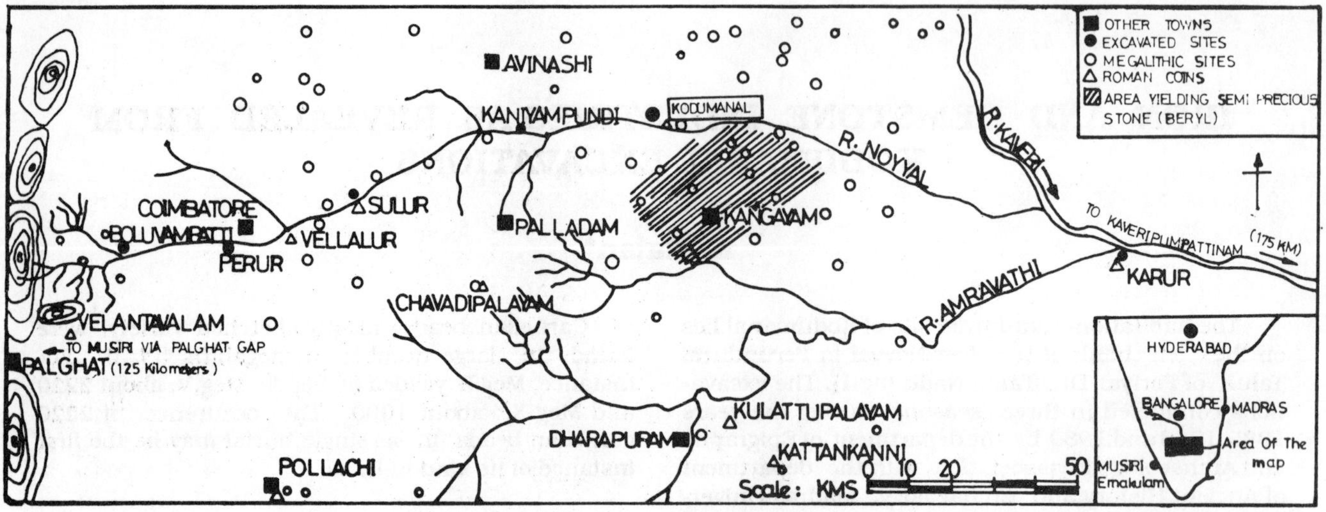

Iron Industry

Numerous iron slags scattered in an area of about 100 sq.m was found on the southern edge of the habitation mound. One of the three trenches laid at this place yielded a circular base of a furnace at the depth of 65 cm right on the natural soil. This circular portion was distinguished by white colour, caused perhaps due to high temperature. The circular portion had a diameter of 115 cm. Around this circular base numerous iron slags were found. Some of the iron slags stuck to the wall portion of the furnace had a smooth surface. Some of the slags also had the burnt clay embedded with the slag. Vitrified brickbats also were recovered. Many tuyere pieces (terracotta pipes) with vitrified mouth were also collected. The total length of the available tuyeres is about 15 cm and the thickness is about 6 cm. It has a hole of 1.5 cm in diameter. The length of the tuyeres suggests that the bellows were used quite near to the furnace. The granite slabs found near the furnace might have been used for forging. Since the furnaces were dismantled to remove the bloom after smelting, it is hard to get the furnace intact. The absence of postholes, floor level and less occurrence of potsherds in this (smelting) area suggest that the iron smelting was done on the periphery of the habitation.

Crucible Furnace

Seven trenches laid 300 m north of this iron smelting area yielded a crucible furnace. These were exposed at the earliest level at the depth of 125 cm. The main crucible furnace was found surrounded by more than 12 small furnaces. The big furnace somewhat oval in shape measured 112 cm north-south and 100 cm east-west and had a depth of 40 cm. The burnt clay wall was 20 cm in thickness (Pl. IV). Inside the furnace pit were collected burnt clay pieces with rectangular holes. These pieces were obviously part of the furnace wall. The holes allowed the air to pass through evenly into the furnace. The complete absence of the tuyeres in the crucible furnace suggests that these holes were arranged for a natural draft of air into the furnace.

The small circular furnaces surrounding this big furnace, almost at regular intervals, had 30 cm diameter at the mouth with a small hole or depression in the centre. These might have been used to heat longer crucibles removed from the bigger one.

An important find here is a vitrified crucible, partially broken, found in the small furnace in situ position. This small bowl-shaped crucible had a diameter of 9 cm at the mouth with total thickness of 0.7 cm at the top and 0.9 cm at the base (Pl. V). Besides this, many other fragmentary pieces of vitrified crucibles were also found. Another interesting find is an unused crucible made of well lavigated ferruginous clay.

Dr. Buchchnan who travelled in south India in 1801 has given a graphic description of the steel making industry in the vicinity of the Chennimalai hill, about 15 km east of this site. This also suggests the long survival of an ancient tradition in this region, till at least the early part of the 19th century.

Conclusion

The above facts clearly demonstrate that Kodumanal served as an industrial centre in the period between c. 3rd century BC and c 3rd century AD. Iron and steel might have been exported to other parts of South India while the stone beads were certainly sent abroad as part of Roman trade. A Roman silver coin, a terracotta figurine, of plausibly Roman origin, pieces of rouletted ware, two silver punch marked coins, personal names of prakrit origin written in Brahmi characters and beads of carnelian and lapis lazuli found at this site and the large number of Roman coin hoards from the surrounding places clearly suggests that Kodumanal was an active industrial and trade centre in the early centuries of the Christian era.

A RARE IMAGE OF AVALOKITESVARA FROM EASTERN INDIA:

Shashi Asthana*

The National Museum, New Delhi acquired in 1960, a unique stone sculpture representing a Budhist maledeity.

A small stone stele[1] carved in high relief presents a two armed deity seated in *sukhasana* on a double lotus pedestal with left leg pendant, foot resting on a small lotus and right folded on the pedestal. Both of his hands are partly damaged, but their posture and location against the chest clearly reveal that they were in the dharmachakra mudra. A stalk of the full blown lotus is emerging from the main bottom stem, passing through the left elbow and blossoming on top near the shoulder on his left side. In order probably to balance this another lotus was carved in the same style. However, the flower is now lost but its stalk is still intact which is shown passing through the right elbow. The deity is bejewelled with necklace, armlets, bracelets, eardiscs, anklets and beaded sacred thread. The hair is arranged in *jata mukuta* with two ribbons fluttering on either side of the head. He is clad in a *dhoti*.

The image is flanked by two female deities. On his right is seated a two-armed goddess on lotus pedestal. She displays the *abhayer mudra* with her right hand while left holds a stalk of full blown lotus. On her left he is accompanied by a four armed goddess, seated on a lotus pedestal. The main pair of hands is in *anjali mudra* while the other two hands carry the rosary and pot ? She sports jata mukuta on the head. The third eye adorns the forehead.

The most unusual feature of this image fs the representation of a large serpent lying against the main stem of the lotus with the head raised. On his long tail six male figures are shown standing. All of them are in different postures, including *anjali mudra, vismaya mudra* etc. While the first one is in aggressive mood forwarding towards his head, the others are only marginally animated. On either side of this scene is found a devotee in *anjali mudra* (Pl.I).

On the top of the stele there are the images of five Dhyani Buddhas with amitabha in the centre.

As the image has been bought from a dealer, its exact find spot is not known. However, stylistically it can be assigned to the pala period of eastern India and dated to the 10th century A.D.

As there is no Dhyani Buddha image present in the crest of the deity to give us some clue for exact identification, the focus will be mainly on the *Dharmachakra mudra* and lotus for this purpose. The lotus is a very common attribute in Buddhist pantheon, therefore its appearance with the deity displaying *dharmachakra mudra* will be considered. At the same time two female companions of the deity will be taken into consideration.

A casual look at the sculpture suggests this deity to be Manjughosha or Manjuvara, the two forms of Manjusri, the god of wisdom. Both of them display the *dharmachakra mudra* and lotus. However, a close look at the image and its detailed iconographic study reveal the fact that it was a different deity.

According to the Sadhanamala[2], both the deities, Manjughosh and Manjuvara, should ride lion. The hands of Manjughosh are engaged in forming *Vyakhyanamudra*. He displays the right lotus in his left and bears the image of Akshobhya on his crown. On his right should be Sudhana Kumara and on left Yamantaka. Manjuvara also displays *dharmachakra mudra* and holds the lotus on one side or on either side but it should have the manuscript Prajnaparamita on top. He is also accompanied by Yamantaka. The present image is shown riding neither a lion nor holding the lotus with manuscript on top. Therefore, his identification with Manjuvara is to be ruled out. Similarly as it has the lotus on either side, which is prohibited in the case of Manjughosh his identity with manjughosh is also doubtful. Moreover in place of Sudhan Kumar and Yamantaka, the presence of two female figures also creates problems for these identifications. Two images of Manjuvara, housed in the Indian Museum, Calcutta, are similar to our image in posture but both these are with the lotus and manuscript on the top.

There is only one image of Avalokitesvara found at Kurkihar[3] presently housed in the Indian Museum Calcutta giving the clue for its correct identification (Pl.II) This two armed image of Avalokitesvara seated in *sukhasana* with hands displaying the *dharmachakra mudra*. A lotus stalk is passing through the left elbow and blossoming on top. He is flanked by Tara and Bhrikuti on either side. Five Dhyani Buddhas adorn the stele. A small stupa is carved between the Dhyani Buddha and Avalokitesvara. But the most important feature which gives us the due is the presence of Dhyani Buddha Amitabh on this crest.

* Keeper, National Museum, Janpath, New Delhi.

As Amitabh is shown in the crest, his identity as one of his Vemanations' is beyond doubt. Beside Aralokitesvara, Mahabala and Hayagriva are the only two male emanations of this Dhyani Buddha. Both are ferocious in form, therefore Avalokitesvara is the only choice left with us. Sadhanas do not prescribe *dharmachakra mudra* for any form of Avalokitesvara. However, these is a supporting evidence available for this feature, one of the 108 forms of Avalokitesvara painted at Manchhandar Vahal monastery, Kathamandu, Nepal, displays the *dharmachakra mudra*, inscribed below as Sukhavati Lakesvara[4] The other attributes of this six armed deity are however, completely different. The *dharmakosasamgraha* of Amritananda[5] while referring to Sukhavati Lokesvara does not mention this mudra for him. However, it does mention a feature which is present in this image of Avalokitesvara i.e. the presence of chaitya, and Tara a well known companion of Avalokitesvara flank him in his various forms. Therefore, the identification of this image as Avalokitesvara is beyond doubt.

Now to certain extent this image helps us in identifying the present image in question. Like the above mentioned image, our image is also two armed, seated in *sukhasata* with hands in *dharmachakra mudra*. A stalk of full flown lotus is emerging from the bottom, passing through the elbow and blossoming up. Five Dhyani Buddhas are on top with Amitabha seated in the centre. He is flanked by Tara on right and Bhrikuti on left. Their identification is quite certain as they appear in this posture in a large number of sculptures. The difference lies in the presence of a lotus on the right side, absence of Amitabh in the crest and depiction of the serpent and human figures underneath the lotus pedestal. The presence of a lotus on the right side might be just to balance the depiction of lotus on the left, this was a usual practice with the artist of that period. Several Pala sculptures are found displaying this phenomenon. The absence of Amitabha in the crest can be explained with his presence on top in the centre. Several times when all the five Dhyani Buddhas were depicted on stele, the parental Dhyani Buddha was always represented in the centre. This may be applicable to this image also.

The depiction of serpent alongwith the human being is most peculiar and probably has been noticed for the first time in the whole gamut of Buddhist art, though serpent were always very popular and prominently depicted in early Buddhist art. Its identification is still a mystery. No textual reference could be found so far for this image. Could this scene be related with the Krishna legend as male figures appear to be the childrens and leader of the group seems to be Krishna himself? The assimilation of Hindu theme in Buddhism is not very unusual in the world of Buddhist art. Could we name the image as Krishna Lokesvara on the analogy of Vishnu Lokesvara as his identity as Avalokitesvara is by and large established ?

REFERENCES

1. *National Museum* New Delhi, Acc No,60,1501.
2. *Sadhanamala* pp, 109-111.
3. *Indian Museum* Calcutta, old ACC No. 58-59.
4. Bhattacharya, B. *Indian Buddhist Iconography*, Calcutta, 1968, p.395.
5. Ibid p. 142.
6. Ghosh, M. *Development of Buddhist Iconography in Eastern India* New, Delhi, 1980, plates 42-50.

ARCHAEOMETALLURGICAL STUDIES AT KANKRAJHOR AND DHULIAPUR

Sudhin De* and
Pranab K.Chattopadhyay**

The archaeological work at Kankrajhor and Dhuliapur in the Midnapur district, West Bengal (IAR-1983-84:93-94) revealed that the neolithic culture was succeeded directly by the Iron Age culture. The two sites excavated by us, are located in the Tarapheni valley which is geographically an extension of the Chotanagpur plateau.

Kankrajhor (86°36' 30" E - 22°41' 30" N)

Two digging operations were carried out at Kankrajhor-I and Kankrajhor-II. The latter is a mound. In the west of the site, a small stream flows down to Kharosoti, a tributary of Suvarnarekha. A trial trench, measuring 2 m x 2 m was laid at the top of the Kankrajhor mound to a depth of 0.72 m. The cultural strata, counting from the top, have been revealed as follows :

Layer-1 is humus, now much eroded. Layer-2 is as thin as 5 cm of medium compact brown earth, yielding potsherds of dull red colour and unslipped black ware alongwith iron collyrium stick and slags. Layer-3 is sterile, composing a medium compact brown earth with a thickness of 6 cm. From layer-4, neolithic ground celts have been found. In this layer hand made bowls with featureless rim of black-and red ware, rim portion of a vessel of dull red were, etc. have also been found. The thickness of this deposit is about 30 cm.

Dhuliapur (86° 51' E, 22° 31' 30" N)

Trial digging at Dhuliapur reveals that the site witnessed the activities of man right from the lower Paleolithic time to the medieval period - with some intermittent cultural gaps during and in between middle palaeolithic, chaicolithic and early historic periods. A trial trench of 2 m x 2 m was put on the site located on the southern bank of the river Tarafeni. The iron age occupation layers yielded iron implements like nails, sickle arrowheads, points, spearheads, knife, sword etc. alongwith red ware. Large quantity of iron slag and ore have also been found. The amount of slag along with iron implements evidently proves that the site was an iron smelting and forging centre. Lump of burnt clay has also been found from this occupational level which was due to open-furnace activities for smelting iron ore on platforms. Four 'tuyers' terminal end of a pipe through which air is injected in a furnance were also found in this level.

Analysis of the Findings

Metallurgical and chemical analyses were carried out on four selected iron implements, a tuyer and two slag specimens excavated from the two sites. The specimens are as follows : a) sword, b) Shapeless bit, c) rectangular nail, d) oval nail or rod, e) tuyer and f) slag specimens.

a) *Sword* : The portion of the sword recovered at Dhuliapur is 114 mm in length. It consists of the handle and a part of the cutting edge. The handle portion is rather thin with a thickness of 5 mm. The middle part of the handle is 21 mm in breadth. The rear portion is curved in shape, with a maximum of 44 mm. The remaining part of the cutting edge is 55 mm in breath. One side of the edge is projected out side with a ridge, and the purpose is not clear from the present corroded remains. However, it might be the midrib. A point to be noted is that the sword is a straight one but it is considerably curved which is rather unusual.

b) *Shapeless bit* : The specimen, though not much corroded, is covered with a dark brown and thin oxidised layer. It is 42 x 20 mm in length and width respectively with a maximum thickness of 7 mm. Most probably it was an ingot. It may be assumed that an intermediate or unfinished product is most likely be found in an area where metal manufacturing had been in practice. The specimen was recovered below the eroded surface in the iron-bearing horizon at Dhuliapur.

c) *Nail* : A rectangular nail of 70 mm in length with a maximum cross section of 9 mm x 7 mm gradually tapers to a thinner section.

d) *Nail or rod with oval cross-section* : The nail which is like a piece of iron rod was recovered from Kankrajher, (KKNJ II/87). This is about 6 mm in diameter with a length of 46 mm. The two edges of this rod has been rounded off by wear and corrosion. This had perhaps been used either as a nail or a semi

* Directorate of Archaeology, Government of West Bengal 33 Chittaranjan Avenue, Calcutta - 700 012.
** Training Centre, Alloy Steels Plant, SAIL, Durgapur - 7132108

finished product to be used for further processing.

e) *Tuyer* : As many as four tuyers were recovered, These are in excellent state of preservation. The most complete one is made of hard burnt clay. One end is vitrified and slagged, clearly representing a prolonged use in smelting operations. The peculiarity of the tuyer is that it is not cylindrical but is with a tendency of truncated cone. The present length indicates that it was more than 80 mm. The approximate diameter is about 58 mm. The eroded portion is also slanted and eccentric with an internal diameter of 31 mm and the external diameter 62 mm with a slanting angle of 15°, indicating that the thick portion was placed on the ground.

f) *Slags* : Both the two sites have yielded iron slags. They are similar in physical appearance. One representative specimen from each site is analysed for its chemical composition.

The slag specimens are heavy in density. Their physical appearance indicates that the smelting was conducted at a temperature above 1100° C.

Chemical analysis : Analysis for the metal specimen have been done with Strohlein apparatus for determination of carbon and other elements like copper, nickel, manganese, lead and zinc. It has been done with atomic absorption spectrophotometer in air acetylene flame with PYEUNICAM SP 2900. The main advantage of this technique is that it has high accuracy with a minimum amount of the specimen consumed. Since more amounts of specimen are required for slag analysis by wet method we adopted the same with a view to determine the various constituents as mentioned earlier. In Table-1 analysis of metal specimens is given. The slag analysis carried by wet method is referred to in Table-2.

Table - 1 (Wt .%)

Specimen	Cu	Ni	Mn	Pb	Zn	C	Fe	P
a) Sword	0.06	0.05	0.006	-	0.007	0.40	base	0.255
b) Shape less bit	0.08	0.13	0.006	-	0.006	0.43	base	0.035
c) Nail	0.05	0.13	0.080	-	0.006	0.24	base	0.066
d) Nail/ rod.	0.09	0.09	0.013	0.025	0.008	Not done	base	0.309

From Table-1, the main interferences which can be drawn are that the specimen a, b, and c are similar in nature and the sources are identical. But the specimen d, i.e. from Kankrajhar, our inferences are different with respect to lead (Pb). Moreover, the average value of a, b and c are much different in all other constituent of d.

Table - 2 Composition of slag (Wet) in (Wt. %)

Constituent	Kankrajhar	Dhuliapur
FeO	58.31	28.53
Fe_2O_3	9.72	43.35
MnO	0.89	0.60
Al_2O_3	4.33	4.40
SiO_2	19.89	16.28
CaO	1.40	1.80
MgO	1.00	1.45
P_2O_5	0.30	0.47
TiO_2	0.60	0.50
CuO	Nil	0.02
SO_3	Not done	1.70
Na_2O	Not done	0.07
K_2O	Not done	0.17

The analysis of the slag of Kankrajhor mentioned in Table-2 was done from the sample at natural state. The shortage of about 3.56% was due to the presence of water vapour, carbon or sulphur dioxide in small amount, sodium and potassium oxides are also neglected.

Metallography of the metal specimens :

Metallographic analyses was performed to determine the manufacturing processes or the treatments carried out after finishing the implements. From all the four implements a small portion was removed by a saw. Sawing was carefully done so that the specimen does not get heated due to friction in sawing. The specimens were then mounted in transparent lucite mountings in a mounting press. Later on these were polished by emery papers of different fineness. The final finishing was done as a mirror like polish given by a diamond cloth.

The initial metallographic observations at different regions within each specimen indicate the presence of inclusions- principally silicates in the form of slags. The amount was also considerably less.

The metal's microstructure, as revealed by a 2% nital etchant was non-uniform. The recrystallised grain size was also with little variation, mentioned in the ASTM standard scale for each specimen.

(a) Sword . The microstructure revealed for this specimen is non-uniform in structure and grain size number varies from 6 to 7. Prior to etching, patches of silicate inclusion noticed at places. Structure is mostly ferrite but in some places about 20 to 25% pearlites are seen which are located in grain boundaries and have been revealed at a magnification of 500X. The sword had been air-cooled after forging as indicated by the 'normalised' structure.

(b) Shapeless bit : Microstructure consist of ferrite and pearlite. The presence of a few Widmanstaten ferrite indicates overheating. This has been indicated in the microstructure obtained at a magnification of 500X.

(c) Nail : The microstructure of this implement is also found to be a nonuniform structure consisting of ferrite and non-uniform distribution of tempered martensite. Carbon inhomogenity may be due to nonuniform and preferential decarburisation. In some places ferrite bands are also present probably due to phosphorous seggregation. Grain size variation is from 5 to 6, at 500X.

(d) Nail or rod ? : The specimen represents mostly the martensitic structure, which perhaps followed with a tempering operation. Photomicrograph at a magnification of 500X represents a severe forging and, while manufacturing it, tempering was unintentional.

(e) Slag : Only the slag specimen recovered from Kankrajhor has been analysed for its mineralogical constituents. A small piece of slag was cut out from the lump and digested with Canada balsam and later polished with abrasives. For keeping its opaque quality it was not made into thin section. Observaing with a mineralogical microscope, the microstructure revealed with a magnification of 32X, is a multi-phase structure consisting of dendritic wustite in silicate matrix.

Observations :

1) The archaeology of the two sites clearly indicates that there was direct transition from the Neolithic to the iron age.

2) Slag/smelting techniques at this site are different from that of Pandurajar Dhibi, Bahiri or Dihor. Gangetic sites.

3) Similar transition has been previously noted at Barudih, Dt. Singhbhum, Bihar. Metallographic analysis has been carried on an implement obtained that site.

4) Present sites are closer to a zone where a few megalithic burials had also been discovered earlier. A cist burial inside the cave Devapahar at Laljal along with human skeletal remains, potsherds and iron spearheads were excavated by the present team (IAR 1982 - 83 : 104)

5) The typical tuyers of oblong shape and slanted finish at the bellows' end was a product of long experiment of iron smelting technique. It may however also be observed that the present form of tuyer is unknown to other sites which have revealed the craftsmanship of the ancient smelters. Still, the difference is hardly vital for the iron smelters.

Acknowledgement : The authors are beholden to the scholars Dr. S.C. Mukherjee, Dr. Atul Bhowmick, Dr. Asok Dutta, Sri Dilip Ray and Sri Biswanth Samanta for their generous help in the study of Archaeology; and Shri H.N. Saha, Sri A.K. Roy, Sri D.K. Sengupta, Sri K. Guha, Sri S.P. Bhattachryya, and Sri S.K. Banerji in the field of Metallurgical studies.

ARCHAEOMETALLURGICAL STUDY OF IRON PILLAR AT DHAR

B. Prakash*

The iron pillar of Delhi (5th century, and the massive iron pillars and tridents (trishul) of Kodachari, mount Abu, Tanginath and dhar (11-13th century) as well as the iron beams of Konark (13th century, have kept the historians, archaeologists and technologists busy in studying them for decades.

These iron pillars and beams each weigh between 2000 to 7000 kg each and they are one of the heaviest iron objects of their times in the word. They have fairly uniform chemical composition as well as excellent resistance to atmospheric corrosion. Unfortunately the historical records mention very little about the details of their manufacture including smelting furnaces and fabrication technology. Hafdield[1] Berdgett and Stanner[2] Ghose[3] and Lahiri et al [4] have used modern techniques and studied the Delhi iron pillar to determine its chemical composition and the cause for its excellent resistance to corrosion but the other objects have been only partially studied. Table-I gives the chemical analysis of Delhi's pillar and the iron beams of Konark (Orissa). Clearly, these are of plain carbon steel (0-23-0.45% c) or wrought iron, containing high phosphorous (0.15) to 0.18%) and some slag inclusions. This being the general composition of the iron produced from Indian bloomeries (Table-I) it may be assumed that the chemical composition of the pillar at Dhar may be in the similar range.

Recently tylecote[5] and Prakash and Tripathi[6] have tried to throw some light on the forging technology of the Delhi's pillar but no further information is available on this subject. The smooth surface finish and the ornamental design occurring at the top of the pillar speak volumes regarding the knowledge and skill of the ancient Indian blacksmiths who could produce such massive objects without the availability of any heavy machinery for handling the red hot blooms or heavy forge hammers. Even today, with the availability of very advanced knowledge regarding the deformation behaviour of iron alloys and also the availability of highly sophisticated machinery for heating, manipulating and forging, it requires very high degree of skill to forge such heavy shafts as marine shaft and high bore gun barrels. Recently, ultrasonic study of the Delhi's pillar has been conducted by Bindal[7] and he has concluded that the internal structure of this pillar is very sound and it has only minor structural heterogenity and some unsoundness due to local porosity or presence of slag inclusions. Prakash[8] has done detailed analysis of the iron smelting practice and furnace design, and concluded that the ancient indian furnances were designed following certain norms and they were operated with great skill to produce wrought iron containing 0.1 to 0.5 or more carbon and no cast iron (containing more than 2% C) was allowed to be produced.

The Iron Pillar at Dhar

The iron pillar at Dhar weighs about 7000 kg, 1000 kg more than the Delhi's pillar and it is probably the tallest solid iron pillar of the world. At present it lies broken into three pieces near the 'Dilawar Khan's Lal Masjid' at Dhar (M.P.). The major part of this pillar is square in cross-section, and at the top (the third portion) it has been shaped into octagon and finally finished into a very short length of circular cross section. The three parts of this pillar have been kept in an open place near the Lal Masjid by the Archaeological Survey of India. According to the report of Cousens[9] the total length of this pillar has been 13310 mm and it has an average width of 253 mm at the square section. The measurements and the cross-sectional details of the three pieces are given in table - II.

Historical Review

There is no historical record available regarding the exact site of the manufacture and location where the Dhar pillar was first erected. Cousens[9] is of the opinion that this pillar might have been a 'jayastambha' having a statue of 'Garura' fixed at the top or a 'Trident' or trisula at the top. The inscriptions on the square part of the pillar show that some southern king TILUNGAVIDYA erected a pillar of victory at UJAYAPURI and probably it was first set near a Vaishnava temple at Mandu, and it was intact there till the conquest of Malva in 1304.A.D. There is also an inscription of Akbar, dated in the 44th year of his reign, recording his halt at Dhar on his way to 'Dekhan' (south central India). There are a few other inscriptions of some names, the most prominent being of Jasu Soni (Sonar) for Yashvant Soni. This shows that the pilar was probably intact till the 44th year of the reign of Akbar and afterwards muhamadans had broken it into pieces and one piece (square one) was brought by Dilawar Khan Ghori around 1405 A.D. to erect it near Lal or Lat Masjid at Dhar. The other two pieces were lying for a long time in Lal Baugh and nearby in the compound of High School in Dhar till all the three pieces were shifted and kept horizontally. Cousens also writes that the largest part of the pillar was erected for

Department of Metallurgical Engineering, Banaras Hindu University, Varanasi-221005.

some time near the Lal Masjid till Sultan Bahadur of Gujrat captured Mandu in 1531 A.D. and at that time he was ordered by Jahangir to carry the pillar to Gujrat and in this attempt it broke and fell down near the Masjid.

Visual Examination of the Pillar's Surface

Recently, the author had an opportunity to visit the place and examine the three pieces of the broken pillar. Its surface was found to have a very crude finish as compared to that of Delhi pillar, although it has been manufactured atleast eight centuries latter. The pieces are now kept horizontally on masonary supports and their surfaces are open to the atmosphere due to which slow rusting is in progress. This is evident due to the stains of iron hydroxide formed on the cement floor from the collection of the solution during rainy season. In order to protect these pieces from such decay it is essential that a proper shed is erected on the site.

As described by Cousens[9] the first and the bottom most part is square in cross-section and it has a number of circular holes made on all the surfaces having a diameter of 30 mm and 40 to 75 mm depth. These holes seem to have been made with the help of a cold tapered steel punch hammered into the red hot main body. One of the holes has been blocked either due to fracture of the punch inside the hole or fixing a pin to fill in the hole. From the study of these holes at first Cousens had assumed them to be made to fix pegs to prepare the pillar as 'Deepdan' but later he abondoned this idea in favour of the holes made for fixing crowbars used for tilting and moving the pillar.

The second piece is partly square and partly octagonal in cross-section as described in Table II. The holes continue to be present on the square section, but there are no holes on the octagonal section. The third and the smallest part is octagonal with a circular section at the top end, and it also does not have the holes. The whole pillar has a continuous taper from bottom to top.

The author's examination has revealed the following new features of the pillars :

(a) The four surfaces of the first section and the square part of the second section are covered with 5 to 15 mm thick and 600 to 700 mm long pieces of flat plates.

(b) The above mentioned holes have been punched about 50- 100 mm before the end of each of these plates deforming them and pearsing into the main body, as can be seen in fig. nos. 3 & 4.

(c) From the examination of the surface of the pillar it seems that this pillar has been fabricated by joining 700 to 850 mm long pieces of square cross-section and the plates have been fixed and forge welded as butt welded' re-enforcement on the joints.

(d) The examination of the second part where the square cross-section has been converted into octagonal one or the octagonal section into circular cross-section in the third part indicates that these acts have been accomplished by hot forging the pillar in the horizontal position, i.e. by turning over the corners and hot forging them by heavy hammers. This completely rules out the possibility of changing the cross-section by chisselling out the excess material to give the desired shape.

(e) The fractured end of the third piece indicates porosity, structural heterogenity and also the presence of coarse rough grain size, as well as poor welding of lumps of sponge iron. This also shows a clear circular marking at the centre of the cross-section as if a thick circular pin has been inserted. This type of circular variation in 'ultrasound' reflections in the centre of the cross-section of Delhi's iron pillar has also been reported by Bindal[7].

(f) The fracture of the pillar into three pieces also suggests that either the forge welding of the small lumps of hot sponge iron has not been perfect due to insufficient pressure or there has been too much slag inclusion in the material.

Probable Technology of Fabrication of the Dhar Pillar

On the basis of the afore-mentioned facts it is obvious that the skilled iron smelters must have used the largest capacity furnace then in operation. Fig.6 shows the photograph of a 40 kg. capacity furnace named 'Kothi' which has been in operation in the Nagpur area. The only other large capacity furnace described by Buchnan[10] is the twin hearth furnace of Malabar which had a production capacity of 250 kg. per heat, but this furnace came into operation only in 18th or 19th century. Hence, it is likely that the Kothi type smelting furnace having a capacity of 40 kg per heat was in operation. As mentioned by Elvin[11] Ujjain was very famous as a centre for smelting iron and it is likely that the iron required for construction of this furnace was smelted near Ujjain and first forge welded into square blocks of 700 to 850 mm and then transported to Mandu on some near by area for final fabrication. The hot forged square sections had a circular tapered hole in the centre of the square cross-section. These holes of 40 to 60 mm diameter were punched in these blocks in red hot condition (120°C).

In the second stage of manufacture these 700 to 850 mm long sections were joined together in the hot condition by fixing a common iron pin and the forge welding the two adjoining faces. For such forging operation simultaneous heating of two to four sections was desirable and probably a furnace of the type 1 was used. This four channeled brick lined furnace has been found during excavation near a temple at site No.13. at Nalanda. The construction of the furnace has been described in detail by Joshi[12] and it has been referred as a melting furnace. The four trenches of the furnace have two holes for fixing the bellows and a flue for the escape of the hot gases. Some slag and charcoal pieces have been found in the bed of the furnaces and hence it has been classified as a melting furnace used for producing brass and bronze castings. But this furnace is much different from the crucible melting or smelting furnace described in Rasa Ratna Samuchchaya[13] (8- 12 centuyry) as 'Angar Kosthi' and shown in fig. 2. Hence, it is postulated that the four channelled furnace as shown in fig.1 or its variation was used for simultaneous heating and secondary refining treatment of the sponge iron as described by Krishnan[14]. The slag found in the bed of the furnace must have flown out from the iron sponge during the secondary refining and forge welding of the iron sections.

For handling the hot sponge highly skilled craftmen must have been used and their forging hammers must have weighed in the range of 20 to 40 kg. The author has seen such heavy swing forge hammers being used even today in the cottage industries for the production of heavy forgings. It is also possible that the forging pressure was applied by dropping a heavy forging block (of iron) raised above the ground level with the help of a pully hung from a stout branch of a tree or a wooden structure. Unfortunately no details of the forging technology have been mentioned anywhere in the ancient Indian text, nor any evidence is available for supporting this technique.

It is presumed that by the uses of this tecnnique several 700 to 850 mm long sections were joined together to fabricate a long pillar or shaft which was further forged in the horizontal position to give it a proper shape.

In the case of Dhar pilar, as rvealed from the photographs the joints were further strengthened by 'butt' welding of the iron plates. These plates were forge-welded on the joint and in order to secure them in position as well as weld them with the main body a cold punch was hammered through the hot stock under heavy pressure, which left the holes in the body. These holes must have further facilitated the handling of the iron shaft as suggested by Cousens[9].

Table - I, Chemical analysis of Delhi's Iron Pillar and Iron Beams at Konark (Orissa) and Indian Bloomery Iron.

Place	C%	Si%	P%	Mn%	S%	Others
Delhi Pillar	0.23	0.006	0.18	Nil	Traces	N2-0.0065
Konark Beam	0.27 to 0.45	0.05 to 0.11	0.15 to 0.18	0.04 to 0.015	0.006	Cu, 0.016 Cr, 0.09 NiO-0.16 N2O-0.004
Adivasi Iron (Recent origin)*	0.0016 to 0.043	—	0.021 to 0.2	0.057 to 0.013	0.007	

* Produced at the Vikash Bharati, Bishunpur, by Adivasis.

In the octagonal section either these holes have been plungged in before giving it the present shape of they got filled up during the shaping of the square section into portions with octagonal and circular sections.

Table :II, Measurements and cross-section of Iron Pilllar at Dhar (M.P.)[9]

Sr. No.	Item	Length mm	Cross-section	Remark
1.	Part-I	7391	Square	Width 203-260 mm
2.	Part-II	3531	Square to Octagonal	Octagonal Section Length-940 mm
3.	Part-III	2286	Octagonal to Circular	Circular section length-205 mm
4.	Overall dimensions of the Pillar	13208	Square-octagonal circular	Average width of square section 253. Gross weight 700 kg.

Although the aforementioned technology of manufacture of the Dhar Pillar is based primarily on the visual examination of the object, it is clear that the knowledge of the iron smelters regarding production of consistant quality of iron and its fabrication technology were of very high order. The determination of the fabrication technology requires further detailed examination regarding the chemical analysis of the material, its microstructure and non- destructive examination using Radiography, Ultrasonic and XRF methods. These tests at the site of the pillar should be organised by the Archaeological survey of India to **highlight the advanced skill of the ancient iron smelters and blacksmiths.**

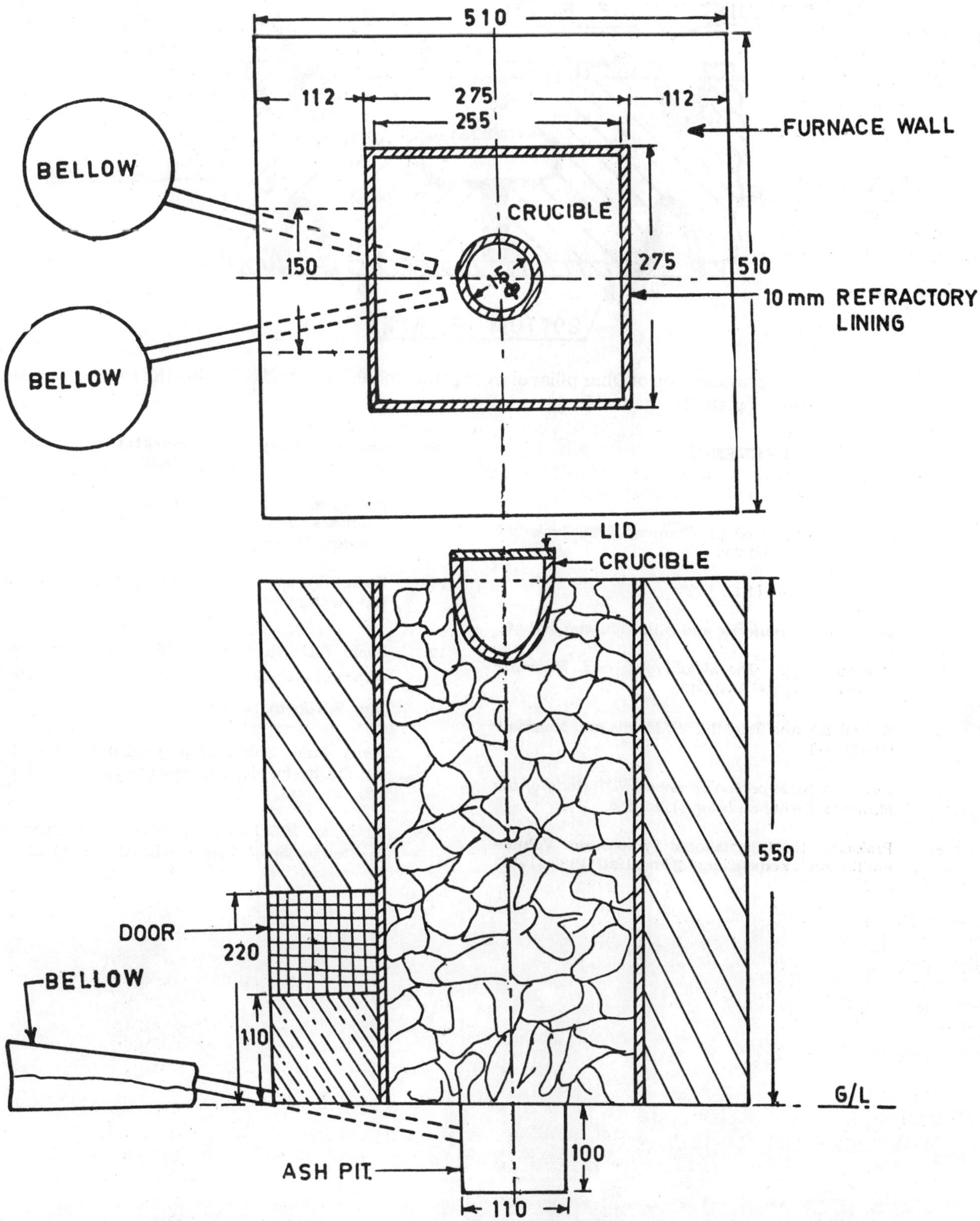

Fig. 2 Angar Kosthi melting crucible as described in *Ras Ratna Samuchchaya* (B. Prakash)

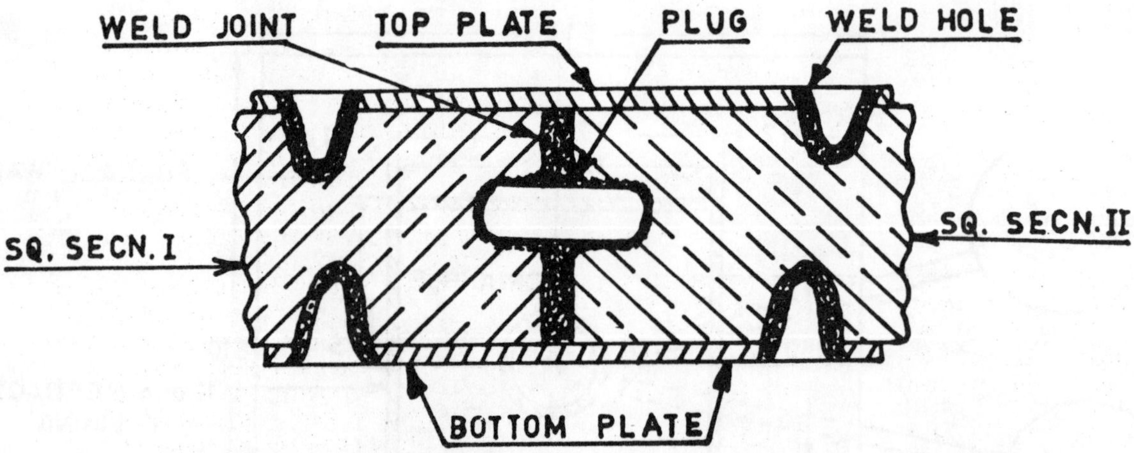

Fig. 1 Longitudinal cross section of Dhar pillar showing the probable method of joining the iron section and the butt welding of plate (B. Prakash)

REFERENCES:

1. Hadfield, R.A., *JISI* 85, (1912)134.
2. Burgdatt ,w.e. AND j.f. Stamers, *NML Technical Journal* v.1. (1963) 24.
3. Ghosh, M.K., *ibid* 31.
4. Lahiri, A.K. T.Banerjee and B.R. Nijhawan,ibid 46.
5. Tylecote, R.F., *The Metallurgist and Materials Technology* July (1984) 343.
6. B. Prakash and Tripathi, V., *Metals and Materials* (1986) 568.
7. Bindal, V.N. *Report on Ultrasonic NDT study of the Historical Delhi Iron Pillar*, (1988-89).
8. Prakash, B. International Symposium Volume entitled *Archaeometallurgy of Iron*, 1967-1987, (1987) 307.
9. Cousens, Henry, *Annual Report of the Archaeological Survey of India (1902-1903), 205.*
10. Buchnan, F.A., *Journey from Madras, Through the Countries of Mysore, Canara and Malabar*, (London, 1807).
11. Elvin, Verier, *The Agaria*, Humphry Milfred, Oxford University Press (India) (1942).
12. Joshi, S.D. *History of Metal Founding on the Indian Subcontinent since Ancient Times*, Published by Mrs. S.S.Joshi, Ranchi (1970).
13. *Rasa Ratna Samuchchya*, English translation by Dr. D. Jhoshi, dept. of Rasasastra, B.H.U. (1987-88), in press.
14. Krishnan, M.S. *Iron ores of India*, Indian Association for Cultivation of Science, calcutta (1955) 23.

BOOK REVIEWS

Stone Age of India by S.A. Sali, Shankar Publications, Aurangabad, 1990

Prior to Independence, studies on the prehistory of India were rather sporadic in spite of the fact that savants like Robert Bruce Foote had made valuable contributions to the subject. At that point of time our knowledge of the Stone Age of India had certain major lacunae. For example, while a good deal was known about the Palaeolithic industries on the one hand and the Neolithic Culture on the other, there was no systematic knowledge of all that transpired in between. For that matter, even though microlithic industries were known to occur in various parts of the country, these were regarded by persons like D.H. Gordon to be very late.

Sustained field-work by Indian archaeologists since Independence has filled many of these gaps. For example, now we can confidently talk of Middle and Upper Palaeolithic stages in the prehistory of India; or we have no hesitation in saying that some of the microlithic industries in the country may be as old as the early part of the Holocene. Bhimbetka has not only given a good sequence of Stone Age industries but has also brought to light a veritable panorama of prehistoric art.

With such systematic work, not only have some missing bones been restore to the skeleton of the Stone Age man, but a good bit of flesh has also been added to the skeleton, with the result that we are now able to visualize that man some what more clearly. There is, however, no scope for slackening our efforts.

A good book summarizing these new discoveries and integrating them with the earlier ones was a great desideratum. The late Professor H.D. Sankalia made an almost heroic attempt by producing his *Prehistory and Protohistory of India and Pakistan* 15 years ago. This is a magnum opus with its own plus points but, I am afraid, it has drawbacks too. For the student community, however, a much more concise and handy book was needed, and this need has been greatly fulfilled by the book of Dr. Sali.

In its earlier part, the book has three chapters. Of these, the first one deals with the geological and geographical background, which is a must for any worthwhile understanding of the lithic industries so intimately connected with the nature of the terrain. The second chapter deals with methodology, for the student ought to know the manner in which the data are obtained and interpreted. The third chapter gives very succinctly an overview of the stratigraphy of the Stone Age as a whole. Having thus prepared the student for what is to follow, the author gives in Chapters IV to VIII a detailed discussion of the various Stone Age cultures, viz. the Pebble-tool industries of the sub-Himalayan region, the Lower, Middle and Upper Palaeolithic Cultures and finally the Mesolithic one. In giving these descriptions the author has taken care to include almost every site that has made any notable contribution to the subject. Thus, the picture on the whole is quite a balanced one. The last chapter deals with the life-style of the Stone Age man, which, for the obvious reason of inadequate data, must for the time being, remain sketchy. The text is supplemented with many line-drawings of the artefacts, sections bringing out the stratigraphy, and maps showing the location of the sites.

A book designed for students has primarily to be information-oriented. Thus, it would not be justified to look into it for in-depth research analyses, though one can catch glimpses of the same here and there.

B.B. Lal

Encyclopaedia of Indian Archaeology, 2 volumes, Edited by: A. Ghosh, Munshiram Manoharlal, New Delhi, 1989. Price Rs. 1200.00

Indian archaeology came of age long back, so much so that it has a history of its own. It threw up in the process so many cultural and chronological nametags, nomenclature and identification marks that a virtual labyrinth was created through which it was difficult to pick one's way. In its development, Indian archaeology did not move from one milestone to another but it represented blanket output of data coming from a variety of cultures, sub-cultures, periods and phases. The result was the breathtaking panorama of a flurry of archaeological activities India witnessed since its independence. While the archaeological data was piling up, there was a longstanding need to bring out a compendium of organized archaeological information that will enable a scholar and a student alike to have clearer picture of India's varied cultural mosaic. To that end, it is gratifying to note that late Sri A. Ghosh made an extraordinary contribution by bringing out the Encyclopaedia.

The book as the blurb declares, "has been planned

in an ambitious manner; it is not mere alphabetical listing of entries with sketchy information on topics". In view of the hazards involved in dealing with a subject as complex and as vast as the Indian archaeology, the first volume contains twenty major heads with sub-heads; from domestication of animals, Archaeobotany and cultures to toilet objects, weapons and writing- in all 371 pages of neatly compiled information.

The section on animals not only contains interesting data on the origins and locale of domestication, but also the fact that dog was first domesticated in Russia as early as the Upper Palaeolithic period, and that the earliest archeozoological evidence in India comes from Adamgarh (5500 B.C.) and Bagor (4500 B.C.). The occurrence of *Bubalus bubalis* or the buffalo at Adamgarh and upper levels of Mohenjo-daro points, according to the Encyclopaedia, to smaller herds of that animal present at these sites. However, recent excavations in Saurashtra suggest that buffalo was considered as important as rest of the cattle by the Chalcolithic farmers. The percentage of the buffalo bones is high at Harappan sites like Kuntasi. Probably in the later part of their existence, the Harappans relied more on buffalo in view of its high milk and meat yields.

As far as the presence of horse at Harappan sites is concerned, doubts persist as the evidence adduced is far from unequivocal. The Wild ass or *Equus hemionus khur* is represented at the Harappan sites along the margins of the Ranns of Kutch. It was probably eaten and no taboo was attached on that score contrary to what the Encyclopaedia has to say.

The section on "Cultures", comprehensively deals with various aspects of prehistoric, protohistoric and historic cultures. However, it needs to be pointed out that the chronological position of the Lower Palaeolithic tools has changed since the Encyclopaedia was conceived some fifteen years. Now the earliest Acheuliar tools from Bori near Poona are dated to early Pleistocene or 1.4 million years. In fact, the Lower Palaelithic of India and Africa have been chronologically rendered so close that early hominids in India may not have lagged behind in coming on the scene compared to their African counterparts. Soan Valley in Pakistan has recently attracted the attention of scholars as the tool- bearing sediments have been dated to two million years B.P.

The Bronze Age cultures have naturally been dealt with some detail, Admittedly, the data given is out of date by almost a decade, yet much useful information has been provided on various aspects of the Harappan culture. However, recent excavations of the pre-Harappan and Harappan settlements have brought to light many new facets which may force us to revise long-held views. For example Mehrgarh has shown that beginning of civilization had derived its initial spark from cultures going back to sixth millennium B.C. This apart, the recent excavations in Kutch and Saurashtra strongly suggest the presence of a pre-Harappan stratum at Nagwada, Dholavira and Surkotada. As far as the Late Harappan Phase is concerned, the transition was gradual and some sites like Rangpur, Rojadi and Kuntasi have the so-called 'Intermediate Phase of Marshall at Mohenjo-daro. It is also increasingly realised that economic settings of these two phases were quite distinct. As a result, the Mature sites are few and far between but well fortified. In comparison the latter sites multiplied in numbers but were smaller in size and sans walls. Even the dates for the Harappan civilization are in for revision. The radiocarbon dates presently available are in most cases uncalibrated. Even a marginal revision can make the Harappan trading activities coeval with the pre-Sargonid period, earlier than 2350 B.C.

The section on Domestic and Misscellaneous objects gives useful inventory for different objects including ploughshares.

The second volume is in the form of a Gazetteer of 469 pages. This is for the first time that the various sites - in fact hundreds of them representing a plethora of cultures - have been put within the confines of a single volume.

Not only archaeological sites have been put alphabetically, but relevant information for each has been given at length. Not since the publication of Marshall's reports on Mohenjo-daro so much painstaking endeavour has been put in the publication of a single book, employing the services of so many scholars. The Encyclopaedia can therefore rank as the most outstanding and durable contribution to the archaeological literature in recent years. Though, Late Prof. Ghosh did not live long enough to see the fruits of his labour on the volumes, the archaeological community shall always remain grateful to him for the two volumes he provided to us and that have easily identifiable work of his masterly editorship.

Y.M. Chitalwala

The External Trade of the Indus Civilization by Dilip K. Chakrabarti, (Munshi Ram Manohar Lal New Delhi, 1990) pp. 183+viii. Price Rs. 220/-

In civilizations Trade has two major areas of operations, an Internal, ie. within the region, both core and peripheral of its extent, and (two) external ie. outside the internal area. It is the former sphere of operation which is the subject matter of this work, the 'internal' trade network of the Harappans which was much more systematized, regulated and wide spread than the 'external' trade that has been by and large marginalised here, although it has been emphasized by the author that without the strong foundation of the 'internal' trade, 'external' trade was impossible, particularly when it was infact the case of 'Long Distance' trade involving the Persian Gulf Countries and Mesopotamia. The author in four major chapters, viz. The Archaeological Evidence, The ordering of the evidence and Chronology, and line, has collected at one place practically all pieces of archaeological evidence which are significant and relevant to the long Distance External trade of the Harappans. He has then attempted chronological ordering of this evidence which spans the period, broadly between 3000 B.C. and 1300 B.C., he is opposed to what we now call 'Shorter chronology' of 2300- 1700 B.C., the author of course, includes the 'Early Indus' phase in it since he places the beginning of the mature phase in 2600 B.C. According to the author, however, first there is no evidence of 'effective' West Asian trade of the Harappans prior to the 'mature' phase, secondly, the long distance trade was not at all the cause of 'birth' of the Indus Civilization, thirdly, agreeing with Dales and Possehl, the Kullis played a major role in this trade as 'middle men', fourthly, the 'maritime trade' existed along with the 'overland trade' and finally, the 'external trade' continued upto 1300 B.C.

The reviewer is in full agreement with the author except for the last point, even though the Indus seals from the Kassite levels of Mesopotamia may prove the point of the author. He feels that if it is accepted as a thesis that 'long-distance trade' exists only on the shoulders of a strong structure of the 'internal trade' then we have hardly any evidence to show that the structure of the 'internal trade' existed till about 1300 B.C.

The author has added in this monograph of observations of 19th century travelogues also as far as the routes between southern Iran and the Indus delta are concerned. This is valuable.

In my opinion this is perhaps the best text book written on the subject. It is lucid, clear to the point and is recommended for all serious students, teachers, and researchers who are interested in the subject. His bibliographic references is extensive and fair treatment has been given to all those who have contributed towards furthering our knowledge about Indus Trade.

S.P. Gupta

One World Archaeology Series, Series Editor Peter J. Ucko,
Published by UnWin and Hyman London.

The World Archaeological Congress (WAC) held in Southampton in September 1986; supposed to have been 11th Congress of the International Union of Prehistoric and Protohistric Sciences (IUPPS), was in many ways unique. Those who were associated with the Congress know and went through all that was enevitable after the Congress was disowned by IUPPS on January 17, 1986. Later for the benefit of all Prof. Peter Ucko wrote a book on the Congress (*Academic Freedom and Apartheid: The Story of the World Archaeological Congress*, 1987; DuckWorth: London). As a matter of fact many in the world around thought that congress was finished and except for two the entire British Executive Committee responsible for organizing the WAC resigned. It entirely goes to the credit of Prof. Peter J. Ucko who rescued the Congress, reorganized the sessions and the Congress was held as planned-from 1 to 7 Sept., 1986. The success of the congress can be imagined by the fact that more than 70 countries were represented by over one thousand participants, 95 percent of them contributing papers, mostly precirculated ones.

It was for the first time that an International Congress was planned with the publication of several volumes resulting from the congress and contract with an established and reputed publisher namely Unwin Hyman was signed in the General Editorship of Prof. Peter J. Ucko. The scholars mostly the session/theme organisers were entrusted the job of selecting the paper and editing them for publication. The result has been the following twenty two volumes.

1. *Animals into Art*
   Edited by: Howard Morphy — £ 50.00
2. *Archaeological Approaches to Cultural Identity*
   Edited by: Stephen J. Shennan — £ 35.00
3. *Archaeological Heritage Management in the modern*
   World Edited by: Henry cleere — £35.00
4. *Centre and Periphery*
   Edited by: T.C. Champion — £ 30.00
5. *Chalcolithic Bronze and Iron Age Cultures in South Asia*
   Edited by: Makkhan Lal — £ 30.00
6. *Conflict in the Archaeology of Living Traditions*
   Edited by : Robert Layton — £ 28.00
7. *Domination and Resistance*
   Edited by: D. Miller, M. Rowlands & C. Tilley — £ 35.00

8. *The Excluded Past*
Edited by: P. Stone & R. Mackenzie £30.00
9. *Food, Metals and Town in African History*
Edited by : T. Shaw, J. ALexander, A. Okpoko, B. Andah & P. Sinclair £ 30.00
10. *Foraging and Farming*
Edited by : D.R. Harris HB £ 50.00
& G.C. Hillman PB £ 19.95
11. *From the Baltic to the Black Sea*
Edited by : L. Alcock and D. Austin £ 30.00
12. *Hominid Evolution, Behaviour and Dispersal*
Edited by : M.H. Day, R. Foley, Wu Rukang & T. Raynolds £ 30.00
13. *Hunters of the Recent Past*
Edited by : L.B. Davis & B.O.K. Reeves £ 30.00
14. *The Meaning of Things*
Edited by : Ian Hodder £ 30.00
15. *The Pleistocene Perspective*
Edited by : A.M. ApSimon & S. Joyce £ 30.00
16. *The Politics of the Past*
Edited by: P. Gathercole and D. Lowenthal £ 35.00
17. *Signifying Animals*
Edited by : R. Willis £ 25.00
18. *State and Society*
Edited by : J. Gledhill, B. Bender and M.T. Larsen £ 35.00
19. *The Walking Larder*
Edited by : J. Clutton-Brock £ 40.00
20. *What is an Animal*
Edited by : Tim Ingold £ 28.00
21. *What's New*
Edited by : S. Van der Leeuw £ 30.00
22. *Who Needs the Past*
Edited by : Robert Layton £ 28.00

As can be seen, each volume has been edited by well known scholars in their field of specilizations. Instead of a detail review of each volume what I propose here is to briefly talk about the series and keep the detail review for a later date.

The Animals in Art deals with the theme-the ways in which people depicted animals in their art covering simple depiction to complex art forms and artistic representation. It has many paper which deal with cultural meanings of their representation in various human societies. Some of the sub-themes dealt with are identification of images, their location in space and time, interpretation of images, meaning of motives etc.

What is an Animal question several assumptions so dearly held in our thoughts about the animals and animality. The book deals with several sub-themes like boundaries between humans and animals between humans and non-human animals, between animals and other life forms and between animates and inanimates. The book offers a better comprehension of our attitudes towards animals and thereby to a broader understanding of what it means to be human.

State and Society, Domination and Resistance and *Centre and Prephery* all three deal with the various aspects of the complex societies. The *State and Society* concentrates on the political centralization and social hiearchy while the *Domination and Resistance's* main concern is the explorations in the realms of the nature of power. It has several interesting papers on various operating agencies within a state system and how they not only complete for greater share of power and profits but also resist the attempts of strong ones who always try to subjugate the weakerones. The *Centre and Periphery* address itself not only with the question of exploitation of weak and poor but also with the trade, diffusion and colonialism.

Foraging and Farming and *The Walking Larder* deal with domestication and exploitation of plants and animals respectively. The long history of interaction between plants and people have been viewed from various angles. The aspects like techniques of harvesting, cultivating storing , cooking, fermenting and detoxifying plant foods have been dealt with in great details at global level beside, of course the question of origins of agriculture. *The Walking Larder* deals with the problem of domestication of animals and their exploitation for energy, food and economy, again on global level. Many paper do bring out clearly the prefarence for a particular animal in a partical glographical area or during a particular cultural period.

What's New, as the title of the book indicates takes a closer look at the process of innovation while trying to expand our knowledge about the various words like acculturation, intensification, change etc. so frequently used in archaeology. We all know that these are not just the words but are concepts which carry meaning both apparently as well as between the lines. The volume also searches the context for the above words and processes.

A very specific session in the Congress was organised which dealt with various political, social and religious forces that work with practicing archaeologist and create a new kind of evidence and literature. The session became all the more relevant in the light of academic boycott of South Africa. *The Politics of Past* is the result of this session. The papers from various parts of the world show that how the archaeology has been used by the rulers, the ruled, the religion and Society to satisfy and prove what they wanted provided one is in position to pressurize the practicing archaeologists. It is really amazing to think that the same past has been used by various groups differently.

Archaeological Heritage Management in the Modern

World has papers from a large number of countries grouped into four major sections- general, regional studies, case studies and training and qualification of archaeologist for heritage managements. The diversity of papers ranges from listing and describing the various archaeological heritage to its state of preservation various efforts and techniques being used for conservations and the training facilites of heritage managements.

Archaeological Approaches to Cultural Identity is a facinating volume giving insight into how various societies or nations have tried to identify their association with various archaeological cultures, thus trying to have an afinity and roots in the past. It is this desire of search for roots which connects archaeological cultures with the communities of the area through various legends. Also many papers go other way round and attempt to identify ethnic groups on the basis of archaeological evidence.

Conflicts in Archaeology of Living Traditions and *Who Needs the Past* deal with the problems in methodology of research, collection of data and its interpretation concerning archaeologist and the one whose past is being investigated. Several papers bring out sharply the perception of archaeologists and some of the tribes indigenous people who claim to be connected with the particular archaeological record. It is important to understand that some of the things like burials, graveyards or various other finds might be just another archaeological findings but may carry a lot of emotional, cultural and religious meaning to the people who feel connected with that archaeological site/ objects. Our interpretation may have totally different meaning that what the connected people themselves feel about the things. Thus a proper understanding among both world yield much result.

Similarly all other volumes dealing with specific themes are the real mine of informations and are must for the archaeologist. It should be mentioned that this is by no means a review of the series but just an introduction. In future volumes we shall have detail review of as many volumes as possible.

The one person who deserves to be congratulated once again for bringing out this splendid volume is Prof. Peter J. Ucko. I am certain that he has set so high a standard for organising an International Congress and their Publishing as many as 22 volumes as its proceedings, it would be difficult if not impossible for anyone to do it in future.

Makkhan Lal

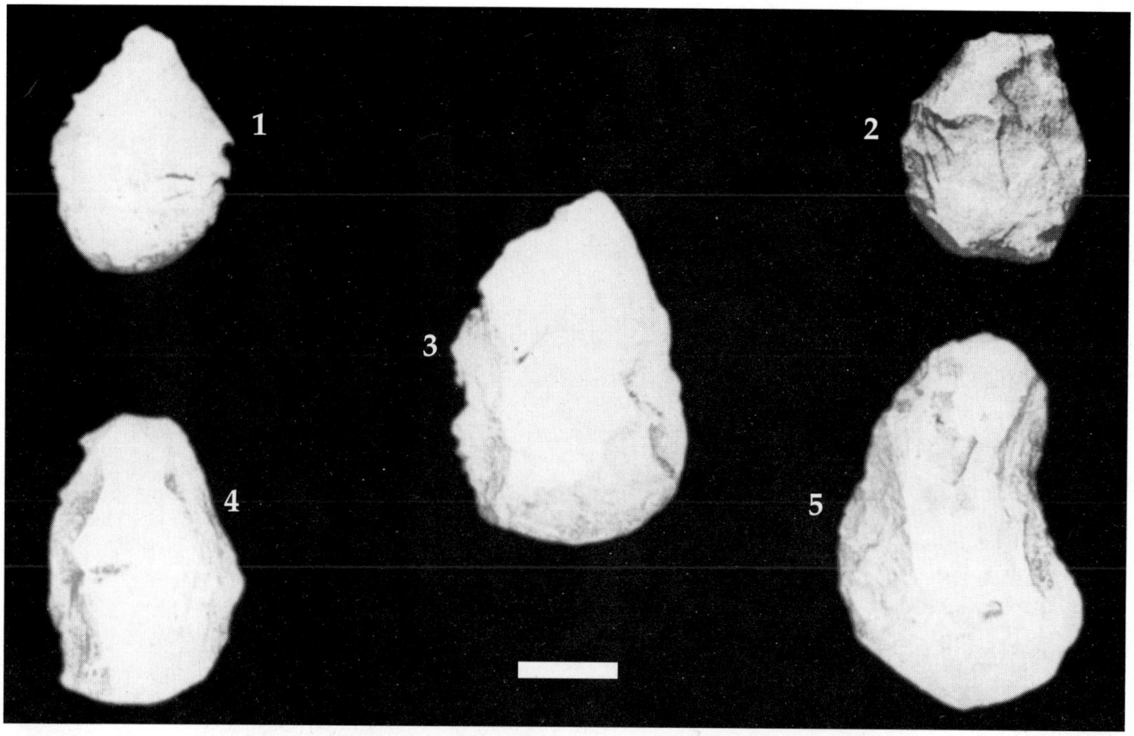

Pl. I. Handaxes from Deogarh. (Lal and Salahuddin)

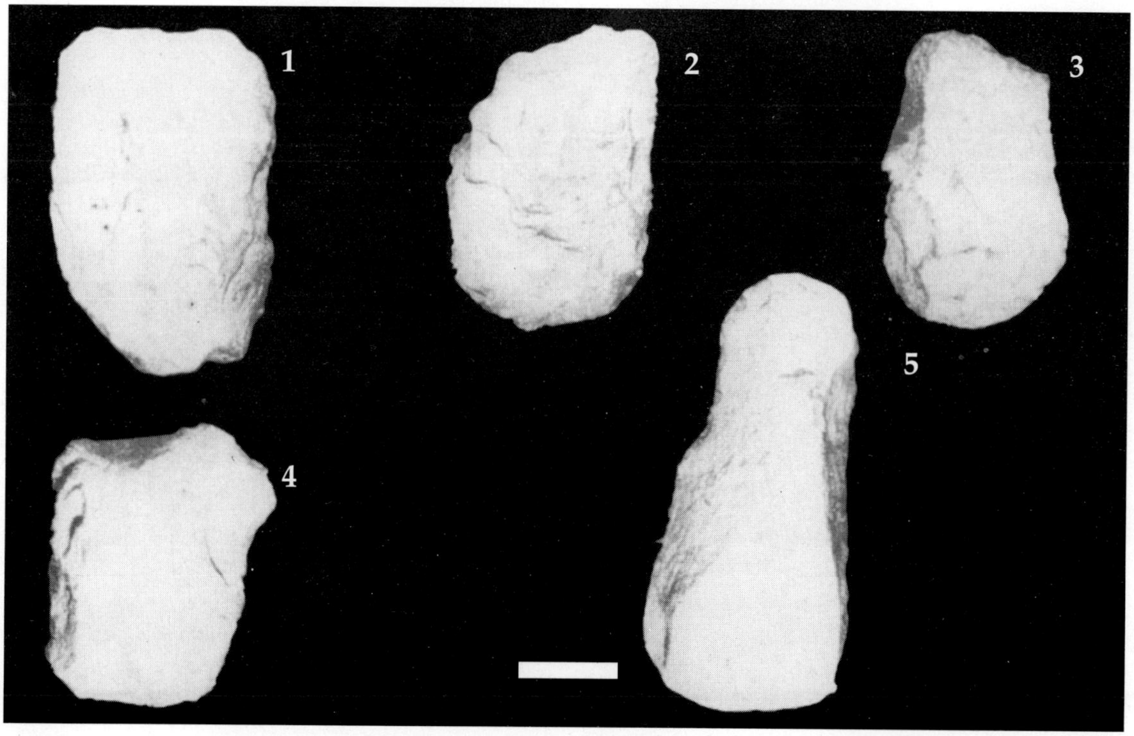

Pl. II. 1-4 Cleavers; 5 Pick from Deogarh. (Lal and Salahuddin)

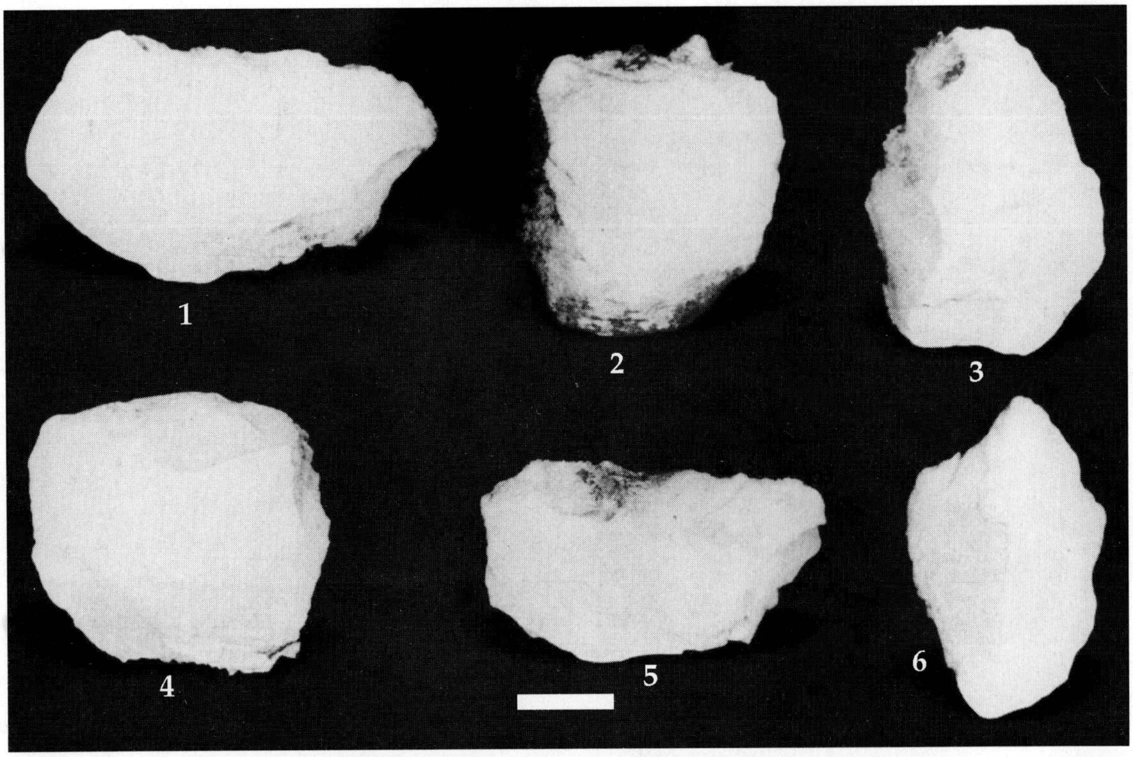

Pl. III. 1-5 Scrapers; 6 Point from Deogarh. (Lal and Salahuddin)

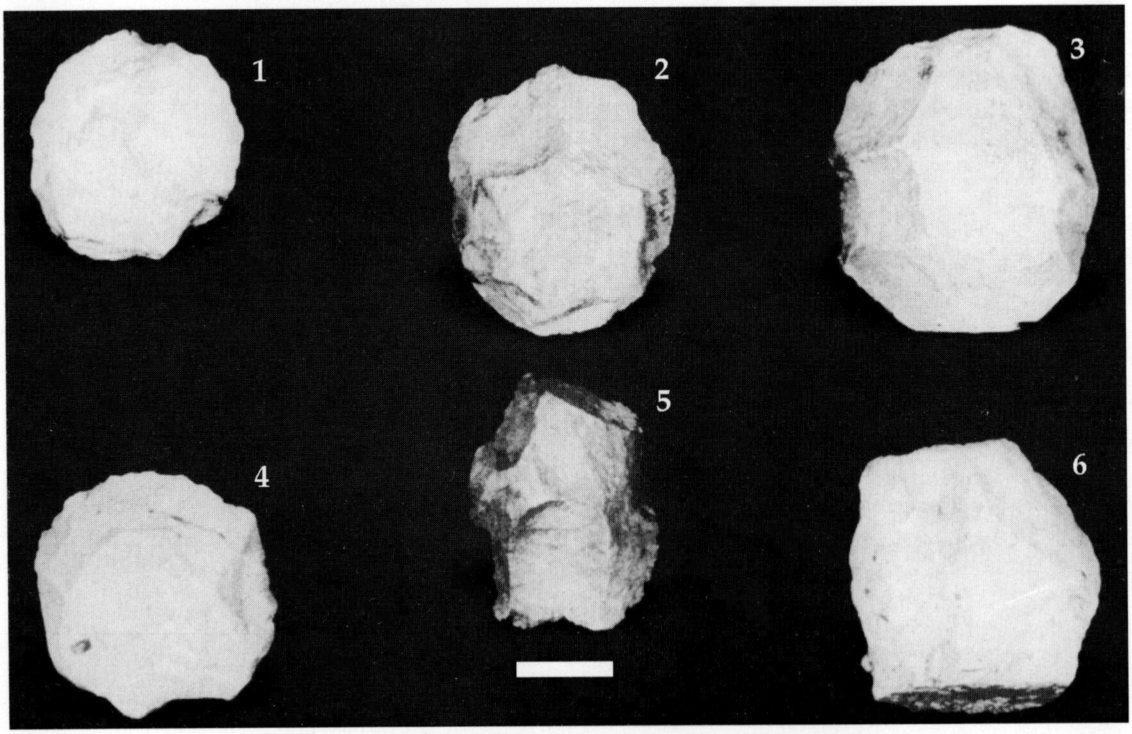

Pl. IV. 1-3 Discoids: 4-6 cores from Deogarh. (Lal and Salahuddin)

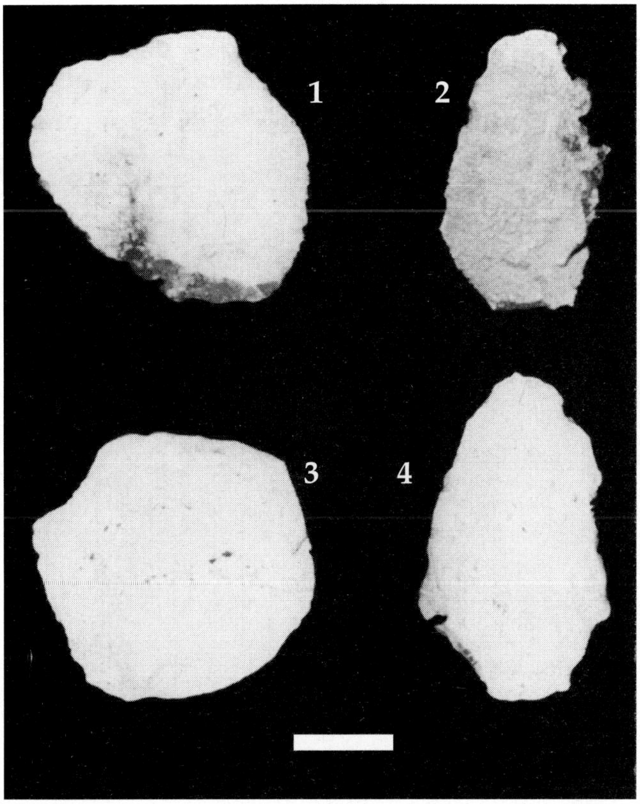

Pl. V. Flakes from Deogarh. (Lal and Salahuddin)

Pl. I. Pre-Harappan deposit underlying first rampart followed by the second rampart (right) of the acropolis. (Bisht)

Pl. II. Pre-Harappan Pottery. (Bisht)

Pl. III. Excavations in acropolis across the southern arm of the fortifications. (Bisht)

Pl. IV. Details of pillar-base, Harappan period. (Bisht)

Pl. V. North-gate complex showing passage way, side-chambers and front terrace, Harappan Period. (Bisht)

Pl. VI. North-gate complex showing a staircase passageway and Western chambers, Harappan Period. (Bisht)

Pl. VII. Outer threshold in passageway of North-gate, Harappan Period. (Bisht)

Pl. VIII. A view of North-gate, Harappan Period. (Bisht)

Pl. IX. A Harappan inscription of nine letters lying in Western Chamber in North-gate, Harappan Period. (Bisht)

Pl. X. Northern bank of Water-Structure with ancient Channel provided with a manhole, Harappan Period. (Bisht)

Pl. I. Adam : Stupa cutting seen through the rampart opening. (Amarendra Nath)

Pl. II. Adam : Pot burial, Period V (Amarendra Nath)

Pl. III. Adam type pottery from Shirkanda. (Amarendra Nath)

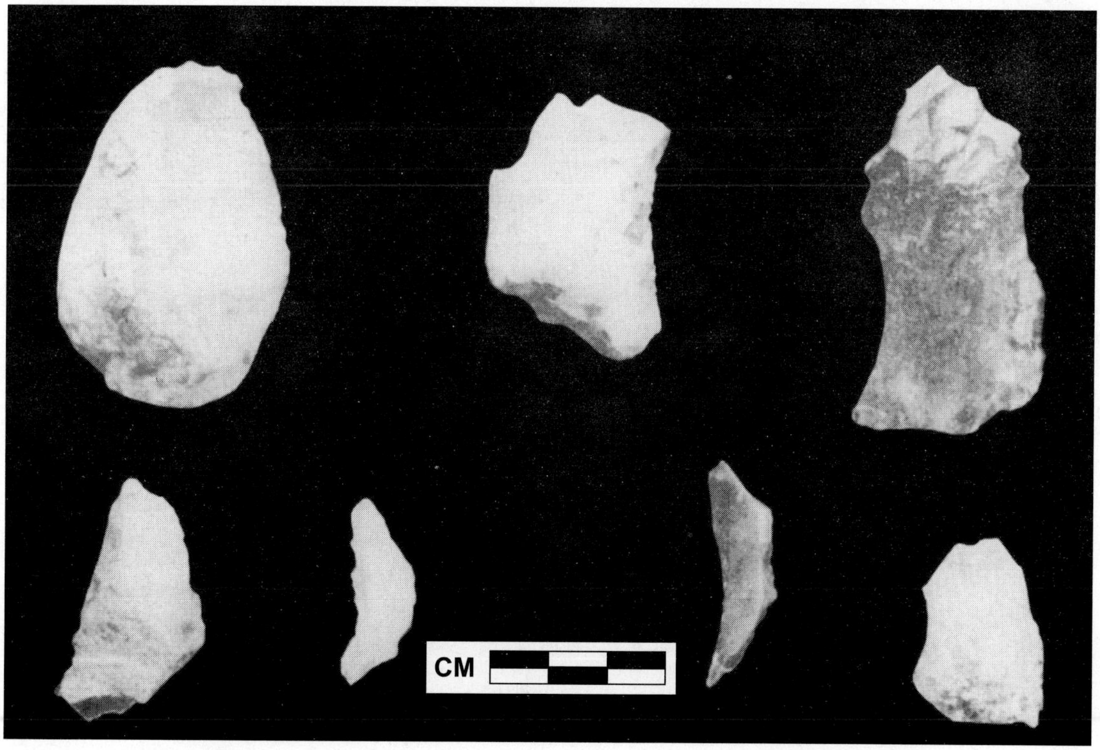

Pl. IV. Stone tools from Shirkanda. (Amarendra Nath)

Pl. I. Human shaped structure exposed in the course of excavations (Dhavalikar)

Pl. II. Fragments of the face of the giant sculpture. (Dhavalikar)

Pl. III. Ear of the giant sculpture. (Dhavalikar)

Pl. IV. The left hand holding *abjapuraka*. (Dhavalikar)

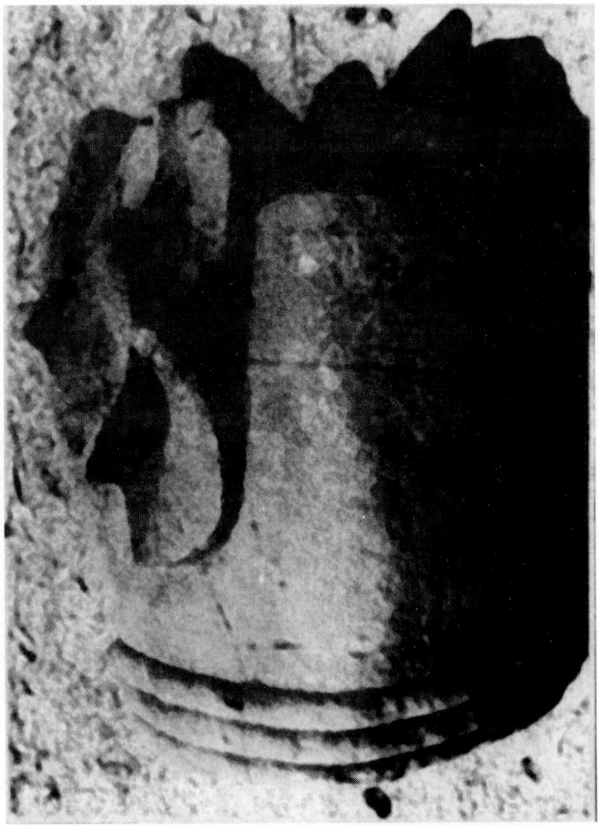

Pl. V. The right hand probably holding *Khadga*. (Dhavalikar)

Pl. VI. The right leg. (Dhavalikar)

Pl. VII. Fragments of smaller hands kept in the fort at Kandhar. (Dhavalikar)

. VIII. Ganesh image found in the field adjacent to the structure; probably Mandala Siddhi Vinayaka of the inscription. (Dhavalikar)

Pl. IX. Entrance of the shin. (Dhavalikar)

Pl. X. Human skeleton in the right half of the front wall. (Dhavalikar)

Pl. I. Goraj : View from east of the excavated plinth of the ancient temple and the Ramesvara Mahadeva temple. (Pande and Vyas)

Pl. II. Goraj : View of the excavated plinth of ancient temple from south and the Ramesvara Mahadeva temple. (Pande and Vyas)

Pl. III. Goraj : Brick mouldingsof the plinth. (Pande and Vyas)

Pl. IV. Goraj : Chandra-sila. (Pande and Vyas)

Pl. V. Goraj : Stone drains with a view of the Runda. (Pande and Vyas)

Pl. VI. Goraj : Signet ring.
(Pande and Vyas)

Pl. VII. Goraj : Matrika image.
(Pande and Vyas)

Pl. VIII. Goraj : Mahishasuramardini.
(Pande and Vyas)

Pl. IX. Goraj : Surya.
(Pande and Vyas)

Pl. X. Goraj : Ganesh.
(Pande and Vyas)

Pl. XI. Goraj : Tirthankara figure.
(Pande and Vyas)

Pl. I. Kodumanal : Etched carnelian beads from the burial. (Rajan)

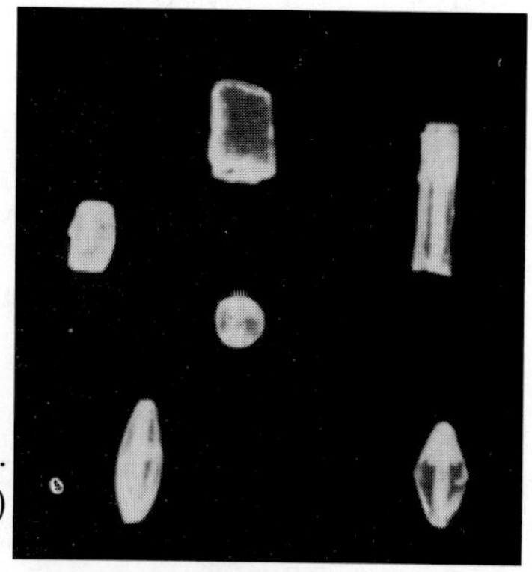

Pl. II. Kodumanal : Quartz beads. (Rajan)

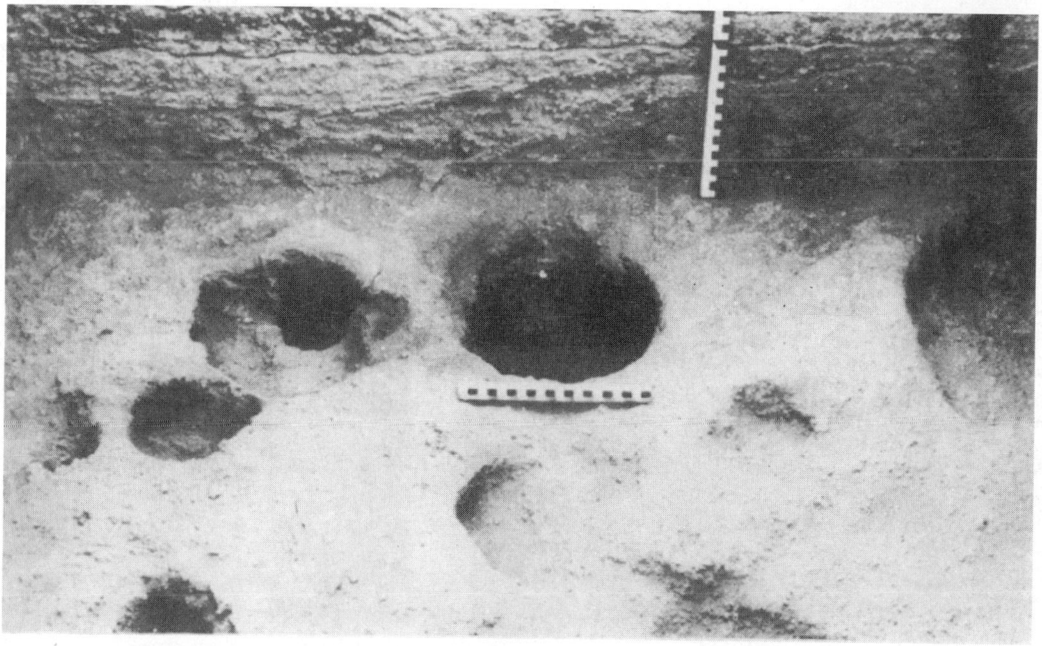

Pl. III. Kodumanal : circular pits dug into the natural soil. (Rajan)

Pl. IV. Kodumanal : Cross section of the crucible furnace. (Rajan)

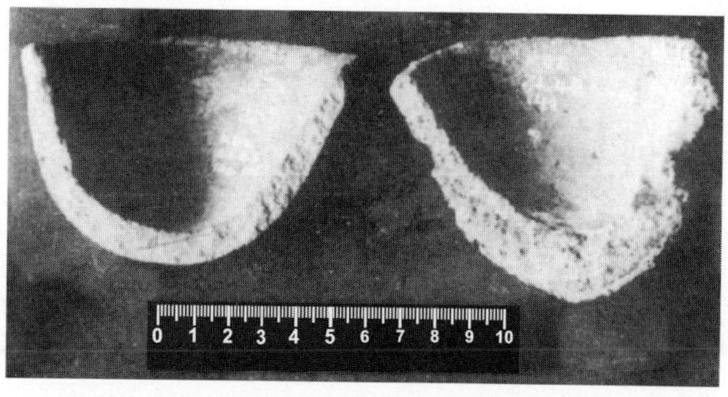

Pl. V. Kodumanal : Vitrified crucible. (Rajan)

Pl. I. Avalokiteswar, Pala 10th Century A.D.
Eastern India. (Asthana)

Pl. II. Avalokitesvar, Pala 10th Century A.D.
Kurkihar, Bihar, Indian Museum, Calcutta. (Asthana)